*A Commentary and Review of
Montesquieu's Spirit of Laws*

Antoine Louis Claude
Destutt de Tracy

A COMMENTARY AND
REVIEW OF

Montesquieu's
Spirit of Laws

Antoine Louis Claude
Destutt de Tracy

TRANSLATED BY
THOMAS JEFFERSON

EDITED AND WITH AN INTRODUCTION
BY JEREMY JENNINGS

LIBERTY FUND

This book is published by Liberty Fund, Inc., a foundation established to encourage study of the ideal of a society of free and responsible individuals.

[cuneiform inscription]

The cuneiform inscription that serves as our logo and as a design element in Liberty Fund books is the earliest-known written appearance of the word "freedom" (*amagi*), or "liberty." It is taken from a clay document written about 2300 BC in the Sumerian city-state of Lagash.

The text of this edition is the translation by Thomas Jefferson published in 1811 by William Duane, Philadelphia.

Frontispiece and image on jacket and cover of Antoine Louis Claude Destutt de Tracy is from a bronze portrait medallion by Pierre-Jean David d'Angers, 1830; courtesy of The Metropolitan Museum of Art, New York, gift of Samuel P. Avery, 1898.

Printed in the United States of America

24 25 26 27 28 C 5 4 3 2 1
24 25 26 27 28 P 5 4 3 2 1

Library of Congress Control Number: 2024940798

ISBN 978-0-86597-923-9 (cloth)
ISBN 978-0-86597-924-6 (paperback)

LIBERTY FUND, INC.
11301 North Meridian Street
Carmel, Indiana 46032
libertyfund.org

Contents

Introduction

Destutt de Tracy's Life

Antoine Claude Louis Destutt de Tracy was born into a wealthy French aristocratic family in 1754. Following the death of his father in 1766, Destutt de Tracy's mother received a generous pension from the French king, and soon afterward, at the age of fourteen, he was able to join the company of guards to the royal household, later studying at the artillery school in Strasbourg. In 1773, to his mother's delight, Destutt de Tracy was admitted to the royal court, hunting with the king in the forests of Fontainebleau. A year later he was appointed counselor to the French ambassador to Savoy in Turin. A life of glamorous parties and dissipation ensued. Then, with the death of his grandfather in 1776, Destutt de Tracy inherited not only the title of Comte de Tracy but also very considerable landed estates in Nivernais and Bourbonnais in the center of France. To complete his social ascent, in 1779 he married the great-niece of the Duc de Penthièvre, Émilie Louise de Durfort de Civrac, at a ceremony attended by many of the French aristocratic elite. The birth of four children followed.

There is little to indicate why Destutt de Tracy might have tired of a life of aristocratic ease and privilege. We know that from an early age he was a devoted reader of Voltaire and that, while living in Strasbourg, he made a pilgrimage to the home of the old philosopher in Ferney. In Strasbourg, he studied classical philosophy and, at some point, came to read the works of physiocrats such as François Quesnay and Pierre Samuel Dupont de Nemours as well as the writings of the *encyclopédistes*. In addition, like many young nobles of his generation, Destutt de Tracy was an enthusiastic admirer of the principles proclaimed by the American Revolution and later supported the administrative reforms announced by Louis XVI's ministers, Anne Robert Jacques Turgot and Jacques Necker.

The dramatic change came in 1788 when Destutt de Tracy found himself drawn into the early stages of the French Revolution, first as a representative of the Bourbonnais nobility at the meeting of the Estates General convened by Louis XVI and then as a member of the newly constituted National Assembly. The rapidly unfolding events of these months posed difficult choices for Destutt de Tracy as a member of the French aristocracy. However, he supported the abolition of the tax privileges of the aristocracy on 4 August 1789 as well as the proclamation of the Declaration of the Rights of Man three weeks later. In June 1790 he backed the hugely controversial legislation enacting the Civil Constitution of the Clergy, a measure that confiscated the property of the Catholic Church and reduced all clergy to employees of the state.

The clearest statement of Destutt de Tracy's political position at this time came in a speech before the National Assembly on 3 April 1790. This was a response to Edmund Burke's first parliamentary attack on the Revolution and was subsequently published as a fifteen-page pamphlet entitled *M. de Tracy à M. Burke.** Burke, Destutt de Tracy countered, had simply failed to understand the Revolution now underway in France. It was not the Revolution that was the source of France's ills but the "vanity" of Louis XIV, the "long despotism of Louis XV," and "the incompetence and depravity of his ministers and favourites." In these circumstances, Destutt de Tracy announced, Burke should not criticize the French for making a revolution but praise them for having the courage to undertake one. Burke's greatest error, Destutt de Tracy argued, was to decry the French for not giving France a constitution that resembled that of England. Rather, Destutt de Tracy concluded, it was for Burke to admire "the love of equality, of moderation, and of justice" that now animated the government that the French had given themselves. Here were themes that were to resurface in Destutt de Tracy's later comments on Montesquieu.

Never a man enamored of the febrile world of revolutionary politics, Destutt de Tracy now found himself drawn into some of the leading intellectual circles of Paris. He joined the Société de 1789, where he met the Abbé Sieyès and the philosopher Condorcet, and later became a member of Lafayette's Club des Feuillants. Ineligible for reelection to the National Assembly, Destutt de Tracy resumed his earlier military career in readiness for the approaching war with Austria but, with the radicalization of public opinion and the ascent of Robespierre's Jacobins, he concluded rightly that it would be best to withdraw from public life. Accordingly, in the summer of 1792, Destutt de

---

* Antoine Louis Claude Destutt de Tracy, *M. de Tracy à M. Burke* (Paris: Imprimerie Nationale, 1790).

Tracy and his family took up residence in the small village of Auteuil to the west of Paris.

This move was to be of considerable significance. Auteuil was home to many of the last generation of Enlightenment *philosophes*. Condorcet moved there in September 1792 and, no less importantly, it was here that Madame Helvétius continued to host her famous salon. Now Destutt de Tracy imbibed the sensationalist psychology of Étienne Bonnot de Condillac as well as Helvétius's maxim that a government should concern itself primarily with the well-being of the majority. He also familiarized himself with Condorcet's view that mathematics should be applied to the moral sciences. It was here too that Destutt de Tracy befriended the physician and medical theorist Pierre Cabanis. Both were to become convinced that a science of man should rest upon a detailed empirical investigation of the human faculties.

Unfortunately, a quiet life of philosophical reflection and conversation was not enough to save Destutt de Tracy from the charges of "*incivisme*" and membership in the aristocracy. Denounced as an enemy of the republic, he was thrown into prison to await the guillotine. There, apart from playing checkers with one of his fellow prisoners, he continued to read Condillac and then moved "back" to the writings of John Locke. Together, Destutt de Tracy wrote, these two writers showed him that what he was seeking was "a science of thought." Only the fall of Robespierre in July 1794 saved him from execution. He was released from prison three months later.

Like many of his generation, Destutt de Tracy was now absorbed with a question that could receive no easy answer. How had it been possible for a revolution that had begun in pursuit of liberty and with a declaration of the rights of man to descend so quickly into fanatical terror and mass murder? For Destutt de Tracy and those of his intellectual associates who came to be known as the *idéologues*, the answer lay in what they saw as a society-wide condition of conceptual and intellectual confusion. The Terror of 1793–94, Destutt de Tracy believed, could only be understood and explained via a thorough analysis of human nature, and this in turn required an examination of the principles of human thought. It was this science that was to be known by a word coined by Destutt de Tracy: *idéologie*. Its subject was the study of the formation of ideas. It was to be through philosophy and education that revolutionary turmoil was to be put to an end and that a moderate republic was to be established upon solid foundations.

Political circumstances now favored Destutt de Tracy and his friends. If the fall of Robespierre marked the end of Jacobin Terror, it also heralded a rightward movement leading to the founding of a five-man directory and the drafting of a new constitution defending freedom of thought, religion, and work. Destutt de Tracy and his fellow *idéologues* were in effect to become the official philosophers of the new regime.*

This was achieved through their membership in the newly created Institut National des Sciences et des Arts. Replacing the various academies (for example, the Académie française) that had existed before the Revolution of 1789, this new body had a vaunting ambition of nothing less than the unification of all knowledge. Accordingly, the Institut National was divided into three classes: the Class of Physical and Mathematical Sciences, the Class of Moral and Political Sciences, and the Class of Literature and the Fine Arts. It was to the second of these that Destutt de Tracy was elected in February 1796.

Of particular interest to Destutt de Tracy was the standardization and improvement of the curriculum to be taught in the Republic's new *écoles centrales*. Recognizing that, of all the sciences, morality was the last to be perfected, he saw that public instruction, along with clear and sensible legislation, was the best means to encourage private virtue and public happiness. To that end, in addition to presenting a series of papers that sought to define the concept of *idéologie*, Destutt de Tracy began the writing of what he hoped would be a set of textbooks that would provide a complete knowledge of our intellectual faculties. The first in the sequence, published in 1801, was entitled *Élémens d'idéologie*. This was followed by a second, *Grammaire*, in 1803 and a third volume, *Logique*, in 1805.

Once again, political developments in France were to shape Destutt de Tracy's intellectual journey. At first, he and his colleagues lent their support to Napoleon Bonaparte after his seizure of power as First Consul in 1799. For his part, Napoleon actively courted their approval, symbolically visiting Madame Helvétius in Auteuil. Destutt de Tracy himself was appointed a member of the

---

* For further reading on Destutt de Tracy and the *idéologues*, see Emmet Kennedy, *A Philosophe in the Age of Revolution: Destutt de Tracy and the Origins of "Ideology"* (Philadelphia: American Philosophical Society, 1978); Cheryl B. Welch, *Liberty and Utility: The French Idéologues and the Transformation of Liberalism* (New York: Columbia University Press, 1984); B. W. Head, *Ideology and Social Science: Destutt de Tracy and French Liberalism* (Dordrecht: Martinus Nijhoff, 1985); and Martin S. Staum, *Minerva's Message: Stabilizing the French Revolution* (Montreal: McGill-Queen's University Press, 1996).

Senate for life (on a very substantial salary). But as he sought to extend his power and authority, Napoleon soon showed that he had little time for what he did not hesitate to denigrate as the idle speculations of a "metaphysical faction." Accordingly, in 1803 the Class of Moral and Political Sciences was closed. In a country where all dissenting opinion was to be silenced, there could be no room for intellectual opposition.

The Writing and Translation of the *Commentary and Review*

It was in these circumstances that Destutt de Tracy decided not to press ahead with the writing of the fourth volume of his *Élémens d'idéologie*, provisionally entitled *Traité de la volonté*, for it was here that he intended to explore the "practical applications" of his general ideas to politics and economics. The intervention of Napoleon's censors would have been inevitable. Instead, Destutt de Tracy retired to his study and in secrecy started to write a commentary on Montesquieu's *Spirit of the Laws*. It was with the completion of this work that, in June 1809, Destutt de Tracy wrote to Thomas Jefferson (recently retired from the presidency of the United States) to suggest that he might have this work translated into English and published anonymously.*

It is possible that Destutt de Tracy first met Jefferson during the 1780s when Americans were welcomed enthusiastically into the highest intellectual and social circles in Paris. The achievements of the American Revolution, and of men like Jefferson, were widely admired in France, and this was to remain the case after the hopes for France's own revolution had been so cruelly dashed. Despite the continued existence of slavery, America's advocates believed that the United States gave living expression to the idea that a society could be transformed, and for the better. Its constitution showed that a government of liberty and of wise leaders was no chimera. Among Destutt de Tracy and his circle, therefore, the election of Jefferson to the office of president was greeted with considerable enthusiasm. Moreover, the manner in which Jefferson left office in 1809, freeing himself voluntarily from the "shackles" of government, only served to increase that admiration. The contrast with the Emperor Napoleon's abuse of autocratic power could not have been starker.

---

* For the relationship between Destutt de Tracy and Jefferson, see Gilbert Chinard, *Jefferson et les Idéologues d'après sa correspondance inédite* (Baltimore: Johns Hopkins University Press, 1925).

One demonstration of this esteem came in 1802 when Jefferson was elected as a foreign associate member of the Class of Moral and Political Sciences. After this, he began a correspondence with several of its members. These included Destutt de Tracy, who, in February 1804, sent Jefferson copies of both his *Élémens d'idéologie* and his *Grammaire*. Destutt de Tracy's hope, he wrote, was that Jefferson would view with "indulgence and generosity" two works whose goal was to ensure "the progress of the human spirit and at last provide a solid basis for all our knowledge" (Chinard, 37). Jefferson, in his reply in February 1806—written to congratulate Destutt de Tracy on his own election to the American Philosophical Society—confessed that the burdens of office meant that the two volumes were "with those things which are to sweeten a retirement" (Chinard, 41).

Two years were to elapse before Destutt de Tracy was to correspond with Jefferson again. Writing to "the man whom I respect most in the world and whose approval I most desire," he sent a copy of the now-completed manuscript of his commentary on Montesquieu, informing Jefferson that it was "a work on the things which are most important for the happiness of men." He also told Jefferson that he would be delighted if Jefferson could have it translated into English, adding that his authorship of the text must remain unknown and that Jefferson should feel free to change and improve the text as he saw fit (Chinard, 43–44).

Destutt de Tracy had made his inquiry to the right person, for, as he rightly surmised, there was much in his manuscript that would appeal to Jefferson, not least his criticisms of the English constitution. Thus, a year later Jefferson was to write to his close friend and supporter William Duane, editor of the *Philadelphia Aurora*, to tell him that he had an "enterprise" to propose to a "good printer." In his possession, he told Duane, he had a manuscript in French "confided to me by a friend, whose name alone would give it celebrity were it permitted to be mentioned." It was, Jefferson continued, a commentary and review of Montesquieu's *Spirit of Laws*, a "great work" having, in Jefferson's words, "much of truth and sound principle, but abounding also with inconsistencies, apocryphal facts and false references." It was to the correction of the latter, he told Duane, that the text was devoted, and this was done "not by criticising words and sentences, but by taking a book at a time, considering its general scope and proceeding to confirm or confute it." And "much of confutation" there was, Jefferson added (Chinard, 54)!

To Duane, Jefferson admitted that he had not yet read the whole manuscript, as it was handwritten in French, but he had read enough to "infer with

confidence that we shall find the work generally worthy of our high approbation, and that it everywhere maintains the pre-eminence of representative government, by showing that its foundations are laid in reason, in right, and in
general good." To help Duane decide, Jefferson forwarded his own translation of Destutt de Tracy's discussion of Montesquieu's Book XI (devoted to
the key question of the relationship between political liberty and the constitution). Jefferson's wish was that the text should be "translated by someone
who possesses style as well as capacity to do justice to abstruse conceptions"
and that this should be "executed with as little delay as possible." He also
offered to revise the translation "if required" (Chinard, 55).

Duane immediately accepted Jefferson's proposal, and a month later
the latter forwarded the French manuscript. Again, Jefferson emphasized the
importance he attached to Destutt de Tracy's text. "Since writing to you," Jefferson commented, "I have gone over the whole, and can assure you it is the
most valuable political work of the present age." Specifically, and in reference
to another work on Montesquieu by David Williams,* he added, "I am glad to
hear of everything which reduces that author to his just level, as his predilec-
tion for monarchy, and for the English monarchy in particular, has done
mischief everywhere, and here also to a certain degree." Clearly, Jefferson's
disagreements with Alexander Hamilton and the Federalists were not forgotten. The intention was that Destutt de Tracy's text would continue the argument for the true principles of republicanism (Chinard, 59).

Not long afterward, Duane reported to Jefferson that progress on the translation and production of Destutt de Tracy's text was not going smoothly. He
readily admitted that the translation was not as good as might be—there were
too many *whys*, *wherefores*, and *moreovers*!—and, to make matters worse, his
workers had gone on strike. For his part, as a letter to Duane of 25 October 1810 makes clear, Jefferson was far from happy with the quality of the
material he was receiving. It is this letter that best allows us to gauge the extent
of Jefferson's involvement in the preparation of Destutt de Tracy's text. It merits being quoted at length.

I now return the translated sheets. You will find in them some pencilled
words, chiefly corrections of errors in the copyist. In one part they are

* David Williams, *Lectures on political principles, the subject of eighteen books in
Montesquieu's Spirit of Laws* (London: Cengage Gale, 1789).

something more, having retained a copy of the part I translated and forwarded to you in my first letter, I was enabled to collate that with the corresponding part now enclosed, and I found in a few instances, changes in the nature of the sentences etc, which tho[ugh] equivalent to the author's own, yet were not exactly in the form he had chosen. Knowing his precision of idea, and his attention to the choice of words, for expressing them, I apprehended he would be better satisfied with our adherence to his forms of expression as far as the genius of the two languages would admit it. I made the notes therefore merely with a view of recommending this generally. (Chinard, 61)

As we can see, Jefferson was no idle spectator: he worked assiduously to correct and improve the material he was being sent.

This he continued to do, as was illustrated by Jefferson's next letter to Duane of 18 January 1811. Again, a lengthy quotation is merited.

I observe that the three last packets of about 130, or 140 pages . . . bear the marks of much hastier translation than those of the preceding. I should be tempted to conjecture a change of translator; sentences incomplete, false syntax, want of perspicuity, and sometimes a suspected mistranslation will require from yourself a rigorous revisal of these packets, with the original in your hand, to enable it to meet public approbation. It would be a subject of much regret that a work so distinguished for perspicuity, and a critical choice of words, should appear disadvantageously exactly in these particulars; and the more so as there will be no original to recur to for correction or explanation. (Chinard, 63)

Duane's confused and confusing reply the following week can only have confirmed all of Jefferson's apprehensions. Citing overwork, Duane reported that the person he had taken on for the job of translation had translated "the whole text but it was not well done, tho[ugh] he is capable." Thus, he explained, he had decided to take on the task as "a practical essay for myself, as well as to enjoy the gratification it afforded me, as to make my knowledge of the French better." Accepting that he "had hurried the whole on depending too much on the translator, or rather not having time sufficient to chasten and arrange the language," he told Jefferson that he felt confident that he would be able "to remedy the defects of the latter part" (Chinard, 67–68).

In brief, the translation of Destutt de Tracy's text was the work of three people: the original unknown translator, Duane, and Jefferson. Jefferson clarified the difficulties this had involved in a letter to Destutt de Tracy of 26 January 1811, where he confirmed that the translation was now complete. "My situation," he wrote, "far in the interior of the country, was not favorable to the object of getting this work translated and printed." Once the project was underway, Jefferson continued, "the sheets came to me by post, from time to time for revisal; but not being accompanied by the original, I could not judge of verbal accuracies." He therefore had found it "impossible to give it the appearance of an original composition in our language." Nonetheless, he assured Destutt de Tracy, he believed the translation to be "substantially correct, without being an adequate representation of the excellences of the original; as indeed no translation can be" (Chinard, 74–75). In a second letter, written seven years later, Jefferson restricted himself to saying that, while he had been able to "correct inaccuracies of language," this had not been possible with "inconformities of sentiment with the original" (Chinard, 202).

It will be remembered that when Destutt de Tracy had sent Jefferson his manuscript, he had stipulated that his authorship of the text must remain unknown. This too presented Jefferson with difficulties. At first he had thought to publish the volume as if it had been written originally in English and not indicate that it was a translation. However, the imperfect quality of the translation convinced him that this ploy would be quickly exposed. So he came up with the ingenious idea of writing a short preface to the book himself but pretending that its author was "a Frenchman by birth and education." This Frenchman, the American audience was told, had been "an early friend to the revolution of France" but had now fled "the tyrannies of the monster Robespierre" and found "safety, freedom and hospitality among you." "Few nations," the imagined exile told his hosts, "are in a situation to profit by the detection of political errors, or to shape their practice by newly developed truths. This is the eminent advantage of the country in which I write." One can easily imagine Jefferson's amusement at the bafflement of the French censors and the self-satisfaction of his fellow citizens.

Discussion with Jefferson

The letter in which Jefferson told Destutt de Tracy that it was his intention to add a "prefatory epistle" so as to preserve the "secret of the author" also provided him with an opportunity not only to praise Destutt de Tracy's text but also to express his disagreement with certain important features of the latter's argument. This in turn encouraged a reply that explains much about the differing perspectives of American and French writers on politics at the time.

"I had," Jefferson began, "deemed Montesquieu's work of much merit; but saw in it, with every thinking man, so much of paradox, of false principle, and misapplied fact, as to render its value equivocal on the whole." A "radical correction" of these errors had therefore been a "great desideratum." This, Jefferson wrote, had now been supplied, "with a depth of thought, precision of idea, of language and of logic" that would convince "every mind." Destutt de Tracy's book, he declared "in the spirit of truth and sincerity," was "the most precious gift the present age has received" (Chinard, 74).

However, Jefferson continued, "one of its doctrines, . . . the preference of a plural over a singular executive, will probably not be assented to here." "When our present government was first established," he explained, "we had many doubts on this question, and many leanings towards a supreme executive council." Such a system had existed at the time in France under the Directory but, Jefferson observed, it quickly failed, and "not from any circumstance peculiar to the times or nation, but from those internal jealousies and dissensions of the Directory, which will ever arise among men equal in power, without a principal to decide and control their differences." A similar experiment, Jefferson confirmed, had been tried in the United States in 1784 with the creation of the Committee of the States, but this too had swiftly fallen into "schisms and dissensions" such as to "render all cooperation among them impracticable." Both these failures, he wrote, had "authorized a belief that the form of a plurality, however promising in theory, is impossible in men constituted with ordinary passions." Likewise, in the United States, "the tranquil and steady tenor of our single executive" had given hope that "this important problem is at last solved." Aided by a cabinet of five or six people, the president "consults either singly, or all together, he has the benefit of their wisdom and information, brings their views to one centre, and produces an unity of action and direction." As might be imagined, Jefferson bolstered this point by reference to his own experience (Chinard, 75–76).

Nonetheless, Jefferson confessed that he remained "sensible to the solidity" of the principle of plurality as a safeguard of "public liberty." The "conservative body" proposed by Destutt de Tracy "might be so constituted as . . . might also be a valuable sentinel and check on the liberticide views of an ambitious individual." But here too the United States had produced its own answer. The "true barriers of our liberty," Jefferson proclaimed, were the nation's state governments, and "the wisest conservative power ever contrived by man, is that which our Revolution and our present government found us possessed." "Seventeen distinct states," he continued, "amalgamated into one as to their foreign concerns, but single and independent as to their internal administration, regularly organized with a legislature and governor resting on the choice of the people, and enlightened by a free press, can never be fascinated by the arts of one man, as to submit voluntarily to his usurpation." In contrast, the republican government of France, "*un[e] et indivisible*," had fallen without a struggle due to the lack of provincial organizations around which the people could rally (Chinard, 77–78).

In retrospect, Jefferson's dismissal of Destutt de Tracy's argument rested upon certain optimistic assumptions that were, with time, to be shown to be ungrounded. There was, Jefferson admitted, one danger that might reasonably be thought to arise from the federal structure of the U.S. constitution: namely, "that certain States from local and occasional discontents, might attempt to secede from the Union." This, Jefferson conceded, was "certainly possible"; but, he contended, "it is not probable that local discontents can spread to such an extent, as to be able to face the sound parts of so extensive a Union; and, if ever they should reach the majority, they would then become the regular government, acquire the ascendancy in Congress, and be able to redress their own grievances by laws peaceably and constitutionally passed" (Chinard, 78–79).

It was to be many months before Jefferson's letter reached Destutt de Tracy in Paris and not therefore before October 1811 that he was to pen his reply. Like Jefferson's message, Destutt de Tracy's response was to run to several pages and to touch many topics. Here we will limit our discussion to just two of the latter.

First, Destutt de Tracy was delighted to learn that his work on Montesquieu had now been published in America. It had always been his "sincere desire," he wrote, to be "useful," but now he had obtained the only "glory" that he could ever have really wanted: "the approbation of the most virtuous and most truly enlightened statesman who had ever presided over the destiny of a great people." Thanks to Jefferson, his ideas had been saved from oblivion and he had the quiet satisfaction of knowing that Jefferson shared his views (and therefore that they were sound) (Chinard, 87).

Second, Destutt de Tracy reflected on Jefferson's praise of American federalism as a bulwark of liberty. In essence, his argument was that, while such a system might work admirably in America, this could not be the case in Europe. In part, this was due to the political culture that existed in the United States. Jefferson's phrase, included in his letter, that he had never "been able to conceive how any rational being could propose happiness to himself from the exercise of power over others" was, Destutt de Tracy remarked, impossible for him to translate, as it "appeared foreign to every European language." That this system seemingly worked in America also had much to do with geography. A federal constitution, Destutt de Tracy contended, was simply not an option for a people surrounded by powerful enemy governments. Had France faced its recent dangers held together only by a "weak federal union," she would have been quickly torn to pieces. "If therefore," Destutt de Tracy wrote, "a federal constitution is an impossibility when one is surrounded by dangerous neighbours; if, at the same time, the unity of executive power is only not dangerous under a federal constitution; and if nevertheless this unity is necessary for a free government to survive; the sad conclusion must be drawn that in our old Europe, and especially in the Mediterranean countries, all moderate and lawful government is not possible in the long run" (Chinard, 89–91). All of this, Destutt de Tracy wrote, made him realize that "liberty was still more difficult to preserve" than he would have thought and that, if this was ever to be attained, it would be in the United States.

Montesquieu's *Spirit of the Laws*

What of the book that Destutt de Tracy has chosen to comment on and its author? Charles-Louis de Secondat, later Baron de Montesquieu, was born on 19 January 1689 near Bordeaux in the southwest of France. As was the case with Destutt de Tracy, he was the scion of a distinguished aristocratic family, but one that also made money through the wine trade. Like many members of his family before him, he served as a member of the *parlement* of Bordeaux, a body responsible for registering royal decrees and edicts, something that brought it into frequent disagreement with the French Crown. In 1716, Montesquieu was elected to the Académie de Bordeaux, and it was here that he began to develop an interest in the development and benefits of science. Nonetheless, until he published his *Persian Letters* in 1721, there was little to differentiate Montesquieu from many another provincial aristocrats with a lively interest in the arts and sciences. The success of the *Persian Letters* changed all of that and turned him into an international celebrity.

Published anonymously, the *Persian Letters* is a novel in the form of a series of letters written by two Persian visitors to Europe to their wives and friends at home. It is set largely in a Persian harem and the literary salons of Paris. Its success derived from the fact that it enabled the French to see themselves as others saw them, and to that extent could be read as a comedy of manners. But there was much more to it than this. Montesquieu's text exposed many of the practices and habits of a supposedly sophisticated Parisian and European society to ridicule, ruthlessly dissecting the human capacity for vanity and self-deception. It also laid bare the perils of despotism, even in its then popular Enlightened form, and gave us a first glimpse of what Montesquieu took to be the conditions in which liberty might flourish.

The Spirit of the Laws was published in 1748.* It is a vast book comprising thirty-one separate books, dealing with a wide array of topics touching philosophy, history, politics, and much else. At first sight, it has no obvious structure or clear purpose. Most famously, it is known for its claim that climate is one of the many factors, along with manners and mores, that govern the behavior of individuals. That said, for all its multiple digressions, there is a division between the first and second parts of the text: the first thirteen books examine the nature of government and the function of law; Books XIV–XXVI look at the relationship of laws to climate, slavery, commerce, luxury, and religion. The final five books (of not inconsiderable length) amount to an appendix analyzing Roman and early French laws of succession and inheritance. As Montesquieu wrote in his preface, "I ask a favour that I fear will not be granted: it is that one not judge by a moment's reading the work of twenty years, that one approve or condemn the book as a whole and not some few sentences" (Montesquieu, xliii).

How, then, might the complex content of *The Spirit of the Laws* be summarized? The most obvious point is that Montesquieu sought to make a distinction between the letter of the law and the spirit of the law. To that end, having told us in his first sentence that "laws, taken in the broadest meaning, are the necessary relations deriving from the nature of things; and, in this sense, all beings have their laws," Montesquieu offered a threefold typology of government. These were republics (in their democratic and aristocratic forms),

---

* Montesquieu, *The Spirit of the Laws*, ed. Anne M. Cohler, Basia C. Miller, and Harold S. Stone (Cambridge: Cambridge University Press, 1989).

monarchies, and despotisms. "Republican government," Montesquieu wrote, "is that in which the people as a body, or only a part of the people, have sovereign power; monarchical government is that in which one alone governs, but by fixed and established laws; whereas in despotic government, one alone, without law and without rule, draws everything along by his will and caprices" (Montesquieu, 10). Following from this, Montesquieu distinguished between the nature of a government ("its particular structure") and its principle ("the human passions that set it in motion"). In democracies, the latter is taken to be virtue; in monarchies, it is the sentiment of honor; and in despotic states, it is fear.

What becomes apparent as the text proceeds is that Montesquieu, in a radical break with the traditions of classical political thought, was of the view that the ancient republics of the past were not appropriate models for an eighteenth-century world and that the existence of a virtuous citizenry prepared to put the general interest before self-interest could not be relied upon. More intriguing still, Montesquieu focused much of his attention upon analyzing the nature of despotism and in using it as the standard by which all other regimes were to be judged.

Montesquieu was by no means the first French writer to address this subject—it had been a common theme since the days of Louis XIV's absolutist regime—but in drawing out the centrality of fear in despotic regimes, he was able all the better to differentiate it from monarchical rule and what he saw as mixed government. The goal of despotic government was to reduce all subjects to a condition of passive obedience where all blindly submitted to the absolute will of the sovereign. Bound by no rules, the despot could take away life and property according to his arbitrary whims and whenever he chose. The activity of government was reduced to that of the preservation of the prince. In such a situation, Montesquieu wrote, "man is a creature who obeys a creature who wants" (Montesquieu, 29).

Crucially, despotic government lacked the all-important ingredient of moderation, and, as Montesquieu was to comment in Book XXIX, he had written his work to prove that "the spirit of moderation should be that of the legislator." That same paragraph also told his readers that "the political good, like the moral good, is always found between two limits" (Montesquieu, 602). Montesquieu's discussion of the nature and meaning of moderation is interspersed throughout the text, and it is never easy to ascertain whether his remarks are intended to be normative claims or factual statements; but they underpin a further significant distinction made by Montesquieu: that between moderate and immoderate governments. Immoderate governments were not only ones where power operated according to the arbitrary wishes of the prince but also where there existed no countervailing forces or institutions capable of limiting or countermanding that abuse of power. Specifically, there was no separation between the executive, legislative, and judicial branches of government. As Montesquieu wrote in Book XI, "So that one cannot abuse power, power must check power by the arrangement of things" (Montesquieu, 155).

From this, Montesquieu concluded that "political liberty is found only in moderate governments" (Montesquieu, 155), and by political liberty he understood "that tranquillity of spirit which comes from the opinion each one has of his security, and in order for him to have this liberty the government must be such that one citizen cannot fear another citizen" (Montesquieu, 157). To that extent, Montesquieu affirmed, in a society where there are laws, liberty "in no way consists in doing what one wants. . . . [It is] the right to do everything the law permits" (Montesquieu, 155).

To justify these conclusions, Montesquieu cited an extraordinary array of cases drawn from classical Greece, Rome, China, Persia, the Italian republics, and far beyond. When, for example, he wanted to illustrate the nature of despotism, he invariably cited the Ottoman Empire. Where did he look for examples of moderate government? In his own age, he looked to monarchies. The monarchies we know, he wrote in Chapter 7 of Book XI, "do not have liberty for their direct purpose. . . . They aim only for the glory of the citizens, the state and the prince. But this glory results in a spirit of liberty that can, in these states, produce equally great things and can perhaps contribute as much to happiness as liberty itself" (Montesquieu, 166). Did Montesquieu place the French monarchy in this category? The answer is that he worried that the absolutist monarchy could descend into despotism; and it was this that led Montesquieu to develop one of the most important themes contained in *The Spirit of the Laws*: the need for limitations to the power of the prince. As he wrote in Chapter 4 of Book II, "Intermediate, subordinate, and dependent powers constitute the nature of monarchical government, that is, of the government in which one alone governs by fundamental laws" (Montesquieu, 17). These intermediate powers might take several forms—an independent judiciary and the clergy, for example—but, as a member of both the so-called nobility of the robe and the provincial *parlement* of Bordeaux, Montesquieu arguably gave pride of place to the aristocracy. To quote Book II again: "The most natural intermediate, subordinate power is that of the nobility. In a way the nobility is of the essence of monarchy, whose fundamental maxim is: *no monarch, no nobility: no nobility, no monarch*; rather one has a despot" (Montesquieu, 18). It was in this context that Montesquieu voiced his admiration for the monarchy of England, a country he had visited in 1729. Rightly or wrongly, he now concluded that England was the only country whose "political constitution has political liberty for its direct purpose" (Montesquieu, 156) and that this was obtained by the rule of law and the separation of powers between the executive, legislative, and judiciary. Whether Montesquieu's description of the workings of that constitution was accurate was something questioned by many of his contemporaries.

Such is the all-encompassing nature of Montesquieu's inquiry that there are many other important themes discussed in his text, but to conclude this overview, two further subjects should be mentioned. There were, Montesquieu believed, several counterweights to despotism, and one of the most important of these was the activity of commerce. Here Montesquieu had in mind not merely the sale and purchase of goods but the beneficial and moderating effects commerce had upon society and the uses to which power was put. "Everywhere there is commerce," Montesquieu wrote in Book XX, "there are gentle mores" (Montesquieu, 338). Commerce cured our destructive prejudices; it led to peace among peoples; and it produced a feeling for "exact justice" that encouraged us to take the interests of others into account. Moreover, in the right conditions, "the spirit of commerce" brought with it "the spirit of frugality, economy, moderation, work, wisdom, tranquillity, order and rule" (Montesquieu, 48).

The second issue follows from Montesquieu's statement in Book XIX that "many things govern men: climate, religion, laws, the maxims of government, examples of past things, mores and manners" (Montesquieu, 310). Much of the latter half of his text is devoted to exploring the impact of these various factors. So, for example, Montesquieu concluded that the climate of England encouraged the English to commit suicide even "in the very midst of happiness." The important point was that, when combined, these different elements governing men produced a general spirit of the nation. To this Montesquieu added that the prudent legislator would be wise not to seek to change the general spirit of a nation through legislation. As he wrote, "One must not correct everything" (Montesquieu, 311). There were therefore distinct limits to what could be achieved through the activity of politics, and government should reflect the mores and manners of society rather than be an instrument for its transformation. There could be no uniformly applicable propositions capable of defining the character of good government, nor could there be a blueprint for the good society.

Responses to Montesquieu

Montesquieu died in 1755. Contrary to his wishes, *The Spirit of the Laws* has ever since been largely read in parts rather than as a whole. Accordingly, it has been subject to a wide variety of interpretations, some positive and some negative. The positive response built upon Montesquieu's key idea that liberty could only be safeguarded through the checking and balancing of central power and that a polity lacking intermediary bodies could provide no safeguards against despotism. Many French liberals in the nineteenth century, including Benjamin Constant and Alexis de Tocqueville, were to find this a convincing argument. Later still, Montesquieu's ideas provided the foundation for what Judith Shklar was to define as a liberalism of fear, a liberalism grounded in a distrust of all governments. In his day, Montesquieu was immediately criticized by supporters of the French monarchy such as Voltaire, for whom estates, *parlements*, and similar intermediary bodies were seen as feudal remnants voicing private and corporate interests that, even in Montesquieu's description of them, came to be conflated with aristocratic power and what was known as the *thèse nobiliaire*. Later *philosophes*, as evidenced in Destutt de Tracy's use as appendices to his *Commentary* of texts by Condorcet and (supposedly) Helvétius, were critical of both the style and content of *The Spirit of the Laws*. As will be seen, for Condorcet, Montesquieu's text amounted to one confusion after another, thus obtaining the approval of "all the prejudiced people, of all those who detest light, of all the protectors and participators in abuse" (CR, 222). For Helvétius, the charge was a simpler one: Montesquieu was incapable of transcending the interests of his own class.

In the early stages of the French Revolution, Montesquieu was cited extensively and, as the French grappled with writing a new constitution, usually in admiration. However, with the radicalization of the Revolution, he faded from view. Aristocracy and the English constitution now had few admirers. Where Montesquieu continued to be debated was in the United States. In the latter half of the eighteenth century, he was arguably the most extensively cited author in America and, as is well known, in 1787 he had a profound influence over the American Founders. The irony is that both those who supported the Constitution and those who opposed it drew sustenance from Montesquieu's text. For James Madison, as he wrote in Federalist 47, he was "the celebrated Montesquieu," "the oracle who is always to be consulted." Thomas Jefferson shared this admiration, but, as we have seen, he had doubts about many aspects of Montesquieu's thinking. This is where Destutt de Tracy's *Commentary and Review of Montesquieu's Spirit of Laws* enters the story.

Destutt de Tracy's *Commentary and Review*

Like most of his writings, Destutt de Tracy's text is a complex and challenging read.* This in part follows from his decision, explained in the Preliminary Observations, not to examine Montesquieu's text thematically but to analyze it in sequential order, book by book. To that end, Destutt de Tracy frequently announces that a particular book of *The Spirit of the Laws* is without interest and can therefore be passed over in silence. The tone of Destutt de Tracy's *Commentary and Review* is set out in its very first sentence. "Laws are not," he writes, "as Montesquieu has asserted, 'necessary relations originating in the nature of things.' A law is not a relation, nor is a relation a law: the definition is not clear nor satisfactory" (CR, 13). Moving swiftly on, he next states that Montesquieu's all-important distinction between republican, monarchical, and despotic governments appears to him to be "essentially erroneous" and "every way defective" (CR, 16, 18). There is, Destutt de Tracy affirms, "no government which in its actual nature can be called *despotic*" (CR, 17). Despotic government, he contends, generally signifies a "monarchy where the manners are savage or brutal" (CR, 18) and, as he remarks later in the text, "monarchy in a state of stupidity" (CR, 35). Similarly, he argues that Montesquieu's comments on the "principles" of government are not "sufficiently perspicuous" and do not withstand "the test of sound criticism." If, for example, we can talk of "true honor, which covets applause for the good it produces alone," so too we can speak of "false honor." Is it certain, he asks, that virtue is the principle of republican government? If so, what is the virtue that is applicable to republics alone? As for Montesquieu's highest virtue, moderation, Destutt de Tracy is equally dismissive. Moderation, he writes, "according to the circumstances in which it is exhibited, or the motives by which it is dictated, is wisdom or weakness, magnanimity or meanness" (CR, 22). Much more is said about the "errors" of Montesquieu's classifications—it would be "tedious and difficult,"

* Page references are to the Liberty Fund edition and are cited in the text as CR.

Destutt de Tracy comments at one point, "to examine them separately" (CR, 39)—but in these circumstances, he felt that he had no alternative but to outline his own classification.

In short, Destutt de Tracy sets out a twofold classification of "the fundamental principles of political society." He does this by dividing all governments into two distinct classes: "*national*" and "*special.*" The first consists of governments that "recognize the principle, that all rights and power originate in, reside in, and belong to, the entire body of the people or the nation" (CR, 19). Such governments, Destutt de Tracy states, may take "any form"—be it pure democracies, representative democracies, aristocracies, or hereditary monarchies—but "so long as the fundamental principle of sovereignty remains in the people, and is not called into question, all these forms so different have this common characteristic, that they can be at any time modified, or even cease altogether." The second type of government extends to all governments where the sources of "power or right" are anything other than "the general will of the nation" (CR, 20). This would include divine authority, conquest, birth, and so on. Again, such governments might take a democratic, aristocratic, or monarchical form, but all are regimes where "particular or exclusive rights" are recognized in opposition to "general or national rights." As Destutt de Tracy remarks, "the general rights of men have no being here" (CR, 26). His preference for national over special governments is immediately apparent.

Building on his rejection of Montesquieu's tripartite classification of governments, Destutt de Tracy next seeks to examine the diverse forms taken by national and special governments. With regard to the former, Destutt de Tracy establishes that its first instantiation takes the form of a "simple democracy." This, he immediately concludes, is "an impracticable order of things," amounting to little more than "a government of savages" appropriate only to "the infant state of society" (CR, 48). Moreover, such democracies could only exist "in territories of small extent" (CR, 24). These, Destutt de Tracy suggests, might develop in several ways. They might be converted into "an aristocracy of some species." Here a privileged class and a common class would emerge, the pride and knowledge of the former and the humility and ignorance of the latter serving to preserve it as a form of government. Similarly, pure democracy might be transformed into one or another form of monarchy, the people submitting themselves to the authority of a single chief. In this case, the government is maintained by "the pride of the monarch, the exalted idea he entertains of his dignity, his superiority over those who surround him" (CR, 26).

Both these forms of government are included by Destutt de Tracy in the category of national governments and are so because it is possible that in both cases "the general principle of respect for the rights of men" might predominate. However, Destutt de Tracy recognizes that this fundamental principle is soon "forgotten or disavowed" in such regimes "almost universally" (CR, 26). They quickly turn into forms of special governments.

It is therefore Destutt de Tracy's considered view that the only form of national government that can remain true to the principle of the sovereignty of the people is representative democracy. Such a form of government, he states, is a new invention and had been unknown in Montesquieu's time. Here is a form of government where "all the associates called citizens, concur equally in choosing their representatives, define the authorities with which they are entrusted, and fix limits beyond which they must not trespass." This, he added, "is democracy rendered practicable for a long time and over a great extent of territory." The principles that sustained it were "love of country, and equality of rights, and, if you will, the love of peace and justice." Its citizens would display a "disposition to simplicity and independence" (CR, 24–25).

It is only later in Destutt de Tracy's text that he seeks to set out what he describes as "the principles of a truly free, legal, and peaceable constitution" (CR, 93) and thus to describe how he envisages that a system of representative government would work in practice. True to his stated intention of following the order of Montesquieu's own text, he next turns his attention to laws relating to education, but in doing so, he is again able to develop his distinction between national and special governments. In a hereditary monarchy, Destutt de Tracy writes, the prince is bound "to inculcate and propagate the maxims of passive obedience, and a profound veneration for the established forms, a confidence in the perpetuity of the political establishments, and a great dislike for the spirit of innovation and enquiry, or the discussion of political principles" (CR, 31). In aristocracies, education serves a similar purpose but with two notable differences. Having less claim to divine authority, aristocracies need to use the educative power of religion with "great circumspection and discretion" lest the priesthood should emerge as "formidable rivals" and "destroy" the power of the aristocracy. Nor should the aristocracy seek to combat religion by "enlightening the people," for to do so would be to "destroy the spirit of dependance and servility" and plunge the people into "disorder, intemperance, and vice." Rather, a sound education, encouraging "a disposition to study, an aptitude for business, a capacity for reflection," should be made available only to "the superior order of society," to the aristocracy itself (CR, 33–34).

As for "the class of governments denominated *national*, under the monarchical, aristocratical, and representative forms," Destutt de Tracy's opinion was that all should respect their people, "since their authority is delegated by the general will." It is not, he writes, in "their interest to debase or deprave the people, nor entirely to enervate or vitiate the minds of the higher class; for if they should succeed, the rights of men would soon be forgotten or misunderstood, and they would thereby lose the character of a national or patriotic government" (CR, 35). It is, however, to representative government that Destutt de Tracy again devotes most of his attention. Here, he writes, is a form of government that can "in no respect fear truth" since it is "founded solely on reason and nature." It ought therefore "constantly to attend to the propagation of accurate and solid knowledge" and combat "the worst of inequalities, . . . the inequality of talents and information, among the different members of society." In so doing, "the love of order, of industry, of justice, and reason" would be established (CR, 35–36).

An equally clear endorsement of representative government is found in Destutt de Tracy's discussion of Book V of *The Spirit of the Laws* devoted to the laws appropriate to different types of government. Once again, Destutt de Tracy does not hide his dissatisfaction with the arguments put forward by Montesquieu. On this subject, he writes, "many of the ideas which he offers, are unworthy of the sagacity of our illustrious author" (CR, 39). The comments on representative government are extensive and can therefore only be summarized here. Representative government, Destutt de Tracy begins, should be considered "the democracy of enlightened reason." "This form of government," he continues, "does not call for nor need the constraint of the human mind, the modification of our natural sentiments, the forcing of our desires, nor the excitement of imaginary passions, rival interests, or seductive illusions; it should, on the contrary, allow a free course to all inclinations which are not depraved, and to every kind of industry which is not incompatible with good order and morals: being conformable to nature, it requires only to be left to act" (CR, 42–43). It is a regime that tends to equality, eschews violent means, encourages talent, and ensures that wealth is "duly distributed, so as to go into the general mass, without any violation of the rights of nature." It does nothing "to impede men in their reasonable pursuits or natural inclinations" (CR, 43).

The next sections of Destutt de Tracy's commentary continue the discussion of these themes, if only tangentially. In brief, the structure of Montesquieu's own text obliges him to address inter alia issues relating to civil and criminal laws, the role of juries, the appropriate severity of punishments, the use of torture, and the utility or otherwise of sumptuary laws. In this context, he also examines the question of the appropriate size of a polity, pointing out correctly that the United States shows that a republic does not have to be small in territorial scale.

It is only when Destutt de Tracy comes to examine Book XI of *The Spirit of the Laws*, devoted to the relationship of law to public liberty, that he is able to return fully to the questions that most interest him. Again, such is the complexity of Destutt de Tracy's argumentation that only a sketch can be provided. Crucially, Destutt de Tracy seeks to define the meaning of liberty, recognizing that it is only when it is properly defined that we are able to assess the impact of a constitutional and political form upon its members. Again, Destutt de Tracy contradicts Montesquieu's definition of liberty. "The idea of liberty," Destutt de Tracy tells us, "is nothing more than the idea of the power to do that which the mind wills; and in general, to be free is to be enabled to do what we please" (CR, 85). Liberty, then, "is nothing else than the power of executing the will, and accomplishing our desires" (CR, 86). It follows that liberty and happiness are the same thing, and thus that "entire liberty" is "inseparable from perfect happiness" (CR, 86). This, Destutt de Tracy remarks, explains why people are so passionately fond of liberty. The argument entails a very important conclusion: namely, that the government under which the greatest liberty exists is the best government because "the greatest number of people are the happiest" (CR, 88). Not surprisingly, this would be the case under a regime that provided "a great facility" (CR, 88) for the people to make their wishes known.

It is precisely at this point that Destutt de Tracy addresses what he terms Montesquieu's "prepossession in favor of English institutions" (CR, 90). In brief, Destutt de Tracy is unconvinced by the accuracy of Montesquieu's description of the English constitution and in particular by the claims he made for the tripartite division of powers as a protector of individual liberty. "The great problem, therefore, of the distribution of the powers of society, so that neither of them may trespass on the authority of the other, or the limits assigned them by the general interests," Destutt de Tracy writes, "is not . . . resolved in that country." This "honor," he states, rests with the United States of America (CR, 93).

As Destutt de Tracy's text shows, his next move is to seek to establish what he describes as "the principles of a truly free, legal, and peaceable constitution" (CR, 93). These principles, he states unambiguously, are not to be found in the institutions of hereditary monarchy. "To hope for liberty and monarchy," Destutt de Tracy writes, "is to expect two things each of which excludes the other" (CR, 111). Rather, Destutt de Tracy opts for a regime based upon universal male suffrage (women, he writes, "are certainly destined for domestic duties, and men for public functions" [CR, 102]) that follows a complicated pattern of indirect election. To overcome possible conflicts between the legislative and executive branches of government, he recommends the creation of "a preserving power" or "conservative body" (CR, 114) to be "composed of a small number of persons elected for a limited time, and partially renewing itself at fixed periods and numbers" (CR, 112). This body, he writes, is "the keystone of the arch, without which the edifice of society has neither strength nor durability" (CR, 115). There would be no bicameral legislature, but Destutt de Tracy insists on the independence of the judiciary. Destutt de Tracy ends this part of his account by stating that political liberty "cannot subsist without individual liberty and that of the press; and that for the preservation of this last, all arbitrary seizure and detention should be proscribed, and the use of trial by jury adopted" (CR, 120). These, he reflects, are freedoms the French had been willing to give up "without the least murmur, and almost with pleasure" (CR, 116). Destutt de Tracy's concluding point is that constitutional questions will only be resolved by "never giving to a single man, any more power than can be taken from him without violence; and that when he is changed, all shall not change with him" (CR, 124–125). Here too the French had failed to set a good example.

At this point in his discussion, Destutt de Tracy declares himself to be "desirous of resting a while." This is so because, like many of Montesquieu's readers, he recognizes that the focus of *The Spirit of the Laws* is about to change. Matters relating to the organization of society and the distribution of its powers are now to be superseded by "a multitude of subjects for our contemplation." These, Destutt de Tracy writes, include "taxes, climate, the nature of the soil, the state of intelligence and habits, commerce, money, population, religion, the successive revolutions of certain laws, civil and political, in particular nations" (CR, 128–129). Once more, our discussion must be brief, and the focus will fall upon points raised in the earlier discussion of *The Spirit of the Laws*.

Immediately noticeable is that Destutt de Tracy finds little of interest or merit in Montesquieu's opinions. Arguing that as societies become more civilized, the influence of climate becomes less, he comments that "Montesquieu has not perceived all the causes of the influence of climate, and . . . has exaggerated its effects" (CR, 159). Of Montesquieu's views on commerce, he likewise suggests that he has "not the least idea of the manner in which the riches of nations are formed and distributed" (CR, 179). Why, he asks of the comment of Montesquieu that all errors should not be corrected, should this be so (CR, 165)? Of Books XXVI–XXX of *The Spirit of the Laws* Destutt de Tracy simply declares that he has nothing to say.

Instead, Destutt de Tracy focuses upon a series of questions that he would later address at greater length in his *Treatise on Political Economy*. In essence, Destutt de Tracy jettisons Montesquieu's emphasis on geography and climate as causal factors in societal development and replaces them with a vision of society as "nothing more than a continual exchange of mutual succours, which occasion the concurrence of the powers of all for the more effectual gratification of the wants of each" (CR, 169). In doing so, he discards the economic theories of both mercantilism and physiocracy, replacing them with those of Adam Smith and his fellow *idéologue* Jean-Baptiste Say. Destutt de Tracy also abandons what was the then-fashionable enthusiasm among economists for population growth. Our "principal object," he writes, "should be to render [men] happy, and not to encrease their numbers to an excess" (CR, 202).

The questions that preoccupy Destutt de Tracy in the final sections of his text therefore are those of the creation of wealth and who its creators are. This first entails a lengthy disquisition on the principles of taxation. Destutt de Tracy's conclusions might best be gleaned via a reading of the following quotation:

> All those imposts upon merchandize, whatever they may be, require a multitude of restraints, precautions, and formalities. They occasion a variety of ruinous interruptions in the pursuits of the active citizen, and are very much subject to be arbitrary; they cause actions indifferent in themselves, to be converted into crimes, which are often expiated by inhuman penalties. Their collection is expensive, requiring almost an army of officers, and producing a multitude of peculators, all of whom become lost to society, and maintain against it real civil war, and all the consequences fatal to social economy and public morals. (CR, 136)

In short, it was absurd to believe that high taxation could be a good in itself. Rather, it was the "most economical" government that was the best, and this was so not only because taxation was a restraint upon the free action of the individual but because "almost all public expenditure" could be classified as "sterile and unproductive" and thus "ruinous" to the well-being of society in general.

As for commerce, an activity that, in Destutt de Tracy's view, consists in exchange and as such is an attribute peculiar to human beings, it is "the foundation and basis of society" (CR, 169). It can only ever be a good and of use because it enables man "to procure that which he is in want of" (CR, 169) and does so with reciprocal benefit. Moreover, Destutt de Tracy seeks to extend the category of those engaged in commerce to include all those involved in productive labor. "In all cases," Destutt de Tracy writes, "there is a complete similitude between the labor of the trader, and that of the farmer or the manufacturer: the one is not more or less *essentially productive* than the other" (CR, 175). To that extent, if society is commerce, "labor is wealth" (CR, 170). This is so because, apart from the manufacture of luxury goods and unnecessary merchandise, all labor, be it in the manufacture or transport of products, results in a new utility.

The greater part of this discussion is devoted to topics such as the division of labor and the balance of trade. In particular, Destutt de Tracy advocates the merits of internal free trade as opposed to foreign trade. It might be fitting to conclude this brief exposition of Destutt de Tracy's ideas by citing his views on a theme that was undoubtedly dear to Montesquieu: the moral effects of commerce. "It is easy to perceive," Destutt de Tracy writes,

> that commerce, that is exchange, being in truth society itself, it is the only bond among men; the source of all their moral sentiments; and the first and most powerful cause of the improvement of their mutual sensibility and reciprocal benevolence: we owe to it all that we are possessed of, good or amiable; it commences by uniting all the men of the same tribe; it afterwards unites those societies with each other, and finishes by connecting all parts of the universe: it excites, extends, and propagates information, as well as reciprocal intercourse: it is the author of all social good. (CR, 188)

Publication of the *Commentary*

Destutt de Tracy's *Commentary and Review of Montesquieu's Spirit of Laws* was published by William Duane in Philadelphia on 4 July 1811. As we have seen, Destutt de Tracy was delighted with the volume, and so much so that it was not to be long before he was to write again to Jefferson to suggest that he might oversee the translation of another work: his recently completed *Traité de l'économie*. As he told Jefferson in a letter of 15 November 1811, this contained "a more methodical and detailed exposition of the principles" in the *Commentary and Review* (Chinard, 99). Jefferson agreed to this proposal and consequently found himself engaged upon another time-consuming and energy-sapping undertaking. The book finally appeared under the title *A Treatise on Political Economy* in March 1817, some two years after it had been published in France as *Élémens d'Idéologie: IV partie: Traité de la volonté*. The significance of this is that this new volume replicated (at times verbatim) large parts of the argument devoted to taxation, luxury, commerce, population, and money to be found in the later sections of the *Commentary and Review*.

It was also in 1817 that the first edition of Destutt de Tracy's *Commentaire sur l'Esprit des Lois de Montesquieu* was published in French. It was printed in Liège, in what was then the United Kingdom of the Netherlands, and the author's identity again remained a secret, the publisher maintaining the pretense that the author lived in the United States. In a letter to Jefferson, dated 10 March 1819, Destutt de Tracy indicated that the edition had been produced with his "tacit consent" but not under his "supervision," with the result that the editors had taken "many liberties with the text" and had frequently changed its style. This, he commented, was of little importance: what mattered was that the book was now freely on sale in France (Chinard, 192).

It was when this edition was reprinted by the Parisian publisher Delaunay in 1819, again anonymously, that Destutt de Tracy resolved to publish an accurate and faithful edition identifying himself as the author. This he did in July of that year, adding his earlier essay of 1798, *Quels sont les moyens de fonder la morale d'un peuple?*, as an appendix.* The new preface recorded that the book had originally been written for Jefferson, "the man of the two worlds," Destutt de Tracy wrote, "that I most admire." There was, however, one very serious difficulty faced by Destutt de Tracy. The First Empire of Napoleon Bonaparte was a thing of the past and France was now a constitutional monarchy: How might the forthright criticisms of monarchy contained in the *Commentaire* be received? Destutt de Tracy neatly sidestepped this issue by adding a lengthy footnote to clarify his position. "I am quite convinced," he wrote,

---

* Antoine Louis Claude Destutt de Tracy, *Quels sont les moyens de fonder la morale d'un peuple?* (Paris: Agasse, 1798).

"that constitutional monarchy, or government represented by a single hereditary ruler is and will be for an extremely long time, and despite its imper-
fections, the best of all possible governments for all the peoples of Europe,
especially for France." This, he continued, was not to contradict himself but
"to establish the very important difference that all wise men cannot but recognize between the abstractions of theory and the realities of practice."*

Although heavily criticized in the royalist press, the book met with immediate success, with seven editions being published in France by 1827. German, Italian, and Spanish translations swiftly followed. Destutt de Tracy's salon
now came to attract many of the rising stars of the Parisian intellectual world.
These included Charles Dunoyer and Charles Comte, both of whom became
advocates of the doctrine of *industrialisme*. It was via this route that the ideas
of the *Commentaire* became integrated into the radical economic liberalism that
emerged in France during the 1820s. Tracing the influence of Destutt de
Tracy and his *Commentary and Review* in the United States is less easy, despite
the obvious appeal of his praise of the American constitution. Perhaps, therefore, the last word should be given to Thomas Jefferson. Destutt de Tracy's
Commentary and Review and the *Treatise of Political Economy*, he wrote in
December 1820, "will become the Statesman's Manuel with us, and they certainly shall be the elementary books of the political department in our new
University. This institution of my native state, the hobby of my old age, will
be based on the illimitable freedom of the human mind, to explore and to
expose every subject susceptible of its contemplation" (Chinard, 203).

* Antoine Louis Claude Destutt de Tracy, *Commentaire sur L'Esprit des Lois de
Montesquieu* (Paris: Desoer, 1819), 211.

Note on the Text

As has been seen in the introduction, Thomas Jefferson was not happy with the finished translation of Destutt de Tracy's text. Yet, in a letter written on 28 November 1813, he told Destutt de Tracy that someone had taken Jefferson himself to be the author and that this person was translating what was mistakenly believed to be the original English text into French! "In a letter which I am now writing him," Jefferson explained, "I shall set him right about myself . . . and shall discourage his perseverance in translating into French . . . a translation . . . where the author's meaning has sometimes been illy understood, sometimes mistaken, and often expressed in words not best chosen."*

The truth of the matter, as Jefferson also acknowledged, is that the translation of a text from one language to another is never an easy and straightforward task. Moreover, Destutt de Tracy's original manuscript would have presented even the most experienced translator with some serious challenges. To that extent, Jefferson and his colleagues should be congratulated on doing a good job in difficult circumstances.

That said, the translation is far from perfect. At times it is poor and there are also errors. For the most part, it conforms to the meaning of the French version, but both the paragraph and sentence construction of the latter are frequently changed. In some cases, what were footnotes figure as part of the text. Italics are used fairly randomly, and quotations in Destutt de Tracy's text are often not acknowledged as such or misquoted. Commas are used in a haphazard fashion and certainly not in line with contemporary usage. Many paragraphs are littered with ellipses between or within sentences. Occasionally, parts of the French text are missing.

It would, however, have been a mistake to seek to change the translation in order to remove these weaknesses. The document is itself a historical

---

* Gilbert Chinard, *Jefferson et les Idéologues d'après sa correspondence inédite* (Baltimore: Johns Hopkins University Press, 1925), 119.

document, and therefore corrections to grammar, spelling, and punctuation have been kept to a minimum. Inappropriate ellipses have been removed throughout. I also provide a series of notes that at times point out errors in the translation and certain textual infelicities but also provide additional information on Destutt de Tracy's references to historical figures, events, literary sources, and so on. The footnotes written by Thomas Jefferson are numbered consecutively throughout the book, and those written by me are referenced with symbols or are within brackets.

A

COMMENTARY AND REVIEW

OF

MONTESQUIEU'S SPIRIT OF LAWS.

PREPARED FOR PRESS

FROM

THE ORIGINAL MANUSCRIPT,

IN THE HANDS OF THE PUBLISHER.

TO WHICH ARE ANNEXED,

OBSERVATIONS ON THE THIRTY-FIRST BOOK,

BY THE LATE M. CONDORCET:

AND

TWO LETTERS OF HELVETIUS,

ON THE MERITS OF THE SAME WORK.

Ignorance of the signification of words, which is want of understanding, dispos-
eth men to take on trust, not only the truth they know not, but also the errors,
and which is more, the nonsense of them they trust: for neither error nor sense
can, without a perfect understanding of words, be detected.

HOBBES' LEVIATHAN, CHAP. 11.

The most certain means of rendering a people free and happy, is to establish a
perfect method of education. BECCARIA.

PHILADELPHIA: PRINTED BY WILLIAM DUANE.

NO. 98, MARKET STREET.

1811.

Contents

CONTENTS

CONTENTS

CONTENTS

> Certain climates have different inconveniencies, for man: institutions and habits may remedy them to a certain point: good laws are those which effect this end.
>
> SPIRIT OF LAWS, BOOK XIV.

> The progress of wealth and civilization, multiplying the chances of inequality among men; inequality is the cause of servitude, and the source of all the evils and vices of human society.
>
> SPIRIT OF LAWS, BOOK XVIII.

> For the best laws the mind should be prepared: wherefore, the legislative power should be exercised by delegates freely chosen for a limited period, from all parts of the territory.
>
> SPIRIT OF LAWS, BOOK XIX.

> Merchants are the agents of certain exchanges; money is the instrument employed to effect it; but this is not commerce, which really consists in simple exchanges. Commerce is society itself; it is an attribute of man; it is the source of all human good; its principal use is in stimulating industry; it is thus it has civilized the world: it weakens the spirit of devastation. The pretended balance of commerce is illusive and trifling.

APPENDIX.

CONTENTS

CONTENTS

The Author,

TO HIS FELLOW CITIZENS OF THE
UNITED STATES OF AMERICA.

I am a Frenchman by birth and education. I was an early friend to the revolution of France, and continued to support it, until those entrusted with its helm, had evidently changed its direction. Flying then from the tyrannies of the monster Robespierre, I found, and still enjoy, safety, freedom, and hospitality, among you. I am grateful for these boons, and anxious to shew that gratitude, by such services as my faculties and habits enable me to render. Reading and contemplation have been the occupations of my life, and mostly on those subjects which concern the condition of man. Montesquieu's immortal work on the Spirit of Laws, could not fail, of course, to furnish matter for profound consideration. I have admired his vivid imagination, his extensive reading, and dexterous use of it. But I have not been blind to his paradoxes, his inconsistencies, and whimsical combinations. And I have thought the errors of his book, the more important to be corrected, as its truths are numerous, and of powerful influence on the opinions of society. These opinions attemper the principles on which governments are administered, on which so much depend the happiness and misery of man. Few nations are in a situation to profit by the detection of political errors, or to shape their practice by newly developed truths. This is the eminent advantage of the country in which I write. Had its language been more familiar to me, I should with pleasure have made it the original medium of submitting to you my reflections, and of explaining the grounds of my cordial esteem for the principles of your government. Their translation, however, is committed to one well skilled in both languages, and, should it be desired at any future time, the original composition shall be at the command of those for whom it has been written.

A Commentary and Review
of The Spirit of Laws.

✦

Preliminary Observations.

MY object in undertaking this work, was to examine and reflect on each of the great objects which had been discussed by Montesquieu; to form my own opinions, to commit them to writing, and in short, to accomplish a clear and settled judgment upon them. It was not very long before I perceived, that a collection of these opinions would form a complete treatise on politics or the social science, which would be of some value, if the principles were all just and well digested. After having scrutinized them with all the care that I was capable of, and reconsidered them well, I resolved to arrange the whole in another manner, so as to form a didactic work, in which the various subjects should be disposed in their natural order, consistent with their mutual dependence on each other, and without any regard to the order pursued by Montesquieu; which in my opinion is not in every respect the best: but I soon perceived, that if he had been mistaken in the choice of his order of discussion, I might be much more likely to deceive myself in attempting a new one, notwithstanding the vast accumulation of light, during the fifty *prodigious* years which have intervened between the period when he gave his labors to his contemporaries, and this at which I now present the result of my studies to mine. It was plain too, that in proportion as the order which I should have preferred differed from that of Montesquieu, the more difficult it would have been for me to discuss his opinions and establish my own; our paths must cross each other continually; I should have been forced into a multitude of repetitions, in order to render to him that justice which properly belongs to him; and I should then find myself reduced to the unpleasant necessity of appearing in opposition to him, without my motives being clearly perceived. Under such circumstances, it is questionable whether my ideas would ever have had the advantage of a sufficient examination: these considerations determined me to prefer the form I have adopted of a commentary and review of Montesquieu's Spirit of Laws.

Some future writer, if my effort be fortunate, may profit by the discussion, in giving a more perfect treatise on the true principles of laws: it is by such a course, I think all the sciences ought to proceed; each work commencing with the soundest opinions already received, and progressively receiving the new lights shed upon them by experience and investigation. This would be truly following the precept of Condillac: *proceeding rigorously from the known to the unknown.* I have no other ambition, nor does my situation admit of more, than to contribute my effort to the progress of social science, the most important of all to the happiness of man, and that which must necessarily be the last to reach perfection, because it is the product and the result of all the other sciences.

BOOK I.

Of Laws in General.

Positive laws ought to be consequent of the laws of nature: this is the spirit of laws.

MONTESQUIEU'S SPIRIT OF LAWS.

LAWS are not, as Montesquieu has asserted, "necessary relations originating in the nature of things." A law is not a relation, nor is a relation a law: the definition is not clear nor satisfactory. The word law has its special and appropriate sense: this sense is always to be found in the original meaning of words, and to which recourse must be had in order to their being rightly understood. Here law means a rule of action, prescribed by an authority invested with competent power and a right so to do: this last condition is essential, and when it is not possessed, the rule is no longer a law, but an arbitrary command, an act of violence and usurpation.

This idea of law comprehends that of a penalty consequent of its infraction, of a tribunal which determines the penalty, and a physical force to put it into execution: without these attributes laws are inefficient and illusory.

Such is the primitive sense of the word law; it was not, nor could it be formed, until after society had commenced: after which, and when the reciprocal action of sensible beings upon each other was perceived, when the phenomena of nature and of reason were discovered, and when it came to be found out, that they operated in an uniform manner in similar circumstances, it was said that they followed or obeyed certain laws. These were metaphorically denominated the *laws of nature*, being only an expression significant of the manner in which the phenomena constantly act. Thus with reference to the descent of heavy bodies, we say that it is the effect of gravitation, one of the laws of nature, *that a heavy body abandoned to itself, falls by an accelerated motion proportionate to the series of odd numbers, so that the spaces passed through are as the squares of the times of its movement.*

In other words, we mean to say that this phenomenon takes effect, as if an irresistible power had so ordained it, under the penalty of inevitable annihilation to the things subjected to this law of nature. We likewise say, it is the law of nature, that an animated being must be either in a state of *enjoying* or *suffering;* thereby implying that one or the other sensation takes place in the individual, through the medium of his perceptions, upon which he forms a judgment; which is only the consciousness of the individual to the feeling of pleasure or pain; that in consequence of this judgment, a will and a desire are produced to obtain or to avoid the operation of those perceptions, and to be happy or unhappy as the will or desire are gratified, or the contrary; by which we also imply, that an animated being is so constituted in the order of its nature, that if it were not susceptible of such perceptions and their consequent effects, it would then not be what we call an animated being.

Here we behold what is meant by the *laws of nature.* There are then laws of nature, which we cannot change, which we cannot even infringe with impunity; for we are not the authors of our own being, nor of any thing that surrounds us. Thus if we leave a heavy body without support we are subject to be crushed by its fall. So if we do not make provision for the accomplishment of our wishes, or, what will amount to the same, if we cherish desires that are unattainable, we become unhappy; this is beyond doubt, the supreme power, the infallible tribunal, the force irresistible, the inevitable punition, that follows, in which every consequence arises as if it had been so predetermined.

Now society makes what we call positive laws, that is laws which are artificial and conventional, by means of an authority purposely constituted, and with tribunals and an executive power to inforce them. These laws should be conformable to the laws of nature, originating in the same source, consequent of the natural laws, and no wise repugnant thereto; without which consonance, it is certain that nature will overcome them, that their object will not be accomplished, and that society must be unhappy. Whence originate the good or bad qualities of our positive laws, their justice or injustice? The just law is that which produces *good,* the unjust that which produces *evil.*

Justice and injustice therefore had an existence before any positive law; although it is only to laws of our own creation we can apply the epithets of just or unjust; since the laws of nature being simply necessary in the nature of things, it belongs not to us to question them any more than to act contrary to them. Unquestionably justice and injustice existed before any of our laws, and had it not been so we should not have any, because we create nothing. It does not appertain to us to constitute things conformable or contrary to our nature. We can ascertain and explain what is right or wrong, only according to our right or wrong comprehension of it; when we declare that to be just which is not so, we do not thereby render it just; this is beyond our power; we only declare an error, and occasion a certain quantity of evil, by maintaining that error with the power of which we have the disposal: but the *law*, the eternal truth, which is opposed thereto, remains unchanged and the same.

But it must be understood, that what is here said by no means implies, that it is at all times just to resist an unjust law, or always reasonable to oppose with violence what is unreasonable. This must depend upon a previous consideration, whether the violent resistance would not cause more evil than passive compliance: this however is but a secondary question, always dependent on circumstances, the nature of which will be discussed in the sequel. We are yet a great way in the rear of that subject.

It is sufficient that the laws of nature exist anterior and superior to human laws; that fundamental justice is that only which is conformable to the laws of nature; and that radical injustice is that which is contrary to the laws of nature; and consequently that our posterior and consequent laws should be in unison with those more ancient and inevitable laws. This is the true spirit, or genuine sense, in which all positive laws ought to be established. But this foundation of the laws is not very easily explained or understood: the space between the first principles and the ultimate result is immense. The progressive series of consequences flowing out of the first principles are the proper subject of a treatise on the spirit of laws, which should be perspicuously pointed out, and its maxims modified to the particular circumstances and organization of society. We shall now proceed to examine these different principles.

BOOK II.

Of Laws Originating Directly from the Nature of the Government.

There are only two kinds of government: those founded on the general rights of man, and those founded on particular rights.

SPIRIT OF LAWS, BOOK II.

THE ordinary division of governments into republican, monarchical, and despotic, appears to me essentially erroneous.

The word *republican* is itself a very vague term, comprehending in it a multitude of forms of government very different from each other: from the peaceable *democracy* of Schwitz,* the turbulent *mixed government* of Athens, to the concentrated *aristocracy* of Berne, and the gloomy *oligarchy* of Venice. Moreover the term republic cannot be contrasted with that of monarchy, for the United Provinces of Holland, and the United States of America, have each a single chief magistrate, and are yet considered republics; beside, that it has always been uncertain whether we should say the *kingdom* or *republic* of Poland.

The word monarchy properly designates a government in which the executive power is vested in a single person: though this is only a circumstance which may be connected with others of a very different nature, and which is not essentially characteristic of the social organization. What we have said of Poland, Holland, and the *American government,* confirms this; to these Sweden and Great Britain may be added, which in many respects are regal aristocracies. The Germanic body might also be cited, which with much reason

---

* A reference to the Canton of Schwyz, one of the original members of the Swiss Confederation. It was known for its tradition of direct democracy.

has been often called a republic of sovereign princes:* and even the ancient government of France; for those perfectly acquainted with it, know that it was properly an ecclesiastical and feudal aristocracy, a government of the gown[†] and sword.

The word despotic implies an abuse; a vice more or less to be met with in all governments, for all human institutions are, like their authors, imperfect: but it is not the name of any particular form of society or government. Despotism, oppression, or abuse of power, takes place whenever the established laws are without force, or when they give way to the illegal authority of one or several men. This may be every where perceived from time to time. In many countries men have been either not sufficiently prudent or too ignorant to take precautions against this evil; in others the means adopted have proved insufficient; but in no place has it been established as a principle, that it should be so, not even in the East: there is then no government which in its actual nature can be called *despotic.*

If there were such a government in the world, it would be that of Denmark;[‡] where the nation, after having shaken off the yoke of the priests and nobles, and fearing their influence in the assembly, if again convened, requested the king to govern alone and of himself, confiding to him the care of making such laws as he might judge necessary for the good of the state: since which period he has never been called upon to give an account of this discretionary power. Nevertheless this government, so unlimited in its legislation, has been so moderately conducted, that it cannot with propriety be said to be despotic, for it has never been contemplated even to restrain its authority. Yet notwithstanding this moderation, many persons have continued to consider Denmark as a despotic state.

The same may be said of the French government, if we view it in the sense given by many writers to the celebrated maxims: "The king depends on himself and God alone," and "As the king wills so does the law."

These are the maxims to which the kings of that country have frequently referred in using the expression "God and my sword," inferring that they

---

* A reference to the Holy Roman Empire.

† This is usually translated as "robe."

‡ During the course of the eighteenth century, Denmark became an absolute monarchy, but monarchs remained weak, with non-noble landowners becoming the real rulers of the country.

acknowledged no other superior right. These pretensions have not indeed been always admitted, but if we suppose them to be acknowledged in theory, yet France, notwithstanding the enormous abuses which existed, could not be called a despotic state; on the contrary it has always been cited as a tempered monarchy. This is not then what is to be understood by a despotic government, and the denomination is not correct as a specific term, for generally it signifies a monarchy where the manners are savage or brutal.

Hence it is inferred that the division of governments, into republican, monarchical, and despotic, is every way defective, and that all of these classes, containing very opposite and very different forms, the explanation of each of them must be very vague, or not applicable to all the states comprised in the class; nor shall I adopt the positive decision of Helvetius in his letter to Montesquieu:[1] "I know only two kinds of government, the good and the bad; the good, which are yet to be formed; and the bad, the grand secret of which is to draw by a variety of means, the money of the governed into the pockets of the rulers," &c.

FIRST. If we only look to the practical effects, in this, as in all other circumstances, we find good and evil every where, and that there is no form of government which may not at some time be classed among the good or the bad.

SECONDLY. If, on the contrary, the theory only be regarded, and the principles alone on which governments are founded, be taken into our consideration, without enquiring whether they operate conformable to their theory or not, it would be necessary then to arrange each government under a good or a bad class, that we may examine the merit or justice of its principles, and thereby determine which are true, and which are false; now this is what I do not undertake to do, I will only, like Montesquieu, exhibit what exists, and point out the different consequences arising from the various modes of social organization, leaving it to the reader to form such conclusions as he may think fit, in favor of the one or the other.

1. This letter, however, in my opinion, appears to contain many excellent things, as well as that to Saurin, and the notes of the same author on the Spirit of Laws. To the abbé de la Roche, we are indebted for having preserved the ideas of so worthy a man, on subjects so important, and for having published them in the edition which he has given the world of Montesquieu's works, printed by P. Didot, Paris. [These letters are translated for, and inserted at the end of this work.]

Confining myself, then, wholly to the fundamental principles of political society, disregarding the difference of forms, neither censuring nor approving any, I will divide all governments into two classes, one of these I denominate *national*, in which social rights are common to all; the other *special*, establishing or recognizing particular or unequal rights.[2]

In whatever manner governments may be organized, I shall place in the first class, all those which recognize the principle, that all rights and power originate in, reside in, and belong to, the entire body of the people or nation; and that none exists, but what is derived from, and exercised for the nation; those, in short, which explicitly and without reserve, maintain the maxim expressed in the parliament of Paris,* in the month of October, 1788, by one of its members, namely, *Magistrates as magistrates, have only duties to perform, citizens alone have rights;* understanding by the term magistrate, any person whatever who is invested with a public function.

The governments which I call *national*, may therefore take any form, for a nation may itself exercise all the necessary powers, and then it would be a simple democracy; it may on the contrary delegate the whole effective power to functionaries elected by the people for a limited period, subject to a renewal from time to time; then it would be a representative democracy; the nation may also abandon its power, wholly or partially, to numerous, or select bodies of men, either for life, with hereditary succession, or with the power of nominating their colleagues in cases of vacancy; and these would be different kinds of aristocracies: the nation may in like manner intrust all its power, or only the executive power, to one man, either for life, or in hereditary succession, and this would produce a monarchy more or less limited, or even without limits.

But so long as the fundamental principle of sovereignty remains in the people, and is not called into question, all these forms so different have this common characteristic, that they can be at any time modified, or even cease altogether, as soon as it shall be the will of the nation; and that there is no one who can have any right to oppose the general will when manifested according to the established form: now this essential circumstance, is in my opinion,

---

2. We might also say *public* and *private*, not only because some are founded in the general interest, and others in particular interests, but because some in all their deliberations affect publicity, others mystery.

* This is a reference to the *parlement* of Paris, which was a law court rather than a parliament.

sufficient to discriminate between the various organizations of society, and to designate a single class of the species of government.

On the other hand, I call all those *special* governments, whatever may be their forms, where any other sources of power or right, than the general will of the nation, are admitted as legitimate; such as divine authority, conquest, birth in a particular place or tribe, mutual articles of agreement, a social compact manifest or tacit, where the parties enter into stipulations like powers foreign to each other, &c. It is evident that these different sources of particular rights, may, like the general will, produce all forms, the democratic, aristocratic, and the monarchical; but they are very different from those of the same name, which are classed under the denomination of national. In this practical class there are different rights known and avowed, and as it were different powers or sovereignties exercised in the same society. Its organization can only be considered as the result of convention, and formal or tacit stipulations, which cannot be changed without the mutual consent of all the contracting parties. These properties of governments are sufficient to authorise the denomination of *special*.

I again repeat, that it is not my purpose to determine, nor even to enquire, at present, whether all these particular and general rights are equally respectable, whether the special can prescribe in perpetuity against the common rights; or whether they can be legitimately opposed to the general will, properly expressed. These questions are too frequently resolved by force, and besides do not come within the scope of my views. All these modes of government exist or may exist. Every existing body has the right of self-preservation. This, with Montesquieu, is the point I set out from; and with him, I will examine which are the laws that tend to the conservation of each of them. I persuade myself that in the course of this enquiry it will be perceived, that the classification which I have made is better adapted for penetrating the depths of the subject than that which he has employed.

BOOK III.

Of the Principles of the Three Forms of Government.

Principles of the governments founded on the rights of man and reason.

SPIRIT OF LAWS, BOOK III.

WITH Helvetius, I think Montesquieu would have been more judicious had he entitled this book *Consequences of the nature of governments:* for what does he here propose but to enquire, what sentiments ought to animate the members of society, in order to ensure the existence of the government established; now this may, it is true, be called the conservative principle, but not the moving principle, which is always united with some species of magistracy exercising power and giving it impulsion. The cause of conservation in a commercial association, is interest, and the zeal of its members; but its principle of action is found in the agent or agents charged with conducting its concerns, whose skill and zeal excites its determinations and ultimately accounts for their success. It is the same with all societies, unless we should at once conclude that the general principles of action are interest and necessity, which indeed is true, but in so general a sense that it becomes trivial in each particular case.

Under every circumstance it is apparent, that those different sentiments which Montesquieu considers as the *moving principles of each government,* should be analogous to the nature of the government established, otherwise they must overturn it. But is it certain, as he says, that virtue is the principle of a republican government, honor that of a monarchy, fear that of despotism: are these characteristics sufficiently perspicuous and appropriate?

There can be no doubt that fear is the cause of despotism, because the most certain means of producing oppression is the exhibition of cowardice. But we have already remarked, that despotism is an abuse, from which no description of government is wholly exempt. Now if a reasonable man resolves often, or very often, to endure abuses, through a desire to shun worse consequences, he wishes to be determined in his conduct by reason and not by fear; besides that it is not to be supposed that any man will seek the means of perpetuating or increasing the abuses under which he suffers. Montesquieu himself says, that *although the manner of obeying be different in these two governments (monarchy and despotism) the power is still the same; to whatever side the monarch inclines he destroys the equilibrium and is obeyed, all the difference is this, in the monarchy the prince is enlightened, the ministers possess more talents, and are better acquainted with the affairs of government, than in a despotism.* But these are not two different kinds of governments, the one is only an abuse of the other, as we have already said; and in this sense a despotism is only a monarchy, with savage or brutal manners: we shall therefore say no more of despotism, or a government of fear.

With respect to *honor* accompanied by *ambition*, which is said to be the principle of monarchy; and *virtue* the supposed principle of a republic, which is transformed into *moderation* when the republic is aristocratic; will the descriptions stand the test of sound criticism? What is honor? Is there not a true honor, which covets applause for the good it produces alone, and requires only to be exempt from unjust reproach? Is there not a false honor which exhibits merely a glittering exterior, indifferent to vice, and entitled only to contempt? And what is ambition? Is there not also a generous ambition, which aspires only at promoting the good of equals, and is satisfied with its success and the gratitude which it produces? And is there not another sort of ambition, which thirsts after power for its pomp, and is alike indifferent to every means by which its ends can be accomplished? Is it not equally notorious, that *moderation*, according to the circumstances in which it is exhibited, or the motives by which it is dictated, is wisdom or weakness, magnanimity or meanness.

Then what is this virtue which is applicable to republics alone? Can true virtue be any where out of its place? And has Montesquieu seriously dared to advance this as a truth! Vice or false virtue is as frequently found in a monarchy, as qualities really meritorious; but because he draws a frightful picture of courts, in Chap. V. is it certain that it must be desirable or inevitable that they should be so. I cannot assent to such an opinion.[3]

3. The following are the expressions of the man so often quoted as the great partisan of monarchy.

Ambition in idleness, meanness in pride, the desire of becoming rich without industry; aversion from truth; flattery, treason, perfidy, infidelity to engage-

In truth what Montesquieu has said on this subject, may be reduced to two points. First, in governments where there are, and must be from their form, distinct and rival classes, interests distinct from the general body of society may answer the purpose of accomplishing the ends of the association. Second, by supposing, that in what Montesquieu calls a monarchy, the authority may be more compact and powerful than in what he calls a republic, it can without the same danger employ vicious persons, and profit by their talents without taking their motives into consideration; to which we may add with him, that on this account there must be a greater proportion of vice in the nation at large, than under a different order of things. This appears to me, all that is plausible in his opinion; to go beyond this would evidently be to err.

As, for reasons already given, we could not adopt the classification of governments laid down by Montesquieu, so we shall not follow him in the details arising out of the subject, but make use of that which we have adopted for the elucidation of our own ideas; beginning with the governments which we denominate national; that is to say, those which are founded on the maxim, that all rights and powers belong to and emanate from the people or body of the nation.

Among the various forms which this class of governments may assume, a simple democracy is almost impracticable. It can exist but for a short time, and among hordes of savages, or among nations but a little more civilized, in some insulated corner of the earth, where the bonds of society are not closer drawn than among savages. In every other circumstance, where the social relations are more intimate and multiform, it cannot exist for any considerable time, and soon ends in anarchy, which brings on aristocracy or tyranny through the

----

ments; contempt for the duties of a citizen, apprehension from virtue in the prince, and hope from his imbecility; above all, the invariable ridicule thrown upon virtue; constitute I believe the characteristics of the greater number of courtiers in all places and times: now it is very improbable that the greater part of the leaders of a state should be dishonest, and those under them honest; that those should be deceivers and these consent to be dupes.

If among the people there should unfortunately be some honest man, Cardinal Richelieu, in his political testament, intimates that a monarch ought to be cautious of him; so certain it is that virtue is not the spring of this government.

After this it is not easy to conceive what kind of honor that is, which is the spring of action in monarchies.

necessity of repose. History in all times confirms this truth:[4] besides actual democracies can only exist in territories of small extent: we shall therefore say no more concerning them.

After this form of society, which is the infancy of a state, comes the representative democracy, that in which, according to forms expressed in an act or law freely deliberated, and agreed upon, and called a CONSTITUTION, all the associates called citizens concur equally in choosing their representatives, define the authorities with which they are entrusted, and fix limits beyond which they must not trespass. This is democracy rendered practicable for a long time and over a great extent of territory. Simple democracy is the true state of nature; representative democracy is that of nature, in a perfect state, without having been sophisticated, and which acts neither by stratagems nor expedients. Representation, or representative government, may be considered as a new invention, unknown in Montesquieu's time; it was almost impossible to put it into practice before the invention of printing, which so much facilitates the communication between the constituents and the representative, and renders it so easy for the former to control, and the latter to account for his conduct; and above all, which averts those sudden storms, so often excited by the force of an impassioned and popular eloquence. It is by no means surprising, that it should have remained undiscovered until about three hundred years after the discovery of that art which has changed the face of the universe: it was necessary that other great effects should have been produced, before such a conception could be matured.

It is evident that the principle of preservation, in this form of government, is love of country, and equality of rights,* and if you will, the love of peace and justice.

The people, under such a government, would seem to be naturally more engaged in preserving and enjoying what they already possess, than solicitous

---

4. Particularly the History of Greece. The democracies of Greece, so much boasted of, never existed by their own internal power, but through the protection of a confederation by which they were united; yet their duration was short; and besides, they were actually aristocracies in relation to the great mass of the population, and among them was a prodigious number of slaves who had no share in the government.

* Here the French text has "liberty and equality" rather than "love of country and equality of rights."

of acquiring what was not necessary to their security or happiness; or, at least, that they should resort to no other means of acquiring it than the exercise of their individual faculties; nor think of obtaining authority, or power, by the invasion of the rights of other individuals, or an improper appropriation of the public wealth; that from the principle of attachment to the rights which vest in them all, each citizen should feel and be affected by the injustice done to his neighbor by the public force, as a danger which menaced and concerned them all, and for which no personal favor could compensate. A people, under such a government, who should once overlook the wrongs of their fellow citizens, or prefer their individual advantages to the security of the rights of the whole, would soon be found willing to place the government itself in a situation to dispose of the public liberties according to its caprice, if there should appear a prospect of individual benefit accruing from the perfidy.

Simplicity, habits of industry, a contempt for frivolity, the love of independence so inherent in every being endowed with a rational will, naturally dispose men to such sentiments. If these had been the definitions of republican virtue, given by Montesquieu, there would be no difficulty in assenting to his principle; but we shall see in the next book, that he makes this virtue to consist in voluntary privations, in self-denials. Now as no human being is so constituted by nature, it is impossible to found any general or even rational principles thereupon, because we cannot renounce our nature, but momentarily or through fanaticism: so that this principle requires of us a false and a fluctuating virtue.

That disposition to simplicity and independence which I have just described, is so conformable to our nature, that a little habit, sound sense, a few wise laws, the experience of only a few years, which may shew that violence and intrigue are too often successful, will infallibly and necessarily excite it in us.

Let us now continue the examination of the different forms of government which we have denominated national, or of common right, in opposition to those which we have styled special, or of partial or exclusive rights.

When the primitive democracy, through the want of a well organized representative system, or through whatever cause, is unable to maintain itself, and submits to be converted into an aristocracy of some species, and thereby establishes a higher, or privileged class, and a lower, or common class, it is evident that the pride of the one, and the humility of the other, the ignorance of these, and the knowledge of those, ought to be considered as the principles of conservation in an aristocratical government, since the dispositions of mind in each class, are exactly adapted to preserve the established order of that form of government.

In like manner, when a democracy resolves to transform itself into a monarchy, by submitting to the authority of a single chief, either for life or in hereditary succession, it is obvious, that the pride of the monarch, the exalted idea he entertains of his dignity, his superiority over those who surround them, the importance attached to the honor of approaching him; on the other hand, the haughtiness of the courtiers, their devotedness, their ambition, even their superciliousness to the lower class; and added to all these circumstances, the servile or superstitious respect for all this artificial grandeur, and their eagerness to please those who are clothed with it; all these dispositions, I say, contribute to the maintenance of this form of government, and consequently, in such an order of society, must be deemed useful to the ends to which they appertain, whatever may be our opinion of them in a moral view, or whatever may be their effects on society at large.

It must be kept in view, that we only speak of the different forms of government which we have denominated *national*, and which are to be understood as professing that all rights and power are inherent in the body of the nation; now in these it is not necessary that all the different particular opinions favorable to the formation of an aristocracy or a monarchy, should be defined, and expressly established; it is sufficient that the general principle of respect for the rights of men always predominates, without which predominancy the fundamental principle will soon be forgotten or disavowed, as almost universally has been the effect.

We shall now proceed to the examination of the governments which we have called *special*; that is to say, those in which various legitimate sources of particular or exclusive right are recognized, and which are acknowledged to exist, though inconsistent with general or national rights. It is evident that the different forms, to which this principle is applicable, admit of the same opinions and sentiments which we have pointed out as favorable to the analogous forms of national government; and even in these, such opinions and sentiments, instead of being subordinate to the principle of the rights of men, can and must be limited, only by the respect due to the different legitimate particular rights established: the general rights of men have no being here.

This is, I believe, all that can be said, on what Montesquieu calls the principles of the different governments. But to me it appears of much more moment to enquire into the nature and tendency of the opinions and sentiments which each kind of government forms and propagates, than to enquire into those which are necessary to the support of each. I have taken notice of them only in conformity with the order which Montesquieu has thought proper to follow, in his immortal work. The other description of enquiry is much more important to human happiness; and may probably be treated of in the sequel of this work. Let us now return to our model.

BOOK IV.

The Laws Relating to Education, Should Be Congenial with the Principles of the Government.

Those governments which are founded on reason, can alone desire that education should be exempt from prejudice, profound and general.

SPIRIT OF LAWS, BOOK IV.

THE title of this book, is the declaration of a great truth, which is founded on another, no less true, which may be expressed in these terms: *government is like every thing else, to preserve it you must love it.* Our education, therefore, ought to instil into us sentiments and opinions in unison with the established institutions, without which we may become desirous of overturning them: now we all receive three kinds of education: from our parents, from our teachers, and from the world. All three, to act properly, should tend to a common end. These sentiments are correct, but they comprise all the utility which is to be found in this book of Montesquieu; who declares, that in despotic states the children are habituated to servility; that in monarchies, at least among courtiers, a refined politeness, a delicate taste, an artificial sensibility of which vanity is the principal cause, are contracted; but he does not inform us how education disposes them to acquire these qualities, nor which of them are common to the rest of the nation.

To what he calls the republican government he gives as its principle *self denial,* which he says, *is a principal thing.* In consequence he manifests for many of the institutions of the ancients, considered with regard to education, an admiration in which I cannot participate: I am much surprized to see this in a man who has reflected so much: the strength of first impressions must have been very great on his mind, and is an exemplification of the importance of a correct elementary education.

For myself, I avow, that I will not blindly adopt all that was said to me in explaining Cornelius Nepos,* Plutarch, or even Aristotle. I frankly acknowledge, that I do not admire Sparta, any more than La Trappe,† nor the laws of Crete,‡ (even if I were satisfied that we are well acquainted with them) any more than the rules of St. Benedict.§ It does not accord with my conceptions, that in order to live in society, a man must render violence to himself and to nature, and speak only the language of mystics. I look upon all the effects of that gloomy enthusiasm, as false virtue, as splendid imposition, which, by exciting men to hardihood and devotedness, renders them at the same time malignant, austere, ferocious, sanguinary, and above all unhappy. This, in my opinion, never was nor ever can be the object of society. Man requires clothing, not hair cloth; his dress ought to comfort and protect him, without causing pain, unless for some useful and necessary end: the same principles apply to education and to government.

Now if all this were not true, or if no attention were paid to it; and if happiness and good sense (inseparable things) were to be considered of no account; and that institutions were, according to Montesquieu, to be regarded only as relative to the duration of the established government, I should equally condemn those forced passions, and unnatural regulations. Fanaticism is itself a state of violence, and by address, under favorable circumstances, it may be kept up for a longer or a shorter period; but in its nature it cannot last; nor can any government erected on such a foundation, long endure.[5]

Montesquieu informs us, that in reserving to himself the right of judging on the different forms of political society, he only notices in laws what appears

---

* Cornelius Nepos was a Roman biographer (c. 110 BC–c. 25 BC).

† A reference to the austere lives of Trappist monks.

‡ The island of Crete was one of the earliest places to produce law codes. The laws covered property and the family in particular.

§ St. Benedict was the founder of Christian monasticism.

5. This is the place, to recall to mind what we have said of the laws of nature and of positive laws; these last should never be contrary to the first. Had Montesquieu, as we have done, commenced with analysing the word law, instead of giving an obscure definition, he might have saved himself much labor and avoided many pernicious mistakes.

favorable or unfavorable to each of the several forms. He then reduces them all into three kinds, despotic, monarchical, and republican; the last of which he subdivides into two species, democratic and aristocratic, describing the democratic as essentially republican; after which he describes the despotic government as abominable and absurd, and precluding all laws: the republican, by which is understood the democratic government, he describes as insupportable and almost as absurd; at the same time that he expresses the greatest admiration of the principles of this form of government: whence it follows, that the aristocracy under several chiefs, to which however under the name of *moderation* he attributes so many vices, and the aristocracy under a single chief, which he calls *monarchy,* and to which under the appellation of *honor* he imputes a still greater portion of vices, are the only forms which meet his approbation: indeed these two are the only kinds among those he describes, which he says are not absolutely against nature. Of this enough, since it will be admitted that nothing can prove more clearly the errors of the classification of governments: we shall therefore return to our own, and offer a few considerations on the subject of education, which Montesquieu has thought proper to leave untouched.

I lay it down as a fundamental principle, that in no case has the government a right to take children from their parents, to educate or dispose of them without their consent or participation, it being contrary to our natural feelings, and society ought to follow and not resist nature; beside that whenever we attempt to alter any thing from its natural direction, it is sure to return with celerity to its primitive position; we cannot long contend with it, either in the physical or moral order of the world: he must therefore be a very rash legislator who dares to oppose the paternal instinct, much more the maternal which is still stronger; no example can excuse his imprudence, particularly in our times.

This being established, the only counsel that can be given to government on the subject of education, is to provide such gentle means of regulation, as that the three kinds of education, which men successively receive, from their parents, from their teachers, and from intercourse with society, shall be in unison with each other, and all tend towards the maintenance of the principles of the government.

With regard to the second stage of instruction, that derived from teachers, it may have a very powerful and direct influence, through the various public institutions for education which are established or favored, and by the elementary books which are there admitted or excluded; for whatever may be the character of such establishments, it generally happens through necessity or habit, that the greater part of the citizens are educated and their minds formed in public seminaries of education: and as for the smaller number who receive a private education, even they are strongly influenced by the spirit of the public institutions.

The education received from parents and from intercourse with the world, are altogether subject to the force of public opinion: the government cannot dispose of these despotically, because they cannot be subjected to command; but it may attach them in its favor, by means which are always in its power to influence public opinion; and it is well known how effectual these means are, particularly when employed with address and allowed due time to operate; for the two great principles of moral action, fear and hope, are always more or less within the power of the government, and in every sense and relation.

Without having recourse to those violent and arbitrary acts, too much admired in certain ancient institutions, and which, like every thing founded on fanaticism, or enthusiasm, can have but a temporary duration, governments possess a multitude of means, by which they may direct every kind of education so as to conform to their views. It only remains to enquire how each form of government should employ its influence, commencing with those which we have called *special*, or which admit of exclusive rights, and amongst them that denominated monarchical.

In a hereditary monarchy, where the prince is acknowledged to possess particular rights (and consequently interests) distinct from those of the nation, which are founded either on conquest, or on the respect due to an ancient possession; or on the existence of a tacit or express compact, where the prince and his family are considered as a contracting party; or on a supernatural character, or a divine mission; or on all these together; he ought to inculcate and propagate the maxims of passive obedience, and a profound veneration for the established forms, a confidence in the perpetuity of the political establishments, and a great dislike for the spirit of innovation and enquiry, or the discussion of political principles.

With these views he ought above all things to call to his view, religious ideas, which taking possession of the mind from the cradle, make durable and deep impressions, form habits, and fix opinions, long before the age of reflexion; nevertheless he should take care previously to attach the priesthood to his interests, by making them dependent upon his favor; otherwise they being the propagators of those ideas, may employ them to their exclusive benefit, establish an interest in the state hostile to his, and form a source of distraction instead of a means of stability. This precaution taken, among the religions out of which he may have to select, he ought to give the preference to that which imposes the most effective submission on the mind, and prohibits all enquiry; which gives to precedent, custom, tradition, faith, and credulity, the force of authority; and propagates the greatest portion of dogmas and mysteries; he ought by every means to render his selected sect exclusive and dominant, though in such a manner as not to excite alarms or too great prejudices against it; and if he cannot find a sect which completely fulfils all these objects, he should, as in England, give the decided preference to that which approaches the nearest to this description.

These first objects accomplished, and these first ideas established in the mind, the second care of the prince should be to devise such attractions as may render the people affable and gay, light and superficial; the belles lettres and fine arts, works of imagination and dramatic exhibitions; the taste for society, and the advantages of those accomplishments best adapted to succeed in the fashionable world; all these afford ample means in the hands of the government capable of contributing powerfully to the intended effect: erudition and the exact sciences can produce no bad consequences, therefore those amiable and useful studies, may be encouraged or honored; the brilliant career of the French in all these elegant acquirements, the admiration which has followed them, and the vanity which has arisen out of them, are certainly the principal causes which have for a long time diverted them from serious business and philosophical researches, propensities which a prince should always repress and discourage. If he succeeds in these courses, he has nothing more to do, to insure the stability of his reign than to encourage in all classes a spirit of individual vanity, and a desire for distinction; for this purpose, it will be only necessary to establish a variety of ranks and titles, privileges, and distinctions, attaching the greatest value to such as permit the holder to approach nearest to his person.

Without entering into any more details, this I believe is the manner in which education in a hereditary monarchy ought to be conducted, always keeping in view the precaution to disseminate information very moderately among the lower classes of people, confining them almost exclusively to religious knowledge; for this class requires to be kept in a state of mental inferiority and ignorance, and the indulgence of their animal passions, lest from attending to and admiring what is above them, the desire of altering or changing their miserable condition should grow up in their minds, as well as to prevent their entertaining ideas of the possibility of a change, which would render them the blind and dangerous instruments of fanatical or hypocritical reformers, any more than of those reformers whose views may be benevolent and enlightened.

Nearly the same may be said with respect to an elective monarchy, but with this difference, that it approaches nearer the hereditary aristocracy, of which we shall presently speak. For an elective monarchy, always a government of little stability, would be without any solidity unless supported by a strong aristocracy, and otherwise would soon become a popular and turbulent tyranny, and of short duration.

The government in which the nobles are acknowledged to be in possession of rights of sovereignty, and where the rest of the nation is considered as legally under their subjection, have in many respects the same interests relative to education, as the hereditary monarchies: they differ however in a remarkable manner. The institution of a nobility is not so imposing as that of a monarchy, which partakes something of the nature of religious superstition; nor is their power so concentrated or firm; they cannot with the same confidence or plausibility employ the machinery of religious ideas; for if the priesthood should attain too much influence, they might become formidable rivals, as their credit with the people might balance the authority of the government; and by forming a party among the nobles, the priests might divide them, thereby destroy their power, and assume it themselves: such a government, therefore, must use this dangerous means with great circumspection and discretion.

If, as at Berne,* they have to deal with a clergy destitute of wealth, power, ambition, or enthusiasm, professing a simple religion, which possesses little power over the imagination, they may, without danger, make use of religious means, peaceably to direct the people, and to keep them in a mixt condition characterised by innocence and reason, and conformable to their interests, in an insulated position, admitting but of few relations with foreign nations, and favoring the system of moderation and half confidence.

But if, as at Venice, the nobles have to act with a rich, ambitious, turbulent clergy, dangerous on account of their dogmas and dependance on a foreign sovereign, they must above all things provide against their enterprizes. They should not suffer the spirit of religious institutions to obtain too great

---

* Berne was one of the first Swiss cantons to embrace the Protestant movement of Calvinism.

influence, for it would soon be turned against them; nor dare they combat it by enlightening the people, for this would soon destroy the spirit of dependance and servility; they can, therefore, only weaken the force of superstitious power, by plunging the people into disorder, intemperance, and vice; neither dare they to make a stupid flock of them under the direction of their pastors, but they must rather degrade them into a miserable and depraved mob, subject to the constant yoke of a rigid police, but still sufficiently prone to superstition; these are the only means of preserving their authority: contiguity to the sea, the influence of extensive commerce, and various laborious occupations, are useful in these circumstances.

Here we may perceive, that an aristocracy, with regard to the education of the people, ought to act like a monarchical government; though it is not the same, with respect to the superior order of society; for in an aristocracy, the governing body requires, that its members should obtain instruction, as solid and profound as possible; a disposition to study, an aptitude for business, a capacity for reflection, a temper disposed to circumspection and prudence, even in its amusements; grave and even simple manners, at least in appearance, and as much as the national spirit requires. The nobles ought to be perfectly acquainted with the human mind, the interests of different conditions, and a knowledge of human affairs at large, were it only to be prepared to counteract them, when brought in hostility to their body. As they are the sole governors, political science in all its compass ought to be their principal study, their incessant occupation; care should be taken, not to instil into them that spirit of levity, vanity, and thoughtlessness, which is infused into the nobles of a monarchy; for it would be the same in effect, as if a monarch were to make himself as frivolous, as it is his interest his subjects should be, the evil effects of which would soon be felt; nor must we forget, that the authority of an aristocracy is always more easily overthrown, than that of a monarch, and is less competent to resist a powerful shock: this last consideration shews the interest, which the members of an aristocracy have in confining all information to themselves, and that they have yet much more cause to fear an enlightened people, than the monarchical authority; although in the end it is always from that quarter, that attempts really dangerous proceed, after having once overcome the feudal anarchy.

This, I believe, is nearly all we have to say of aristocratical governments in regard to education. To pursue with exactness all the parts of the classification which I have adopted, and complete what concerns the class of governments, which I denominate special, I should now treat of that democracy, which is established on particular rights and stipulations, but of which I shall now say nothing; nor of the pure or simple democracy, which is founded on the rights of the nation, these two conditions of society, being almost imaginary; nor could they exist but among an uncivilized people, where no attention can be paid to education of any kind; and indeed to perpetuate such a state, all education, properly so called, should forever be banished. The same may nearly be observed with respect to what is commonly called despotic government, and which is nothing else than monarchy in a state of stupidity: for which reason I shall in like manner pass it over, and proceed to the examination of the class of governments denominated *national,* under the monarchical, aristocratical, and representative forms.

The two first, in as much as they have the same interest, and should observe the same conduct, as those which we have already spoken of; but in so much as they are national, they should have more respect for their people, since their authority is delegated by the general will; and they can also place more confidence in them, as they professedly exist only for the greater good of all.

It is consequently not so much their interest to debase or deprave the people, nor entirely to enervate or vitiate the minds of the higher class; for if they should succeed, the rights of men would soon be forgotten or misunderstood, and they would thereby lose the character of a national or patriotic government, which constitutes their principal strength; and in the end would be obliged, in order to support itself, to assume particular rights more or less disputable, and thereby reduce it to the condition of those governments which we have called *special;* this would never be freely consented to and avowed in a nation, where the true national and individual rights had once been established; hence these governments should never endeavor to lay reason and truth altogether aside; they ought only in some respects, and on certain points, to obscure the one and violate the other; in order that from certain principles, certain consequences too rigorous may not be constantly inferred. There remains no other particular advice relative to education, to be given them.

The pure representative democracy, can in no respect fear truth, its best interest is to protect it; founded solely on reason and nature, its only enemies are error and prejudice; it ought constantly to attend to the propagation of accurate and solid knowledge of all kinds; it cannot subsist unless they prevail; all that is good and true is in its favor; all that is bad or false, is repugnant to it: it ought then by all means, to propagate and favor instruction, and its general diffusion, for it stands yet more in need of rendering knowledge accurate and general, than of encreasing the variety: knowledge being essentially united with justice, equality, and sound morality, the representative democracy should prevent the worst of inequalities, comprising all others, the inequality of talents and information, among the different members of society: it should endeavor to prevent the poor class from becoming vicious, ignorant, or miserable; the opulent class from becoming insolent and fond of false knowledge; and should cause both to approach that middle point, at which the love of order, of industry, of justice, and reason, naturally establish themselves; for by position and interest, it is equally distant from all excesses: whence it will not be difficult to perceive what is to be done by this form of government, relative to education, and it would be superfluous to enter into any details.

Thus we terminate the chapter, to follow Montesquieu, in the examination of the laws proper for each particular form of government.

BOOK V.

Laws Formed by the Legislature Should Be Consistent with the Principles of the Government.

Governments founded on reason, have only to leave nature to act.

SPIRIT OF LAWS, BOOK V.

THE laws given by the legislator, should be analogous to the principles of the government.*

We have said at the commencement of the fourth book, that the laws relative to education, ought to be also analogous to the established principles of government, if it be intended to prevent its downfall; and certainly no one would pretend to assert the contrary: now this truth, so generally admitted, actually comprehends all we contemplate saying in this chapter, for education embraces the whole period of life, while laws are only a part of the education of manhood; there is no law of any kind which does not induce some new sentiment, and resist some other; which does not tend to produce certain actions, or to restrain others of an opposite tendency; whence laws in process of time form our manners, that is to say, our habits of acting. Our business here will be only to examine, what laws are favorable to one or other form of government, without attempting to prejudge their general effects on society, and consequently without attempting to determine the degree of merit of either form of government, to which they may be applicable: this will be the object of a separate discussion, which we shall not for the present touch.

---

* Inexplicably, the title of Book V was relocated to be the first paragraph of text in the original.

37

Montesquieu, throughout this book, forms his reasonings according to the system or classification of governments which he has himself approved, and on what he calls the principles proper to each of them; he makes the political virtue of his democracy agree so well with the self denial and renunciation of all natural sentiments, that the rules of the monastic orders are presented as models, and particularly those which are the most austere and best calculated to eradicate in individuals every human feeling. To perfect his theory, he approves without restriction, of means the most violent, such as the equal distribution of land, so that one person may not be allowed to possess the portions of two; to render it obligatory on a father to leave his portion to one of his sons only, causing the others to be adopted by citizens destitute of children; to give but a small dowry to his daughters, and when heirs, to oblige them to marry their nearest relation; or even to require that the rich should marry the daughters of poor citizens, &c. To this he annexes the greatest respect for all that is ancient; the most rigid and despotic censorship; paternal authority so unlimited, as to possess the power of life and death over children; and even that every father should possess the right of correcting the children of another: without however explaining by what means.

In like manner he so earnestly recommends moderation in an aristocracy, as to require that the nobles should avoid offending or humbling the people in their own eyes, that they should not arrogate to themselves any personal, pecuniary, or exclusive privileges; that there should be little or no compensation for the exercise of their public functions; that they should renounce all means of augmenting their fortunes, all lucrative pursuits, such as commerce, imposts, &c. and among themselves to avoid inequality, jealousy, and hatred; they should admit no rights of primogeniture, majority, entails, or adoption, but that all property be equally divided; a regular conduct, great exactness in paying their debts, and a prompt determination of legal process. Nevertheless he recommends in these governments so moderated, a state inquisition the most arbitrary and tyrannical, and the most unlimited use of spies and secret information: he assures us that these violent means are necessary; we must believe him.

In conformity with his principles, he recommends in monarchies, that all which tends to perpetuate the lustre of families, an unequal distribution of property, entails, the right of testamentary bequests, the power of redeeming estates, personal proscriptive rights, and even of fiefs: he also approbates the delay of legal processes, the conferring of great power on those to whom the administration of the laws is entrusted, the purchase and sale of public employments, and generally every usage or advantage which can tend to maintain the superiority of the privileged classes.

Under what he calls despotism, he rather describes the evils which arise out of it, than informs us how the government should be conducted; which undoubtedly would have been impracticable, after he had previously given this definition of despotic government: *When the savage of Louisiana is in want of fruit, he cuts down the tree to obtain it:* all that could be added to this would be superfluous.[6]

Such are the views which Montesquieu presents to us, on the subject of laws in general, introductory to those books, in which he enters more particularly into the different principles of laws and their various effects: we cannot but say, that many of the ideas which he offers, are unworthy of the sagacity of our illustrious author; and that there are others which are inadmissible; while it must be observed of them generally, that they are neither clearly specified nor accurately defined by the bare use of the terms virtue, moderation, honor, and fear, as significant of so many kinds of government. It would be tedious and difficult to examine them separately, from the base upon which he has placed them, which presents nothing sufficiently solid nor distinct; but we shall be better able to estimate their value, by returning to the distribution of governments into two classes, *national* and *special,* and examining them under their different forms.

Monarchy, or the power of a single person, considered in its cradle, surrounded by ignorance and barbarism (which is what Montesquieu calls despotic governments) employs no system of legislation. With respect to revenue, its resources are pillage, or presents, or confiscations; and its means of administration are the sword or the halter. The person possessing despotic power, ought also to have that of nominating his successor, at least in his own family; the successor should, when seated on the throne, cause all those to be strangled, who might dispute the succession with him; he ought to become either the absolute master, or the subtle slave of the priests, who may possess the highest credit with his ignorant subjects; and, with Montesquieu, we have no other advice to give him, in order to maintain with any security this dangerous existence, but to make use of these miserable resources with address, boldness, and if possible, with plausibility.

---

6. In these few words are comprehended the whole of the thirteenth chapter; followed, however, by comments sufficiently ample, on the same subject, in the four following chapters.

But if the monarch, like Peter the great,* be desirous of changing so abominable and precarious a state of society, or if he be placed among a people already somewhat civilized, and consequently disposed to advance in refinement, then he ought to devise a rational system: First, he should establish the order of succession to the throne in his family; for of all the methods of inheritance, that of lineal succession from male to male, in the order of primogeniture, is the best adapted to perpetuate the race, and the best calculated to prevent internal discord or foreign domination. Peter the great, from circumstances peculiar to himself, could not establish this order of succession in Russia; though eighty years afterwards, the emperor Paul, aided by more favorable circumstances, and sustained by the general custom of European monarchies, accomplished its establishment.

The succession once fixed in the family of the sovereign, a like stability ought to be given to a great number of families, otherwise that of the reigning family would be insecure. A political inheritance cannot subsist long alone in a state, when every thing round it is changeable; when the permanent and perpetual interests of other races do not depend upon its existence for their support, it must be soon overthrown; hence the frequent revolutions in the empires of Asia, and the necessity of a nobility in a monarchy: this is a more certain reason than could be given by the word honor, well or ill understood, well or ill defined: honor is here no more than a cloak; for, in truth, it is no more than the employment of the interests of a great many to secure the obedience of all.

In the class of special governments, under the monarchical form, the prince should support his particular rights, with a great many other particular but subordinate rights; he should be surrounded by a powerful but pliant and passive nobility, who should hold the nation in the same subjection that he holds them; he should make use of bodies in society considered as honorable, and render them dependent on him; he should establish certain forms, and cause them to be respected, and which should have reference to his will; every thing, in a word, should appear as emanating from him or depending on him; great care should be taken to render them plausible, and as little repugnant to reason as practicable, and without admitting of enquiries into the authority upon which they were established, or having recourse to any investigation of primitive rights.

---

* Peter the Great was monarch of Russia from 1682 to 1721. He was famous for introducing a wide range of reforms intended to modernize the Russian Empire.

All this concurs with what we have said of government in the third and fourth books, and this appears to me entirely to justify Montesquieu in the instruction which he gives the monarch in this book. The venality of office, which is without doubt the most questionable, appears to me sufficiently accounted for by these considerations; for, in the first place, the prince, influenced by his courtiers, would not generally furnish better personages than would be provided by the pleasure which he always reserves to himself of giving or refusing to those who present themselves as purchasers; we might also say, that the want of funds produces a first selection which is necessary, which could not be replaced by any other mode of nomination; for in effect it is essential to this kind of government, that the public should attach a great deal of importance to exterior shew. In appointments to office, more attention should be paid to the condition of those who hold them than to their functions; now venality not only keeps out those destitute of the means of paying, but also those who could not sustain the expence of making a figure suitable to their station, or who would be inclined to encourage a contempt for forms, and make themselves esteemed by qualifications less frivolous. Indeed venality has a powerful tendency to repress and impoverish the third and lower classes of the people, and to enrich the treasury at their expence, and to promote the interests of the privileged class by means of the fortunes of those who are introduced to offices; and this is another advantage to be used in this system, for as it is among the inferior orders of people, that industry, economy, genius, and commerce, and all the useful arts, are exhibited, they only have the power of gaining or accumulating riches; and if they were not fleeced by every means, the inferior orders would soon become the most wealthy and powerful; and being, from the nature of their pursuits, already the most intelligent and prudent, their success, or the possibility of their becoming rivals of the privileged class, ought by all means to be restrained.

The words of Colbert to Louis XIV. were fraught with sagacity, applied to this case:* *"Sire—Whenever your majesty creates an office, Providence always creates a fool to purchase it."* If Providence did not continually fascinate the eyes of the privileged orders,† they would soon unite within themselves every advantage

---

* Jean-Baptiste Colbert (1619–83) was first minister of state to Louis XIV from 1661 to 1683.

† Here the French text has "la classe moyenne." This would be better translated as "the middling order" rather than "privileged orders."

that is to be derived from society. The marriage of rich women, of the class of plebeians, with the poor members of the nobility, is also a powerful remedy against the wealth of the lower class; it should therefore be encouraged, and it is one of the circumstances in which foolish vanity is most useful.

Montesquieu's instructions to aristocratic governments, in the same book, appear to me equally prudent. I shall only add thereto, that if the aristocratic class interdicts itself from all means of augmenting their fortunes, they should be sedulous that the lower class* do not encrease their wealth; and for this end they should as much as possible repress their spirit of enterprize and industry; but if they should not be able to succeed in this mode, they should take measures to incorporate successively into their own body, those who appear most dangerous, from amassing great wealth: this is the only means in their power of preventing a general mistrust, nor would this means be without danger, if recourse were to be had to it too often.

It is almost superfluous to remark here, as we have already done in regard to education, that the monarchies and aristocracies called national, in as much as they are monarchies and aristocracies, have absolutely the same interests as these, and should all adopt the same course of conduct, but with more management and circumspection, as they profess to exist for the general good alone. It should not then be too evident, that all those regulations, having only the particular interests of government in view, are repugnant to the general good, or the real prosperity of the community at large; but enough of this subject.

I shall here take no notice of the simple democracy, because, as I have already said, it is but of short duration, and cannot be used in any considerable extent of territory. I will not then amuse myself with enquiring whether the tyrannical and shocking measures thought necessary for its support are practicable, or if even many of them are not illusory and contradictory; but I will pass to the representative government, which I consider as the democracy of enlightened reason.

This form of government does not call for nor need the constraint of the human mind, the modification of our natural sentiments, the forcing of our desires, nor the excitement of imaginary passions, rival interests, or seductive illusions; it should, on the contrary, allow a free course to all inclinations which are not depraved, and to every kind of industry which is not incompatible

* Here the French is "bourgeoisie" rather than "lower class."

with good order and morals: being conformable to nature, it requires only to be left to act.

It tends to equality, but does not establish it by violent means, which never has more than a momentary effect, never accomplishes the whole purposes sought, and is besides generally unjust and oppressive; it confines itself to the diminution as far as practicable of the inequality of the mind, by diffusing information, an inequality the most of all others to be dreaded; it encourages talent, by all the members of society possessing an equal and unrestrained right to exercise their faculties; and it opens to all alike the roads to fortune and to honor.

It should take care that great riches accumulated, be not perpetuated in the same hands, but that wealth be duly distributed, so as to go into the general mass, without any violation of the rights of nature; this must be accomplished without force, and without encouraging profusion or dissipation, which would be in fact corruption instead of oppression. It will be sufficient to prohibit privileges of primogeniture or exclusive birth right, entails, powers of redemption of alienated estates, and all titles or privileges, which are only the inventions of vanity, or of cunning which governs vanity; the practice of demurrer in law, is subversive of right, and incompatible with rational government. An equal distribution of property among children, a regulation interdicting vexatious or unnatural wills, the right of divorce upon rational principles but with rigid precautions; wills and marriages should be prevented from becoming objects of speculation, which though slow in operation, have a sure and certain tendency to subvert industry; and which are too often invited by the vanity of the wealthy and the avidity of the poor.

It is the interest of this government, that the spirit of industry, order, and economy should prevail in the nation; but it is not necessary, as was the custom in some of the ancient republics, that an account should be taken of the actions and circumstances of every individual, nor to constrain any in the choice of their occupations; nor to incommode them with sumptuary laws, which tend to excite discontent, and lead to outrages upon property and liberty. It is sufficient, that no efforts be made to impede men in their reasonable pursuits or natural inclinations; that no aliment be provided for vanity; that pomp and extravagance be not encouraged as means of obtaining public favor; that rapid fortunes may not be suffered to be amassed by the administration of the public treasury; that an act of infamous bankruptcy be the same as a decree of civil death. By such precautions as these, domestic virtue will be found in every family, and the public will maintain a corresponding character; for we often find in private, those virtues in full exercise, even when surrounded by external temptations, and in defiance of the advantages which are too often obtained by renouncing virtue.

For the same reasons, this form of government requires the general diffusion of the most correct and useful knowledge;* information should be promulged constantly, and error exposed and dissipated; popular and moral writers should be rewarded, not by engagement, but by such means as may be devised for exciting a general emulation, without rendering the reward of virtue a business of intrigue on one hand, or of patronage on the other; public professors in the departments of useful sciences, public speakers, exercising representative functions, should be induced to co-operate in this way; and even the drama might be so regulated without violating its freedom, as to render such exhibitions as are repugnant to social virtue, and the manners suitable to a free state, too odious to be admitted, and vice never to be represented but when it should be abhorred: elementary works should be composed, adapted wholly to the promotion of truth and virtue; almanacs and catechisms, moral allegories, and pamphlets accordant with the spirit of public virtue, should be encouraged; periodical journals should be instituted, which by multiplying the means of enquiry, should, through the medium of a bold or free criticism, perform those functions, which under other forms of government, are committed to the inspection of venal censors, or to indefinite restrictions; these would establish new shields for truth, and new incentives to genius and virtue. No one should be placed under any other restraint in the communication of his ideas or opinions, than the contract of moral sentiment, *fari quae sentiat*,[†] for it is indisputable, that wherever opinion is left free with reason only to combat it, truth will ultimately predominate, since being founded in natural principles, it requires no support from remote means, being always as ready to submit to the discovery of error, as to sustain the cause of truth.

The only allowable interference with the exercise of the faculties of the mind, would be such means as would assure the necessary moderation and deliberation in all discussions, but especially in the determinations which may follow.

* The lines below read very differently from the French version. However, the overall message is the same: people should be allowed "to say and to write what they think."

† Translated as "to say what one feels."

The sale of offices should not be suffered under this form of government, which does not require of Providence to create fools, but wise and disinterested citizens; there is no class which it can wish to impoverish, because there is none which it can desire to elevate, and because neither could be of any use to it by its very nature, the greater portion of the public functions, are conferred by the suffrages of the citizens, and the rest by the enlightened choice of those who had been previously elected; almost all the public functions have but a limited duration, and none should have great emoluments nor permanent privileges attached to them; consequently there can be no reason to buy or to sell them.

Much more might still be said on what these governments, and those we have before spoken of, should or should not do, relative to legislation; but I shall confine myself to the objects, which Montesquieu has thought proper to treat of in this book. I have, however, only left it untouched, that I may more effectually demonstrate, in contradiction of this great man, that the direct and violent means which he approves in the establishment of democracies, are not the most efficacious, and that any government whatever, contrary to nature, must be bad. I shall follow the same method throughout this work.

BOOK VI.

Consequences of the Principles of Different Governments, in Relation to the Simplicity of Civil and Criminal Laws, the Forms of Juridical Proceedings, and the Apportionment of Punishments.

First degree of civilization	DEMOCRACY DESPOTISM.
Second degree	ARISTOCRACY under several chiefs.
Third degree	REPRESENTATIVE GOVERNMENT, with one or several chiefs.
Characteristics of the three forms.	{ Ignorance. . . . force. Opinion. . . . religion. Reason. . . . philosophy.
Motives of punishment in the three forms.	{ Human vengeance. Divine vengeance. Prevention of crimes.

SPIRIT OF LAWS, BOOK VI.

NOTWITHSTANDING the great and interesting views, indicated by the title of this book, excite our curiosity and admiration, we do not find the instruction, which we had a right to expect in it, because the illustrious author has not sufficiently discriminated between civil and criminal justice. We shall endeavor to supply this defect; but before we commence this particular subject, we must indulge in some general reflections, on the nature of the governments we have spoken of in the second book; for what we have discussed in the third, fourth, and fifth books, ought to place this subject in a new light.

The division of governments into different classes, presents important difficulties, and suggests many new observations, for it fixes and defines the precise idea we entertained of each of these governments, and the essential character therein recognized. I have already expressed my opinion, respecting Montesquieu's division of them into republican, monarchical, and despotic: I think it defective on several accounts. However, he is so much attached to it, as to make it the basis of his political system; to it he refers every thing, and subjects his entire theory to it; which, I am persuaded, very frequently affects the justness, the connexion, and the profoundness of his conceptions: I cannot, therefore, be too exact in explaining my opinion.

In the first place, democracy and aristocracy are so essentially different, that they should not be confounded under a common denomination; and Montesquieu himself is often obliged to discriminate between them, and then he has four forms of government, instead of three; when he speaks of the republican, we know not which he particularly means: here is a first inconvenience.

Next, what is despotism? We have found that it is only an abuse, and not a kind of government. This will be found true, if we only consider the use of power; but if we regard its extent, despotism is the government of a single person; it is the concentration of all power in one man; it is that state of society, in which a single person possesses all the power, and the other members of society none; it is in fine *monarchy*, taking the word in the extent of its true signification; on which account we have observed, that it is the true pure monarchy; that is to say, unlimited, there being no other true monarchy: for whoever describes a monarchy as tempered or limited, or says that the monarch, though sole chief, yet is not invested with all the power, or that there are other powers in the government besides his, they say no more than this, that *he is a monarch who is not a monarch:* this denomination of limited monarchy, is therefore absurd, and should be exploded, as it implies a contradiction; and instead of republican, monarchical, and despotic, we shall have democratic, aristocratic and monarchical.

But according to this system, what is to be done with what has been called the tempered or limited monarchy? It must be taken into view also, that this limitation of the monarchical power, is never in the hands of the entire body of the nation, for then it would no longer be a monarchical government, as usually understood, but a species of representative or delegated government under a single executive chief, as in the constitution of the United States of America, or as in the constitution formed for France in 1791.*

---

* The next eleven lines of the French text are missing.

But the power of the monarch or chief, in what is called a *tempered mon-archy,* is always limited by a small part of the nation, or by some powerful body or bodies springing up within the nation; that is by some small body forming a party, by some families uniting their interests, or united by birth, by partic-ular functions, or by some common interests, distinct from the general inter-ests of the people; now this is precisely what constitutes an aristocracy, and hence I conclude, that the monarchy of Montesquieu, is neither more nor less than an aristocracy under a single chief, and consequently that his division of governments, well explained, and properly understood, is reduced to this: simple democracy, aristocracy with one or several chiefs, and pure monarchy.

This new manner of considering the social forms, by enabling us to discern more distinctly their essential characters, will suggest to us some important considerations: simple democracy, notwithstanding the eulogiums of pedantry, is an impracticable order of things; pure monarchy is nearly as intolerable; the one is a government of savages, the other of barbarians; neither can pos-sibly endure for any considerable time, being only the infant state of society, and almost necessarily of every nation just forming.

Indeed ignorant and rude men, cannot be presumed capable of combin-ing principles of social organization; two modes of social action or order only could be conceived by them, either that all should take a part in common, in the management of their affairs; or that they should blindly charge one among them, in whom they have confidence, with the sole care of them. The first of these two means, is generally proposed by those whose restless activity have kept up a spirit of independence, and the second by those among whom idleness and love of repose are the predominant passions; in this primitive state of man, the influence of climate is powerful, and generally determines these dispositions; we see every society in a rude state, from North America to Africa, and to the islands of the Pacific Ocean, under one of these two modes of social organization, or passing rapidly from one to the other, according to circumstances; for when a horde of savages have elected a chief to conduct their war, they follow him and obey him implicitly, and thus simple democ-racy is transformed into pure monarchy.

But these two opposite modes of government, severally produce discon-tent; one by the misconduct of the chief, the other by that of the citizens; meanwhile there arises a disparity of talents, wealth, riches, power, among the members of the social body; and those who possess this superiority unite with each other, assume exclusive power, take advantage of the civil and religious opinions which prevail in the community, and turn them to their purposes;

if any resistance be made to the means that are employed in directing the multitude or restraining the despot. This is the origin of direct aristocracies every where, whether with one chief or without any, and their organization is so slow, concealed, gradual, and insidious, their progress is so imperceivable, that they often exist before they are suspected, and their origin is scarcely to be traced, nor can their rights be defined in any other way than by their possession and practical operation. Thus all nations worthy of our attention, are under a government more or less aristocratical; nor has there been any other government in the world, until this enlightened time, when entire nations, renouncing inequality as established, have united themselves by the means of representatives freely elected from among their equals, and constituted the authority of the general will, carefully collected, and clearly expressed: a representative government.

Let us here take leave of barbarians, since we really have only two forms of government to compare with each other, *aristocracy* and *representation,* and their several modifications: our enquiry will thus be more simplified, and produce more determinate conclusions.

Returning to the particular object of this book, we shall commence with the consideration of those laws, which are denominated civil.

Montesquieu remarks, that laws are more complicated in what he calls monarchy, than in what he calls despotism; he pretends that this proceeds from the principle of honor in the citizens of a monarchy, where that sentiment is held in greater estimation and commands more reverence; of course we must take this for granted, since he appears not to perceive this to be another advantage of his favorite monarchy; content with the assumption which he makes, he passes over the heads of democracy and aristocracy, without examination. But there appears to me, another manner of considering this subject; and in the first place, there can be no doubt that the simplicity of the civil laws, is in itself a matter of great importance; but it is also certain, that this advantage becomes more difficult of attainment, in proportion as the society advances from the first stage upwards; for as the social relations become more numerous and delicate, the laws governing them, necessarily become more complicated.

But it must be observed, that the civil laws in a pure monarchy, are generally very simple, for another reason, because these men are not counted as of any more consideration than cattle: and, although Montesquieu does not say so, the same effect is perceptible in the democracy, notwithstanding the respect that is there professed for men and their rights; this is necessarily so in both cases, nor need we seek for the cause in *fear* or in *virtue,* which he gives as principles to those two forms of government; the real reason is, that they are the two conditions peculiar to society in a rude state.

For the contrary reason, these laws are inevitably more complicated in the several forms of aristocracy, which govern civilized nations, only that we must remark, with Montesquieu, that the aristocracy under a single chief, is still more subject than the others to the inconvenience, not because it possesses *honor* for a principle, but because it requires a greater variety of gradations among the different classes of citizens, of which one of the conditions is not to be subject to the same rules, nor judged by the same tribunals; because the same monarch may easily govern provinces, in which the established laws are different; and, in fine, because he may have an interest in maintaining divisions among his subjects, the better to keep them in obedience, by means of each other.

Let us add, in closing this article, that as the representative government cannot subsist, without the equality and union of the citizens, it is that form of all others, among civilized nations, which should most desire simplicity and conformity in its civil laws, and should constantly labor, as much as the nature of things admits, to render them simple and consistent with the spirit of the government.

Respecting the form of judicial proceeding, it appears to me, that in every government, the sovereign, whether it be the people, monarch, or senate, should never decide on the interests of private individuals, either by himself or by his ministers, nor by special commissions, but by judges previously appointed for the purpose; and their decisions should in all cases, be founded on the precise text of the law: this last condition, however, does not seem to me in any manner, to prevent either the admission into courts of those actions which lawyers call *ex bona fide,* nor the judges from giving decisions in equity, when the laws are not sufficiently explicit or applicable.

The criminal laws should be as simple as possible, and under every form of government, judgments literally enforced. The more respect which governments entertain for the rights of men, the more circumspect but liberal the form of proceeding should be in receiving the defence of the accused. These two points are so clear as not to furnish matter for discussion. Various important questions relative to the use of juries, might be treated of in this place; but Montesquieu does not even mention them. I confine myself barely to saying that this institution appears to me more worthy of praise under the *political* than under the *judicial* head; that is to say, I am not satisfied, that trial by jury is always a very certain and efficacious means of ensuring exact justice: nevertheless it is certainly a powerful check upon the tyranny of those who have the appointment of judges; and a certain means of accustoming men to pay attention to their rights, and of witnessing the injustice which may be done to their equals.

This consideration proves that the institution of juries is proper in a government in proportion as its principles are compatible with liberty, the love of justice, and a general concern in public affairs.

It is an excellent institution, under any form of government, that offences shall be prosecuted by the public, and not by particular individuals. To provide such punishments for crimes as will prevent their repetition, should be the true object of corrective justice; but no one should be permitted to employ the public arm to subserve individual passions, for this would not be justice, but private vengeance, and that is despotism in its essence.

With regard to the severity of punishments, the first question that presents itself is, whether society has the right to take away the life of one of its members. Montesquieu has said nothing pertinent on this question, probably because he conceived his plan was always to state facts, but never to discuss rights. Although disposed to be scrupulously exact in following him, I think it unnecessary here to attempt the vindication of capital punishments against the reproaches of injustice, which have been heaped upon it, by men respectable for their motives and intelligence. This severe and afflicting measure, ought not to have too odious a character attached to it, so long as circumstances render it necessary. I acknowledge then, that society possesses the right of previously announcing, that it will punish with death, any person who shall commit a crime, the consequences of which appear sufficient to endanger the existence of society. Such persons as are unwilling to submit to the consequences of such established laws, should renounce the society which adopts it, before they render themselves liable thereto; they should always have full liberty so to do, on this and on all other occasions, without which right there is no law universally just; since there is not one, which has been freely adopted with the previous knowledge and consent of the interested: with such a condition, the institution of the punishment of death appears to me as just in itself, as that of any other punishment.

This admission does not imply, that the culprit is obliged in conscience to give up his life because the law requires his death, or to renounce self defence, because the law attacks him; those who profess such sentiments, are as extravagant as those who deny society the right of punishing with death are in theirs:

both have but an imperfect idea of criminal justice. When the social body announces that it will punish such an action, in such a manner, it thenceforth declares itself in a state of war on such a point, with whoever may commit the action; but the criminal has not on that account, lost the right of personal defence; as no animated being, can be deprived of that, he is only reduced to his individual force; and the social power, which on every other occasion would have protected him, is here arrayed against him.

It remains only to examine, how far this power may be exercised against crimes, so as to effectually prevent them: in this respect, the excellent observation of Montesquieu, cannot be too much admired, that in proportion as the government is animated by the spirit of liberty, the more mild will the punishments be: and what he says on the inefficacy of barbarous, or even of cruel punishments, and the unhappy effects which they have had in multiplying, instead of diminishing crimes, because they render manners atrocious, and sentiments ferocious, are equally deserving of admiration. The necessity of punishment, he properly observes, is in proportion to the magnitude of the crime, or the temptation to commit it; and it should be a particular object of the law, that the guilty should never escape with impunity; for it is the certainty of punishment, which most effectually deters from the commission of crimes; and it should never be forgotten, that the only reasonable motive for inflicting punishment, and the only justifiable cause, is not because the evil is thereby supposed to be repaired, for that is impossible; nor for the gratification of hatred, for that would be promoting vice, and substituting blind passion for justice, but simply the prevention of evil alone.

These reflections, shew the absurdity of the law of retaliation, which gives justice the appearance of savage vengeance: we are therefore astonished, to find in our illustrious author, a particular chapter on this law of savages, and not to find the illustrations which it called for. There are moments, in which the greatest genius appears to doze; Montesquieu furnishes us with an example, in the chapter following, where he approves of dishonoring innocent men, for the crimes of their fathers, or of their children. The same observations would apply to chapter XVIII. where after these words, "Our forefathers, the Germans, seldom admitted of any but pecuniary punishments:" he adds, "Warlike and free men, think their blood should never be spilt but with sword in hand:" nor does he perceive, that if the savages of the forest of Hessia, whom he so much extols, no one knows why, had never accepted pecuniary composition for an assassination, he would have said with more reason, 'These fierce and generous men, estimated the blood of their kindred so highly, that the life of an offender only, could atone for the offence: for they would have despised making a shameful traffic of their blood.' This profound thinker is often mistaken, and, like Tacitus, appears to be too great an admirer of barbarous nations and their institutions.*

Notwithstanding these trivial faults, he cannot be more admired, than he merits: I cannot, however, but reproach him again in this book, for not expressing himself with more indignation against the use of torture and confiscation, though he disapproves of both. It is certain that the power of pardoning is at least necessary, so long as the punishment of death is continued; for while the fallibility of human judges is exposed to imposition, or to be influenced through their passions to violate justice irreparably, there should be some preventative means; and this is the more indispensable, since it is allowed by the common consent of mankind, that laws themselves are at best very imperfect.

I cannot discover upon what principle it is, that Montesquieu says, "Clemency is the destructive attribute of the monarch."† In republics, where *virtue* is the basis of every thing, clemency is less necessary. Nor do his reflections on this subject please me more. In governments where liberty is held in regard, great precautions should be taken, that the power of pardon be not rendered detrimental, and that it shall not become a privilege to certain persons, or classes, for the perpetration of crimes with impunity, as too often happens in monarchies; an exception which Helvetius makes to Montesquieu with great reason.

Let us pass to another subject.

* The Roman historian Tacitus (AD 56–c. 120) was the author of *Germania*, an ethnographic and historical study of the German peoples. It contained the argument that the origins of liberty in Europe were to be found in the forests of Germany. Montesquieu cites Tacitus extensively in his own text.

† The English translation here is mistaken. Montesquieu wrote: "Clemency is the distinctive attribute of the monarch."

BOOK VII

Consequences of the Different Principles of the Three Forms of Government, Relative to Sumptuary Laws, to Luxury, and to the Condition of Women.

The effect of luxury, is the employment of industry, in a useless and hurtful manner.

SPIRIT OF LAWS, BOOK VII.

I REGRET the necessity of being so frequently opposed to the opinions of a man whom I respect; but this necessity has been the cause of the present undertaking, and it is this opposition to opinions, which I deem erroneous, and consequently injurious, which I conceive will constitute the usefulness of my work; consequently, my determinations are already made, and I have resolved not to avoid the danger of a collision with a writer so justly celebrated, but to advance my opinions with the boldness of conscious truth, leaving it to the reader to form his own judgment upon the several subjects.

Helvetius, with reason, reproaches Montesquieu, for not having clearly defined luxury; and consequently for treating the subject in a vague and unsatisfactory manner: it therefore becomes necessary in the first place, to determine with precision, the signification of the term luxury, so much abused. Luxury properly consists in expenditures, which are non-productive, whatever the expenditures may be: as a proof that the nature of the expence is not involved in the question, a jeweller may employ one hundred thousand dollars in cutting a diamond and fabricating other jewels, without any act of luxury on his part, because he calculates on disposing of them with a profit; but if a man purchases a snuff box or a ring for fifty eagles, for his personal use, this to him is a luxurious expenditure. A farmer, a jockey, a waggoner, may keep two hundred horses, without any act of luxury, because they are the tools of their trade; but if an idle person keeps two horses for no purpose but riding for his pleasure, this is luxury. If an owner of a mine or a manufactory, causes a steam engine to be constructed for use, this is an expenditure of economy; but if a person fond of gardening, should cause a steam engine to be erected, merely for the purpose of watering his garden, this would be a luxurious expenditure: no man expends more on fashionable apparel than a tailor, but the luxury is not with him, but with those who wear them.

Without multiplying examples, we may perceive that what really constitutes luxurious expenditures, is their unprofitable nature: however, as we cannot provide for our wants, nor procure any enjoyments, but by expenditures, from which no profits in kind are derived; and as we must subsist, and even obtain enjoyments to a certain extent, which is in truth the object of all our labors, of society itself, and of all its institutions, those expences only can be considered luxurious, which are neither necessary nor profitable; otherwise consumption and luxury would be confounded and mistaken for the same thing.

But absolute necessity has no very definite limits; it is susceptible of extension and restriction; it varies according to climate, season, strength, age, and even according to educated habits, which are a second nature. A man placed in a severe climate, in a sterile district, or who is either sickly or old, is subjected to a greater portion of wants, than a young Indian* in good health who can go almost naked, lie down under a palm tree and nourish himself with its fruit. In the same climate, the objects of real necessity are more extensive, when you refer to a man brought up in ease, who has had little occasion to exercise his bodily strength, and has exercised his intellectual faculties a great deal, than for one who has been brought up in poverty and passed his youth in the exercise of some laborious trade.

There is, moreover, among a civilized people, a sort of conventional necessity, which, though much exaggerated, is not imaginary, but founded on reason: it is in fact of the same nature as the expenditure of a workman for the tools necessary to his trade, for they belong to the profession exercised. The long and warm garment of studious persons, would not suit a herdsman, a hunter, a waggoner, or an artisan, to these it would be a luxury and inconvenience; in the same manner as the cuirass of the ancient soldier, or the

---

* The French text refers to a "young Hindu."

pompous costume of the tragic actor would be to the lawyer. A man whose vocation requires of him to receive a great many people, and cannot go to see them, must be better lodged than the one who can traverse the town; he whose business obliges him to become acquainted with a great many people, to see them, hear them, speak to them, and act with or for them, should be enabled to receive them in his house, and consequently be at more expence than a man without connexions. This is the situation of many public officers. Even a person who does not exercise any public function, but whose fortune is ample, should expend more liberally and give greater activity to consumption, in order that he may not, however benevolent, be reputed parsimonious, or too selfish; because it is a matter of real necessity, for every man to possess the esteem that justly belongs to him, and particularly when it does not mislead him to do what is unjust; such expences are only an employment of means, in a manner somewhat less useful than they might have been. I am aware to what extent vanity, which desires to appear what it is not; and rapacity, which takes possession of what does not belong to it; have often abused considerations like these to color their excesses: but it is nevertheless true, that the empire of necessity has not any very certain bounds, and that luxury, properly so called, only commences where necessity terminates.

The essential character of luxury, is expenditures which are neither necessary nor productive: which is sufficient to shew the absurdity of those who pretend that the encrease of luxury enriches a nation: it is as if a merchant were advised to encrease his household expences, in order to render his affairs more prosperous; such expenses might be indeed a sign, though a very uncertain sign, of his wealth, but it could in no manner be the means of enriching him. It must be evident, that a tradesman by reducing the expences of his business, obtains a greater profit, if the same quantity of merchandize equally good be produced; yet it is said that the more a nation expends, the more opulent it must be: this is most preposterous. But it is said, that luxury encourages commerce and industry, by causing money to circulate rapidly: does it not rather change the wholesome current of circulation, and render it less useful, without at all augmenting it. Let us make a calculation.

My property consists of land, and I have besides a sum of an hundred thousand dollars arising from the produce of those lands. This sum is certainly the product of the labor and skill of those who superintended my farms, who raised produce equal to that value, over and above the expences of their own subsistence and all their workmen, and the just profit of each; certainly this amount produced from the estate is not the fruit of expence, but of economy;

for if the farmers and their assistants, had consumed as much as they had produced, nothing would have accrued to me: the same might be said, if the same amount had been produced by commerce, manufactures, or any other useful employment in society; and had it been expended as it accrued, nothing necessarily could have remained.

I now employ this sum in useless expenditures, and consume it all on myself; I have scattered it abroad; it has passed through numerous hands, who have worked for me; several people have been supported therewith, and this is the amount of the expenditure, for their work is thrown away and nothing remains; it produced me some temporary satisfaction of the same nature, as if the people had been employed in amusing me with fireworks or other spectacles: if, on the contrary, I had employed this sum in useful objects, the money would have been no doubt scattered abroad also, and a like number of men supported from it, but their work would have produced something of permanent utility. The improvement of the soil would ensure a more considerable revenue in future; a house built would receive a tenant; a road opened, a bridge constructed, would encrease the value of the adjoining lands, and open new sources of intercourse, consumption, and commerce, which, by a fair interest, would produce advantage to me, or to the public. Merchandize bought or fabricated, not for my consumption, but for sale, or even distributed to the indigent, would either produce a profit to me, or aid to sustain many who might otherwise have perished through want. This is an exact comparison of the two methods of expending.

If we should suppose, that instead of employing my money in one of those ways, I have lent it, the operation is only indirect, it is not changed; it only requires to be known, how the person who has borrowed employs it, and what use I make of the interest accruing therefrom, and according to that use, it will produce one of the two effects which we have treated of. It is exactly the same in effect, as if I had bought with my hundred thousand dollars, more ground, producing a certain additional revenue.

If we suppose again, that instead of employing or lending my capital, I have buried it, this is the only case wherein it can be supposed that it would have been better had I expended it even fruitlessly, because then some one might have profited by my extravagance.

But here I must observe, first: that this is not a rational course of conduct, but direct folly; and the more so because it affects most the person who acts so absurdly; and it is a course evidently such as can have no influence on the rich generally, nor is it so often met with in countries where the spirit of economy prevails, as in those where luxury predominates; for the productive nature of capital, and the manner of employing it, is there better known.

Secondly: this folly, of so little importance as scarcely to merit our attention, is yet less hurtful than is generally imagined; for it is not goods that are buried but precious metals, and the merchandize which procured it, has been carried into the general consumption, and fulfilled its purposes in society: it is therefore only a quantity of bullion that has been withdrawn from general use; and if it were possible for the quantity to be perceptible, the result would only be that what remains in circulation would possess a proportionately greater value, and represent more of merchandize and the products of industry; and consequently their use would be the same. If any inconvenience could arise from this incident, it would be in relation to foreign commerce, for foreigners might then obtain the products of the country at a lower price, and yet the country would be compensated, in some measure, by the advantage arising to its manufacturers, in enabling them to sell at a lower price than the manufacturers of other countries, which is well understood to be a great principle of superiority in political economy; and this superiority, nations rich in metals cannot counterbalance but by greater skill in fabricating, and greater talents in speculations; capacities which they sometimes possess, not because they are rich, but because such qualifications belong to the long established habits of the nation, and have enriched it: but this is pursuing ultimate consequences to an extreme which they can never reach.

Consequently, I think it may be concluded that luxury relative to economy, is always an evil, a continual cause of misery and weakness; it constantly debilitates by the excessive consumption of some, and the destruction of the produce of labor and industry of others; and these effects are so powerful, though not often understood, that so soon as it ceases for a short space in a country where there is little activity, there is directly perceived an encrease of riches and strength really prodigious.

What is here deduced from reason, history sustains by facts: Holland was capable of efforts almost incredible, when her admirals lived like sailors, and when all her citizens were employed in enriching or defending the state, and in raising tulips and collecting pictures: all subsequent political and commercial events have tended towards its decay: it has preserved the spirit of economy, and yet possesses considerable riches, in a country where other people could scarcely live.

Now let us suppose Amsterdam to be the residence of a splendid and magnificent court, its ships exchanged for embroidered garments, and its magazines converted into assembly rooms; in a few years it would scarcely be able to defend itself against the irruptions of the sea. When was it that England, notwithstanding all her misfortunes and faults, made the most prodigious efforts? Was it under Cromwell or Charles II.? I am sensible that moral causes have a greater effect, than economical calculations: but these moral causes only augment resources, by directing all our efforts towards solid objects; which is the reason, that treasures are not wanting, either to the state or individuals, for great undertakings, because they have not been employed uselessly.

From what cause is it that the United States of America, in their agriculture, industry, commerce, wealth, population, have doubled in less than twenty-five years: it is because, they produce more than they consume. That their position is favorable, and their productions immense, I agree; but if their consumption were greater than their production, they would impoverish themselves, they would languish, and become as miserable as the Spaniards, notwithstanding all the advantages they possess.

Let us resort to a still more striking example: France, under its old government, was not so miserable as it has been represented by many Frenchmen; nevertheless, it was far from flourishing; its population and agriculture were not retrograding, but remained apparently stationary; and if in any particular circumstance the French made some progress, it was less than several neighboring nations, and consequently not in proportion with the progress of general information: it had no credit, and was constantly in need of funds to defray useful expences; its financial resources were inadequate to the common charges of government, still less to support any great external efforts; and notwithstanding the genius, numbers, and activity of its people, the fertility and extent of its soil, and the advantages of a long peace, its rank among its rivals was sustained with difficulty, and had ceased to be respected by foreign nations.

The French revolution commenced, and the nation suffered every evil of which society is susceptible; it was torn to pieces by wars, alternately civil and foreign: several of its provinces were laid waste, and their towns destroyed by flames; every village and hamlet pillaged by lawless banditti or military commissaries; its external commerce was annihilated; its fleets wholly destroyed, though subsequently partially recovered; the colonies, which were held to be essential to its prosperity, were torn from it; and with the additional aggravation that all the men and treasure expended in establishing and conquering them were lost irretrievably; its specie had disappeared with the emigrants. By the enormous creation of paper money, at a period of internal famine France maintained fourteen armies on her frontiers; yet with all these calamities combined, it is now well known that its population and agriculture have augmented considerably in a few years, and now (1806), without any change in her favor in relation to external commerce, to which so much importance had been generally attended; without having had a single moment of peace to recruit its losses, France at this moment supplies immense funds from taxes, expends vast sums in public works, and can accomplish all this without borrowing; such is her power on the continent of Europe, that nothing can resist it; and were it not for the British navy, France might subdue the universe. To what causes are we to attribute these extraordinary effects? The change of a single circumstance in the state of society, has been competent to effect it all.

Under the ancient order of things, the greater part of the useful labor of the inhabitants of France, was employed every year in producing the wealth, which constituted the immense revenue of the court, and all the opulent classes of society; the revenues of the state were almost wholly consumed in luxurious expenditures, that is to say, in supporting a very large proportion of the population, whose labor produces really nothing beyond the gratification of a few individuals. At once this whole system disappeared, and when order was again resumed, almost all these revenues entered into different channels, part into the hands of the new government, part into the hands of the laboring classes; the same number of people have been nourished, but their labor has been employed on objects of general usefulness or necessity; and the product has been found, besides fulfilling all these purposes, competent to defend the state against external attacks, and to encrease its internal productions.[7]

Ought we to be surprized at these consequences, when we reflect, that for a considerable space of time, as a necessary consequence of the general commotion and distress, there was not in France scarcely a single idle citizen, nor one employed on any labor that was not useful? Those who had previously been employed in building coaches, were now occupied in constructing artillery carriages; those who before had wrought in embroidery and lace, now made linens and coarser clothing; those who had ornamented sumptuous palaces, tilled the earth, or toiled in the barn; and even those who during times

7. The suppression of feudal rights and clerical tithes, part of which remained to the farmer, and part went to the coffers of the state, has tended very much to encrease the industry of the agriculturist, and enable government to dispense with various vexatious taxes; and these formed but a small proportion of the revenues of the class that consumed without usefulness.

of peace enjoyed every luxury, were under the necessity of becoming useful in order to subsist. This is the secret, which unfolds the resources of a nation in a great crisis; when every thing becomes useful; when even things before useless and unnoticed, are turned to general advantage: these are the causes which astonish us, only because, from their simplicity, we overlook them.

And thus by a very simple analysis, we discover the emptiness of college declamation on the frugality, sobriety, detestation of pomp, and all those democratical virtues of poor and agricultural nations, which furnish so many themes for those who can comprehend neither cause nor effect. It is not because those nations are poor or ignorant that they are powerful, but because nothing is lost of the natural strength which they possess. A man who owns an hundred dollars and expends them well, is possessed of more means than one who wastes a thousand at the gaming table; now supposing the like to be practised in a rich and enlightened nation, the same effects will be produced as in the French, which have exceeded all that Rome ever accomplished, because they have overcome more formidable and potent obstacles. If Germany, for example, should only for four years, relinquish the revenue now expended in sustaining the pomp of numerous courts of petty princes and rich abbeys, to the laborious and frugal classes, we should soon be sensible what a powerful nation it is competent to become. If, on the contrary, we suppose that the ancient order of things were to be entirely re-established in France, we should soon perceive, notwithstanding the great increase of territory, languor in the midst of resources, misery surrounding riches, weakness in full possession of all the means of becoming powerful.

But it will be objected to me, that I attribute only to the distribution of labor and riches, the effects of a multitude of moral causes of the greatest energy: I do not pretend to deny the existence of such causes, since, with all rational men, I confess their existence, nay more shall undertake to explain their operation: I admit that the enthusiasm of liberty which prevailed within, and the apprehension of menaced desolation from without, the indignation which was universally excited against domestic injustice and oppression, and the still greater execration against unprovoked and premeditated aggressions from abroad, were by themselves sufficient to have effected great changes in France: but it must be admitted that those changes have only furnished the passions with so many means of success, and that even the many errors and acts of horror into which the violence of the crisis plunged them, the effect has been to produce greater energy and a better employment of their faculties and resources. *The good of human society consists in the proper application of labor, the evil in its loss;* by which is implied, that when men are occupied in providing for their wants, they are satisfied; but when time is wasted without utility the effect is suffering: I blush at the idea that there should be any occasion to demonstrate a truth so self-evident; but we must not lose sight of the extent of its consequences, which are very great.

An entire work might be composed on the subject of luxury, and if well executed would be very useful, for it is a subject which has never been properly investigated: we might shew that luxury or a taste for useless expences, is to a certain extent only the effect of a natural disposition in man to seek continually for new enjoyments, when he possesses the means, and the power of habit which renders it necessary to his happiness that he should continue to possess the same enjoyments, even when it becomes difficult to procure them; consequently that luxury inevitably follows industry, the progress of which nevertheless it retards, and the riches which it tends to destroy. For the same reason, when a nation has fallen from its greatness, either by the spirit of luxury or any other cause, the nation may survive the prosperity whence its greatness had been derived, but in such circumstances as to render the return of a like prosperity impossible, unless some violent convulsion produces new impulses of the human faculties, which leading naturally to self-preservation, effects a complete regeneration of society. It is the same with respect to individuals.

From these principles it ought to be shewn, that in the opposite situation, when a nation first takes its place in civilized society, the progress of its industry and information, should be greater than that of luxury, in order that its prosperity may be durable. It is perhaps principally to an attention to this principle, that the great rise of the Prussian monarchy, under its second and third kings, should be attributed: an example which cannot but embarrass those who pretend that luxury is so necessary to a monarchy. It is a due attention to this principle, which, in my opinion, will ensure the duration and prosperity of the United States; and it is reasonable to believe, that any neglect or disregard of the advantages to be derived from the acceleration of internal industry, in a greater measure than the progress of luxury, might render imperfect, if not destroy that prosperity and frustrate the ends of civilization.*

* Instead of "destroy that prosperity and frustrate the ends of civilization," the French text here speaks of "the true prosperity and civilization of Russia."

The kinds of luxury which are most pernicious, might be pointed out to notice: unskilfulness in the manufacture of useful things, may be considered as a pernicious luxury, because it occasions a great waste of valuable time and labor: the principal, and almost only source of luxury, properly so called, that is great fortunes, should be explained, for it would be scarcely possible, if there existed only moderate fortunes: idleness itself, in this case, would hardly appear, which is a kind of luxury, since if it be not an useless waste of time, it is the suppression of productive labor.[8] The branches of industry, which rapidly produce great fortunes, are, therefore, subject to an inconveniency, which strongly counterbalances their advantages: it is not those, which a nation just forming, should desire to see flourishing. Maritime commerce is of this description: agriculture, on the contrary, is preferable, its productions are slow and limited. Industry, properly so called, as manufactures of utility and necessity, are without danger, and very advantageous; their profits are not excessive, success and permanence are difficult, requiring great practical knowledge, besides other estimable qualifications, and producing the happiest effects. A capacity for fabricating objects of the first necessity, is particularly to be desired in a nation. It is not because the manufacture of objects of luxury may be used in the country that produces them, that they are advantageous, but because such productions are like the religion of the court of Rome, of which it was said, it is not calculated for home consumption, but for foreign exportation: but it must be admitted, that there is some danger of our becoming intoxicated with the liquor which we preserve for the gratification of our friends.

All these things, and many others, should be explained in such a work, and which do not properly belong to my subject, nor can I be expected here to give a history of luxury: all that is required of me, is to define it, and point out its influence on the wealth of nations; which I believe I have done.

Luxury is then a great evil, in relation to economy, and still greater in a moral point of view, which is at all times, the most important of all the interests of men, and especially when the inclination for superfluous expence, the principal source of which is the vanity that excites and nourishes it, is in question: it renders the mind frivolous and affects the soundness of the understanding; it produces disorderly manners, which occasions many vices,

---

8. The only idle persons who may be approved of, are those who occupy their time in study, and particularly in the study of man: these only are specified, and for good reasons; they shew how far others are admissable, and they are not those who have the strongest claim.

extravagance, and distraction in families; it easily seduces women to depravity, and men to covetousness, and leads both to disregard delicacy and probity, and to forsake every generous and tender sentiment; in short it enervates the soul by debasing the mind, and it produces these sad effects, not only on such as enjoy it, but also on all who are subservient to, or who from seeing and desiring, learn to admire it.

Notwithstanding these dreadful consequences, we must agree with Montesquieu, *that luxury is particularly proper for monarchies and that it is necessary to such governments;* that is to say, to aristocracies under a single chief: but it is not for the cause he assigns, in order to animate circulation, or that the poor class may obtain part of the riches of the opulent class: for we have seen that in whatever manner these expend their income, they always support the same number of people; the difference being, that in the one case they pay for useful labors, in the other for useless. If the expences of luxury should be carried so far as to require the sale of real property to support it, circulation is not thereby increased, because the purchaser might have employed his money in some more active manner. But this is contrary to the principle established by Montesquieu himself in the preceding book, in which he with reason makes it a necessary condition to the duration of a monarchy, that there shall be established perpetuity of illustrious families.

If then, as must be admitted, the monarch is interested in encouraging and favoring luxury, it is because it is necessary for him to excite vanity, to inspire a great respect for external splendor; to render the mind frivolous and light, in order to divert it from serious occupation; to keep up the sentiment of rivalry among different classes of society; to make all sensible of the necessity of money; and to ruin those of his subjects, whose enormous wealth might render their power or influence dangerous. Without doubt, the monarch is often under the necessity of repairing the disordered affairs of distinguished families, whom it is necessary he should support by pecuniary sacrifices; but with the power which they procure him, he acquires the means of procuring yet greater resources, at the expence of others. Such is the policy of a monarchy, as we have already seen: we shall only add, by way of contrast, the representative government, of which we have also explained the nature and principles. This government can have no motive for encouraging the natural weakness of man in superfluous expences, but quite the opposite interest, and consequently it is never called upon to sacrifice part of the strength of society, for the purpose of governing it quietly. It is not necessary to enter into any more details on this subject.

Should those governments, whose interest it is to oppose the progress of luxury, have recourse to sumptuary laws? I need not here repeat, that sumptuary laws, are always an abuse of authority, an attempt against property, and can never accomplish their object. I shall only observe, that they are useless, when the spirit of vanity is not continually excited by all the institutions of the country; when the misery and ignorance of the lower class are not so great, as to produce in them a stupid reverence for pomp; when the means of acquiring great fortunes with rapidity are rare; when such fortunes, after being acquired, are promptly dispersed by an equal distribution, to heirs of both sexes; when, in short, every thing gives to the mind another direction, and inspires a taste for rational enjoyments; when, in a word, society is happily regulated, or which is the same thing, happy from the absence of unnecessary regulation.

These are the true means of preventing luxury; all other measures are only miserable expedients. I am very much surprized that a man, like Montesquieu, should carry these expedients so far, that in order to reconcile the pretended *moderation* which he has made the principle of his aristocracy, with what he assumes as the interest of the people, he approves of the nobles at Venice expending their riches on courtesans; and applauds the republics of Greece, who expended their treasure in dramatic exhibitions and concerts of music; and that he even discovers, that sumptuary laws are eligible in China, because the women there are prolific.* Fortunately he concludes, that the least important should be destroyed, which if true, does not agree with the principle from which it originates.

Women are beasts of burden among savages, domestic animals among barbarians, alternately tyrants and victims among people addicted to vanity and frivolity: it is only in a country where liberty and reason predominate, that they are the happy companions of husbands of their choice, and the respectable mothers of tender families raised by their care. Neither the Samnites[9] nor the Sunnites marriages, nor the dances of the Spartans, could produce a like

* In both Montesquieu's original text and Destutt de Tracy's text, the word used here is "fertile" rather than "prolific."

9. Voltaire has remarked, in his Commentaries on the Spirit of Laws, that the history of those singular marriages is extracted from Stobaeus, and that Stobaeus speaks of the *Sunnites*, a people of Scythia, and not of the *Samnites*; a matter of little importance. [The example of the Sunnites is drawn directly from Chapter 16 of Book VII of Montesquieu's *Spirit of the Laws*. —Ed.]

effect. It is inconceivable, where every thing was so preposterous and repugnant to nature, that the silliness of these fooleries has not been perceived, any more than the horrible nature of the domestic tribunals of the Romans. Women are no more destined to command or to serve than men; in either station, their smiles are not those of virtue or happiness, and we may safely affirm, that the principle is uniform and universal.

BOOK VIII.

Of the Corruption of the Principle in Each of the Three Forms of Government.

The proper extent of a state, is where it possesses a sufficient power with the best possible limits; the sea is the best boundary of all.

SPIRIT OF LAWS, BOOK VIII.

No book of the Spirit of Laws more clearly proves the erroneous classification of governments, adopted by Montesquieu, than this; and how injurious the systematic use of it has been to the profoundness and extent of his ideas; for by attributing to each exclusively as its only principle, a sentiment which is more or less common to them all, he tortures from them a reason for every thing that is done by or happens to them.

Indeed the first circumstance that strikes us in his eighth book is, that while he announces but three kinds of government, he commences by distinguishing four kinds in substance, materially different from each other; and he concludes by uniting two kinds under the denomination of republican, which have no manner of reference to the extent of territory, which is the topic discussed.

Seeing then that no human institution is exempt from defects, are we to look to him to inform us which are the views inherent and peculiar to each of the social forms, and to instruct us in the means proper for amending them? Not at all! in consequence of his systematic arrangement, he is taken up with abstractions; governments are not yet noticed; their principles alone being taken into consideration; and what does he inform us concerning those principles?

The principles of democracy, he says, are corrupted not only when the spirit of equality is lost, but also when every one desires to be equal to the one that is entrusted with the public authority: the second idea in this sentence he explains by many examples and arguments, which, however true, have no relation to the democratic virtue which he has in another place characterised as *the abnegation of ourselves,* more than any other political principle: but is there any society that can subsist when every one commands and no one obeys?

He tells us that aristocracy is corrupted, *when the power of the nobles becomes arbitrary, and when they do not observe the laws*: undoubtedly these excesses are contrary to that moderation, which he elsewhere assumes, as the supposed principle of this government; but what government is there, whose principles would not be corrupted in principle and in fact, when it has become arbitrary, or when the laws are disregarded.

The article on monarchy is nearly the same, only in other terms: he says that the principle of monarchy is corrupted, when the prince destroys the prerogatives of bodies who enjoy certain rights, such as the privileges of towns or corporations; when he takes from one body their established functions, and transfers them arbitrarily to others; when he follows his inclinations more than the public interests; when he becomes cruel; when under his countenance, a person may at the same time be covered with infamy and invested with dignity: certainly such disorders are pernicious to society, but there is not one of them, excepting only the last, which has any direct reference to *honor,* and even that is as detestable and lamentable under every other form of government, as under a monarchy.

Of the despotic government he tells us other governments perish because particular accidents violate the principle thereof; this perishes by its internal vice, when some accidental cause does not prevent its principle from becoming corrupted; that is to say, that it cannot maintain itself, unless some circumstance compels it to follow some order, or to admit of some regulation. I believe this to be true: it is certain that the despotic government, any more than another, cannot subsist, if there be not some kind of order established; but it must be remarked, that it is rather preposterous to consider the *corruption of fear,* as an orderly establishment: and after all, I must yet ask what information we derive from all that is said in this book?

I may conclude, from the quotations which I have made, that little information is to be drawn from Montesquieu's reflections, on the manner in which, according to him, the three or four assumed principles of government are weakened or destroyed; I shall take no more notice thereof: but I must take the liberty of combating, or at least discussing, an assertion which is the result of all these ideas. He pretends that it is the natural property of small states to be governed by republics: those of a moderate extent to be subjected to a monarch: those of extensive regions to be ruled by a despot: that to preserve the principles of the established government, the extent of the state should not be changed; and that states change their spirit, as their territories are diminished or augmented: this last assertion, I think, is subject to many objections.

I shall in the first place, repeat an observation which I have already more than once made: the word *republic*, is here very equivocal. It is equally applicable to two governments possessing no similitude, excepting their being without a single chief, and which differ very essentially in relation to the object in question. It is true, that democracy can only exist in a small compass, or within a single town; and even strictly taken, it is impracticable every where for any length of time; as we have already said, it is the infant state of society: but for the aristocracy under several chiefs, to which he gives the name of republic, I can see nothing that prevents it from governing as great an extent of territory, as the aristocracy under a single chief, called monarchy; and the Roman republic is a sufficient evidence of its possibility.

I cannot conceive, how Montesquieu could have advanced, chapter XIX., that despotism, that is *pure monarchy*, is necessary for ruling a great empire effectually, after having said previously, that this government exists only by renouncing its principles; which is a contradiction.

This authorises me again to repeat my assertion, that despotism, like democracy, is a state of society yet unformed, and that these two defective orders of things, both impracticable for any considerable length of time, do not merit our attention. There remains then only aristocracy under several chiefs, and aristocracy under one, or monarchy, which both may equally take place in all states, from the smallest to the largest; with this difference, however, that the last, besides the expences and sacrifices, which the maintenance and prerogatives of the higher class or privileged bodies cost the nation, it is also required of the governed to defray the expences of a court, which is a necessary part of its establishment: so that really, in order to be competent thereto, the state should have a certain degree of extent, or at least of riches, honor, moderation, or any other fantastical idea adopted at random: to answer every question without rendering it any more comprehensible, is not the object to be taken here into consideration, but calculations and possibilities; a king could not subsist upon the income arising from a small number of men, not very industrious, and consequently not very rich: for as the amiable and profound Lafontaine says, *A king is not supported by a few.** There is more philosophy and sound politics in these words, than in many systems.

The representative government, with one or several chiefs, which I have always placed in opposition to aristocracy and its several forms, as being that form proper for a third degree of civilization, has, like it, the property of being applicable to all political societies from the smallest to the greatest. It even has the advantage in a greater degree, for by its nature it is less expensive to the governed, and to the support of administration it does not add sacrifices still more burthensome resulting from the privileges of some men; consequently it can subsist more easily in small states; beside joining the physical power of its executive, to the moral power of each of the members of the legislature, deriving their authority from every part of the state, it is better calculated to execute the laws over a vast extent of territory; consequently it can better maintain order in a large state. It only being required that the legislative power be not placed in opposition to the executive power, as it often happens in aristocracies under a single chief, that the privileged classes oppose their chief, and there are many means by which they can effect it: but this is not the subject of our present consideration.

This is, I believe, all that can be said on the extent of territory of a political society; considering it only in relation to the power of government, as Montesquieu has done; but it seems to me that this subject may be investigated under other points of view, overlooked by him, but which afford occasion for many useful observations.

First: in whatever manner a state be governed, it should have a certain extent: if it be very small, the citizens may assemble in a few days, and confer with each other, and bring about a revolution in a week; so that considering the versatility of the minds of men, and their great sensibility to present evil, it would never be secure from sudden changes, and could not calculate with certainty on the permanent enjoyment of liberty, tranquillity, or happiness.

A state should also be possessed of sufficient power: if too weak, it cannot enjoy a true and secure independence; it holds only a precarious existence, dependent on the jealousy of its more powerful neighbors, suffers from all their quarrels, or falls a victim to their reconciliation; their influence is exercised even in the state against its interests, and it often ends by being consolidated with its most powerful neighbor; or what is yet worse, of being left with the

* Jean de la Fontaine (1621–95), known above all for his *Fables*.

shadow of an existence, without possessing the real power of governing itself according to its best interests: it is governed by the policy and interests of its neighboring states; so that it is subject to be overthrown, not only by revolutions within itself, but by those which take place elsewhere.

Genoa, Venice, and all the small states of Italy, and all those of Germany, notwithstanding their confederacy; Geneva, though united in the Helvetic confederation, are so many proofs of these truths; Swisserland, and even Holland, possessed of greater power, are yet more striking examples. It was said, and believed too long, without due reflection, that the one was sufficiently defended by its mountains, the other by its dykes, and both by the patriotism of their inhabitants. But what can such feeble obstacles, even united with zeal, without intellectual or pecuniary resources, accomplish against a nation possessed of both, or the power to bring them forth? Experience has proved, that their existence was to be attributed to the reciprocal deference of great neighboring states for each other; for they were invaded, as soon as one of the powers ceased to feel that deference. I know of no more humiliating or miserable condition, than that of the citizens of a feeble state.

On the contrary, the political body should not exceed certain proportions: it is not the too great extent of territory in itself, that appears an inconvenience. In the refinement of modern societies, relations are so much multiplied, communications so easy; printing particularly facilitates so much the promulgation of laws, the transmission of orders, instructions, and even opinions, and in return with the same ease, the reception of information on the state of affairs in all directions, the instant communication of intelligence, even of the capacities and interests of individuals, that it becomes no more difficult to govern a great nation than a small province, and the distance appears to me a very small obstacle, to the proper exercise of a necessary power or authority. I even think that great extent of territory, is an incalculable advantage, for neither internal troubles nor external aggression, can impede the political machine, because the evil cannot arise in every place, at the same time; there always remains some sound part, whence succor may be obtained for the assailed part. But it is important, that the extent of a state be such as not to contain within itself, people differing too much in manners, character, and particularly language, or which may have particular or opposite interests. This is the principal consideration which should set bounds to the territory of a nation.

There is yet another consideration worthy of our attention: it is essential to the happiness of the inhabitants of a country, that the frontiers be susceptible of an easy defence; that the limits be not subject to dispute, and so circumstanced as not to intercept the outlets of productive industry, or the course which the spirit of commerce naturally takes; for these reasons natural limits are to be preferred, not those imaginary lines which are to be found only on maps.

The sea, therefore, is, of all natural limits, the best; and has also a property admirable and peculiar to itself, that is, the naval power which defends it, employs few men; those men are useful in promoting the public prosperity; and another advantage, they can never in a body take part in civil disorders, nor alarm interior liberty; consequently the advantages of an island for happiness and liberty are very great. This is so true, that if we suppose the surface of the globe divided into islands of a proper extent and distance from each other, it would be covered by rich and industrious nations, who would not stand in need of any land armies, consequently ruled by moderate governments only. Having the most convenient communication among themselves, and scarcely any ability to hurt each other without affecting their reciprocal relations, their differences would soon cease by means of their mutual dependence and wants. If, on the contrary, we suppose the earth without sea, nations would then be without commerce, always in arms, in constant fear of neighboring nations, ignorant of others, and living under military governments: the sea is one obstacle to all kind of evil, and a means of numerous advantages.

After the sea, the best natural boundary is the tops of the highest mountains, taking for the line of demarcation some stream whose waters run from the summit of the points most elevated, and consequently the most inaccessible. This boundary is also very good on account of its exactness, and of the difficulty of communication from one declivity to another. In general, social relations and communications are established by following the course of the waters; and although they may require land forces to defend them, they do not need so many as in level countries, for to defend them it is sufficient to occupy the defiles formed by the principal branches of the great chain.

But when there are neither seas nor mountains, large rivers may answer, commencing where they have obtained a considerable size, and continuing to the sea, but large rivers only; for if the rivers should flow into others, not in the territory, they would be as so many arteries cut, through which there is no circulation, and which may often paralyze a great extent of country; besides small rivers are not considerable enough, at least in part of their course, to become effective barriers against attacks; even large rivers are not boundaries sufficiently exact, for their course frequently changes and occasion many disputes; they are at best insecure defences, an enterprizing enemy being always able to cross them; in short they are better adapted by their nature for uniting than separating those who inhabit their banks; but there are situations in which the rivers must be made use of for defence: in all cases a political society should, for its own happiness, adopt natural limits and never pass them.

The degree of power, necessary for its defence, depends much on the power of its neighbors, to which it must have a relation: this naturally leads us to the subject of the following book.

BOOK IX.

Of Laws Relative to the Defensive Force.

From confederation, there results less strength, than intimate union, but it is better than entire separation.

SPIRIT OF LAWS, BOOK IX.

THE title of this book, seems to announce that we shall here meet with the theory of laws, relative to the organization of the armed force, and the duties which citizens owe to the state for its defence: this is not the subject that occupies the attention of Montesquieu; he speaks only of the political measures, which a state should take to secure itself against the attacks of its neighbors, but we only follow him.

Prepossessed by the idea, that a republic, whether democratic or aristocratic, can exist only as a small state, he can devise no other means for its defence, than an union with others; in this view, he extols the advantages of a confederated constitution, which appears to him the best invention possible, for preserving liberty, internally and externally. It is certainly better for a weak state, to unite itself with several, by an alliance, or a confederation which is the closest kind of alliance, than depend on itself; but if all these united, should form but one, they would certainly be stronger: now this can be perfectly accomplished by a representative government.

The confederative system answers in America, because they have no formidable neighbors: but if the republic of France had adopted this form, as was once proposed there, it is doubtful whether it could have resisted all Europe, as it did by remaining one and indivisible: it is a general rule received, that a nation gains in strength, by uniting with several others; but would it not become yet more powerful, by an incorporation with them; and does it not lose by subdividing itself into several parts, however closely united?

It might be more plausibly maintained, that confederations render the usurpation of the sovereign power, more difficult than a consolidated government; nevertheless, it did not prevent Holland from subjection to the house of Orange. It is true, it was principally *foreign influence,* that rendered the stadtholder hereditary and all powerful: but this topic belongs to a consideration of the inconveniencies to which weak states are exposed.*

Another advantage of confederation, which appears to me incontestible, but of which Montesquieu says nothing, is the more equal distribution of information, and the perfection of administration, by causing a kind of local patriotism, independently of the general one, and that the collective legislature will combine a better knowledge of the local interests of their small states.

Notwithstanding these excellent qualities, confederations, particularly among the ancients, must be considered as mere essays or experiments, of men who had not yet conceived true ideas of a representative system, and who sought to ensure, at the same time, by the confederative medium, liberty, tranquillity, and power, which unquestionably can be united by that form of government alone: if Montesquieu had known it, I dare say he would agree with me.

He with reason observes, that a confederation should be composed of states nearly of the same strength, and governed nearly by the same principles. The want of these two conditions, accounts for the weakness of the Germanic body; and the opposition of the aristocratical principles of Bern and Friburg, to the democratical principles of the small cantons, has often been most pernicious to the Helvetic confederation, particularly of late years.

He also remarks with no less accuracy, that small monarchies are less adapted for forming confederations than small republics: the reason is very evident. The effect of a confederation, is to constitute a general authority, superior to the particular authority of each state, and consequently kings, attempting to confederate, must cease either to be sovereigns or confederates. This is the case in Germany, where the petty princes have only the appearance of sovereignty, and the great sovereigns only the appearance of confederates. If our author had made this reflection, it would have proved his position better

---

* Originally a state functionary, during the sixteenth century the stadtholder emerged as the effective hereditary head of state of the Dutch Republic.

than the precedent of the Cananean laws he quotes, which are of little importance and not conclusive.*

I must here express my surprize, at the number of facts, minute, problematical, and ill detailed, which Montesquieu quotes from authors little respected, and of countries little known, as proofs of his reasonings and principles; for the most part, he wanders from the question, instead of throwing light on it; which to me has always been disagreeable. In the present case, he is so much attached to his proposition of a republic not being able to govern a great extent of territory, without a confederacy, that he cites the Roman republic as an example of a confederation! I will not pretend to question the erudition of so learned a man, I shall only say he does not quote his authorities.

It is true, that at different times, and in different forms, the Romans incorporated the people whom they had conquered, with them; but this cannot be called a real confederation; and if a state ever had the character of unity, it was a republic residing in a single town, which for that reason, was called the head or capital of the universe: *caput orbis.*†

After having spoken of confederations, as the only means of defence in republics, Montesquieu says, that the means of despotic states, consist in laying waste their frontiers, and surrounding themselves with deserts; and that monarchies protect themselves by the erection of strong military works. Thus exclusively attributing these several means, to each specific form of government, is carrying the spirit of system too far: but I shall offer no further observations on this part of the subject, nor on the rest of the book, for I can perceive no instruction that can be derived from it: I shall only notice this fine sentence: "The spirit of monarchy, is war and aggrandizement; the spirit of republicanism, is peace and moderation." Montesquieu repeats the same sentiments in several places. Is this then lavishing praises on a government of one? But let us pass to the next book.

---

* The destruction of the Canaanites because they lacked a common defense is one of the many examples cited by Montesquieu in Book IX.

† "Head of the world."

BOOK X.

Of Laws Relative to the Offensive Force.

The perfection of the laws of nations, would be their confederation. The right of war flows from the right of defence, and the right of conquest from that of war.

SPIRIT OF LAWS, BOOK X.

UNDER this title, the right of making war, and of conquest, are treated of, and the use which may be made of the armed force, and the means of its establishment.

The right which an association of men possess to make war, is founded on the same principle as that of the right of self-defence in every rational being, and comprehends the person and the interests of the man; for it is with the sole view of defending them with less difficulty and more effect, that he has united in society with other men, and that he has exchanged his right of personal defence, for that of assuring the common aid of society upon an emergency.

Nations, as they respect each other, stand in precisely the same relations as savages, who, belonging to no nation, and being bound by no social obligations among themselves, have no tribunal to which they can apply for redress, no public power of which to claim protection, and consequently each, so circumstanced, must submit or make use of his individual strength in self-defence.

These uncivilized men, however, in order not to be continually exposed to passions, that may lead them to tear each other to pieces like ferocious beasts, would at last be obliged to resort to some means, however imperfect, of mutually understanding each other, and of rendering explanations when any variance should arise, without which their quarrels must last for ever; they must agree, by some sort of convention among themselves, to leave each other unmolested, and they must rely to a certain extent, on the pledge or promise that shall have been made to them, although no really sufficient guarantee be given.

Nations act in the same manner. The most brutal employ negotiators, heralds, or ambassadors, who are treated with respect, who make treaties, and exchange hostages. The more civilized go so far as to set bounds to the fury of the passions, while they last. They allow the dead to be buried, the wounded to be taken care of, and the exchange of prisoners, instead of devouring them, or exercising a ferocious vengeance over each other. They usually deem it a duty not to violate a peace without provocation, and not without seeking an explanation of such provocation; and they deem it necessary to make a public declaration, that the explanation offered is not sufficient. All these particulars are comprised in the received usages of every people, and form a kind of law recognized as such among civilized nations; which indeed require some coercive authority to prevent their infraction,[10] but which nevertheless compose what is called the law of nations: *jus gentium.*

This state of things causes nations to rise from that absolute condition of self-dependence, which we have described, and form rude societies; like the savages, who, through mutual confidence, or necessity for defence, have united in a horde, without having been able to organize a public power competent to secure the rights of each of them. In a society already in this state, the best system of conduct is founded in probity united with prudence; because by a discreet management of the means of self-defence, that confidence which is necessary, is secured by the sentiments of attachment and good will, which this course begets. This is what may be said in favor of the observance of the laws of nations; it is the only sanction of which it is at present susceptible.

It may appear invidious to civilized nations, to assimilate their relations to each other, with individuals in a rude and unformed society: it is, no doubt, a great advance to have abandoned the state of self-dependence, and to have reached that point at which society is organized and somewhat more perfect, by the establishment of social duties and rights; it is only requisite further to establish among themselves, a common tribunal, and a power sufficient to enforce its decisions, such as takes place in the interior of a confederation, among the mem-

---

10. This is the true reason why the laws of nations are not positive, though they are founded on the eternal laws of nature. See the definition of the word Law in the first book.

bers of the confederacy; such as takes place in a society, among the members who compose it.

This third state, in civilization, has always appeared impossible and chimerical; however, it is probably less difficult, than the first, or the two first preceding it. When we reflect what time and pains it required, for men, in their primitive state, to form a language, so as to be well understood; to succeed in obtaining mutual confidence enough for forming small communities, and then larger societies; how much was required to render these societies more generous to each other than ferocious animals; to entertain among each other some moral communications and relations. It appears much less difficult to conceive their moral relations producing a rational organization, and assuming the true character of social relations. There certainly was a time when it appeared much more difficult to form a confederate republic, than it is now to establish a real social compact among several great nations; and there is a greater difference between the original state of man and the Achaean league, than between the actual state of Europe and the confederation of all its parts.*
The greatest obstacles arise from the monarchies, of which its governments are composed, they not being so well adapted as republics for such a purpose, for reasons assigned in the preceding book. But why insist upon such a project being possible at present? And why should it be declared for ever impossible? There are more things possible than we may imagine; experience proves it daily. Let time act, and let us not be too eager to realize dreams, any more than to combat or damp the hopes of well meaning men.

I am sorry that Montesquieu, in touching the subject of the right of nations to make war, has not explained the fundamental ideas of *the right of war,* which might have afforded much useful information. But we ought to thank him, at least for having rejected the absurdities of all the older writers on this subject, and for having explicitly declared, that the right of making war has no other foundation than that of the necessity of self-defence; that arms should never be taken up to gratify self-love, or ideas of dignity, much less for what has been called the glory or the vanity of a prince.

From the right of making war flows the right of conquest. A government, by uniting all or a part of the territory of a conquered people, secures to itself a superiority, reaps advantage from its success, diminishes the power of its

---

* The Achaean League was a confederation of Greek city-states dating from the fifth century BC.

enemy, and ensures a future tranquillity. Savage nations do not possess the means of accomplishing the end of war, and establishing peace; this is one of the misfortunes of their condition; consequently their wars are cruel and without any limits; and when there have been any examples of bad faith on either side, there is no certainty of peace but in the destruction of one or the other of the contending parties.

Conquest, therefore, though preferable to this dreadful extremity, is an infraction of the natural rights of man, to choose the society of which he may please to become a member, unless the conqueror shall leave the inhabitants of the conquered country at full liberty to emigrate, as the citizens of every state should have a right to do when they think it proper. But as it respects a conquered people, some precautions may be allowed with them, as annexing some conditions to the liberty of emigration, for a certain time, or according to circumstances, which may prevent a renewal of war: these principles respecting war established, conquest may become perfectly just, if the cause of the war has been just.

Two questions arise: when and for what end should conquest be made, and after peace, how should the conquered countries be treated? Montesquieu explains at large what relates to these two points, in the interests of each of the governments which he has distinguished. He even explains how a nation should conduct itself when it wholly occupies and establishes itself in a country which it has conquered, as the Tartars in China, and the Franks in Gaul.*

I shall reject this last supposition, because it is a continuation of the state of warfare, and remains so until the conquered have been expelled, or the two nations are blended the one into the other by consent or force; consequently this does not apply to the establishment of a state of peace: moreover, this supposition can only take place with a barbarous nation, or a people in a very imperfect state of society: now I shall confine myself to civilized nations.

For this last reason, I shall say nothing of states purely democratic or despotic, noticing only those which are governed by an aristocracy under one or several chiefs, and a representative democracy.

These governments, as we have seen, are alike adapted to rule over a large or a small territory; consequently, this consideration cannot make them fear

---

* Montesquieu indicates that the Tartars established that each body of troops should be composed half of Chinese soldiers and half of Tartars. The Franks allowed marriage with the Gauls.

nor desire an encrease of territory; but the convenience of natural boundaries, appears to me a question of an important nature; and I repeat, that a nation should neglect nothing to procure the best possible boundaries, and when obtained should never pass them: therefore so long as a nation has not obtained this end, it should add to its territory, all the countries it can acquire in peace; but if it has attained thereto, and the necessity of providing for future security obliges it to take from its enemy all or part of his territory, it should cede the superfluous acquisition to some other state, the augmentation of whose power is its interest, or form out of it one or several independent states, to which it may give a government similar to its own; taking care that their power shall be such as to preserve itself from disquietude, while it shall be sufficient for their own defence, and save the protecting state from the necessity of being continually required to protect them, or be the means or pretence of new wars.

Respecting the conduct to be held towards the inhabitants of a conquered country of which possession is retained, I think with Montesquieu, that, like the different kinds of aristocracy, which are not established in exact justice, nor on any principles absolutely fixed, the object of the conquering government should be to employ such means as are best adapted to gain the affection and assure the attachment of the new subjects, and to treat them more favorably than they had been previously treated. But the representative government being founded on invariable equity and moral justice, can render the acquired people no other nor greater advantages than its own citizens already possess, and this being as much as can be coveted or obtained under any circumstances, is well adapted to gratify those who acquire such equal rights, especially if they had not possessed any rights before.

I must here notice the justice of Montesquieu's reflection, that a people often gain a great deal by being conquered: and I must add, that this is particularly true, of those whose fortune it is to be conquered by a representative government, for they thereby gain both liberty and economy, whether they become a part of the social body by which they are conquered, or are formed into a new state, governed by the same principles of virtue and justice. To be thus conquered, is in truth more like a rescue from bondage, than a subjection; and this is what renders the representative form of government formidable to all others; for whenever another form of government is at variance with a representative government, the people under the other form have in fact, a common interest in the prosperity of a government founded on human rights and justice. This is the reason why the great acquisitions of the French, in their republican period, were so easily incorporated with it, notwithstanding the repugnance of their civil and religious prejudices: and the same will happen with Louisiana and the United States of America, though the intrigues of European statesmen may vainly attempt to prevent it.

If France had made as much use as she might of those immense advantages over her assailants, and not deserted equal principles, after fixing her boundaries by natural limits, such as were reasonable and convenient, it would very soon have been surrounded by states like itself, and which, serving as barriers, would have secured its tranquillity and liberty for ever.*

Before leaving this subject, we must notice the profound reflection of Montesquieu, that a republic desirous of remaining free, should have no subjects; this observation is particularly applicable to a representative government, consequently it should have no possessions beyond sea, subject to laws made in the parent country. It might be very useful for her to form colonies, to afford room for superfluous population, or to procure commodious and amicable intercourse, in countries well adapted to maintain advantageous commerce, but they should be emancipated, as soon as they are found competent to exist by themselves, or become a part of the confederation upon common terms with the rest of the society, that is when their population gives them a reasonable title thereto. We have said enough of war and its consequences, let us pass to other objects.

* The French text refers only to "tranquillity" and makes no mention of "liberty."

BOOK XI.

Of the Laws Which Establish Public Liberty, in Relation to the Constitution.

The problem of the distribution of the power of a society, so as to be most favorable to liberty, cannot be solved so long as too much power is given to a single man.

SPIRIT OF LAWS, BOOK XI.

I have thought proper to divide my commentary on this book, into two chapters. The first alone bears directly upon the work of Montesquieu; the second only flows out of the first: but Montesquieu has not gone so far into the subject in his enquiry.

CHAP. I.

IS THE PROBLEM SOLVED, AS TO THE BEST MEANS OF DISTRIBUTING THE POWER OF SOCIETY, SO AS TO BE MOST FAVORABLE TO LIBERTY?*

IN this book, the title of which does not present an idea sufficiently distinct, the degree of liberty which may be enjoyed under each constitution of government is examined; that is to say the effects produced on the liberties of the citizens by the laws forming the constitution of the state. Such laws are those only which regulate the distribution of political power; for the constitution of a society is nothing more than the collection of rules determining the nature, extent, and limits, of the authorities ruling it; so that when these rules are to be united into a single body of laws, serving as the bond of the political edifice, the first precaution to be taken, is not to admit any thing irreconcilable

---

* In the French text, this title appears as the first paragraph of the text.

with the objects proposed to be secured; without which precaution it is not exactly a *constitution,* but an expedient, calculated for a greater or a less considerable portion of the general body of the nation.

To know what influence the organization of society has on the liberty of its members, we should perfectly understand what is meant by liberty. The word liberty, like all others intended to express abstract ideas of a very general nature, is often taken in a multitude of different acceptations, which are so many particular parts of its comprehensive signification; thus we say, a man has become free, when he has finished an enterprize, in which he had been wholly occupied; when he has given up a slavish office; when he has renounced a station, which imposed responsible duties on him; when he has broken the yoke of certain passions, or connexions, which kept him in subjection; when he has escaped from a prison; when he has withdrawn himself from the dominions of a tyrannical government: we likewise say, the liberty of thinking, speaking, acting, writing; that his speech, respiration, and all his movements are free, when nothing constrains him in these respects: then all these particular faculties of liberty are ranged into classes, forming different groups according to their several natures; such as physical, moral, natural, civil, and political liberty; whence it happens, that when forming a general idea of liberty, every one composes it of that kind of liberty, to which he attaches the greatest importance, of a freedom from those constraints against which he is the most prejudiced, and which appear to him the most insupportable; some make it to consist in virtue, in indifference, or in a kind of impassibility, like those stoics who pretended that their sages remained free, even when in chains; others place it in society; others in competency and ease, or in a state unconnected with and independent of any social ties; others again pretend, that to be free is to live under certain forms of government, or generally under one that is moderate and enlightened. All these opinions are just, according to the sense in which liberty is understood; but in none is it seen in all its forms, nor is its proper character embraced in any of their definitions. Let us examine what these different kinds of liberty possess in common, and in what they severally resemble each other; for it is in this way only we can approach the general ideas, abstracted from all the particular ideas which are comprehended therein.

If we consider it attentively, we shall perceive that one property common to all descriptions of liberty, is that it procures for the individual enjoying it, the exercise of his will in a greater extent than if deprived of that enjoyment; therefore, the idea of liberty, in its most abstract form, as well as in its greatest extent, is nothing more than the idea of the power to do that which the mind wills; and in general, to be free is to be enabled to do what we please.

Hence we perceive that liberty is applicable only to beings endowed with will; and when we say of water that it runs more freely when the obstacles opposed to its passage are taken away, or that a wheel turns more freely when the friction retarding it is diminished; it is by comparison we express ourselves, because we presuppose that the water inclines or possesses a quality which disposes it to run, and the wheel a like disposition to turn; or that such is the necessary effect in given circumstances.

For the same reason, this question so much debated, *Is our will free?* should never be urged, for it is an abuse of terms; liberty only relates to the will when formed, and not before the will exists: what has given rise to an enquiry of this kind is, that on particular occasions the motives acting upon us are so powerful, that they determine us immediately to will one thing in preference to or rather than another, and then it is said, we will irresistibly or are necessitated to will; while in other circumstances, the motives not being so strong, or acting with less impulsion, leave us the power of deliberation, to reflect on and weigh them in our minds; in this state, we think we possess the power either to resist or to obey those impulses, and to take one determination in preference to another, solely because we will it; but this is an illusion, for however weak a motive may be, it necessarily determines our will, unless it be balanced by a more powerful motive, and then this is as necessarily determined as the other would have been, if alone; we will or we do not will, but we cannot will to will; and if we could, there would yet be an antecedent cause of this will, and this cause would be beyond the range of the will, as are all those which cause it; and therefore we must conclude that liberty exists only after the will, and in consequence of its unrestrained exercise; or that liberty is no more than the power of executing the will. I ask the reader's pardon, for this metaphysical discussion on the nature of liberty, but it will soon be perceived, that it is neither inappropriate nor useless. It is impossible to speak intelligibly on the interests of men without a previous and due understanding of their faculties; if there be any thing more materially deficient than another, in the writings of the great man on which I comment, it is particularly in this preliminary study, and we may perceive how vague the ideas are which he presents to us of liberty, although he had devoted three chapters to that particular subject. We have made nearly the same exceptions to his idea of the word law, in the first book.

Liberty, in the most general acceptation of the word, is nothing else than the power of executing the will, and accomplishing our desires; now the nature of every being endowed with will, is such that this faculty of willing causes his happiness or unhappiness; he is happy when his desires are accomplished, and unhappy when they are not; and happiness or misery are proportioned in him according to the degree of his gratification or disappointment. It follows that his liberty and happiness are the same thing. He would always be completely happy if he had always the power of executing his will, and the degree of his happiness is always proportionate to the degree of his power.

This remark explains why men, even without suspecting it, are all so passionately fond of liberty; for they could not be otherwise, since whenever there exists a desire, under whatever name it may appear, the possibility of accomplishing that desire is implied, and willed or wished; it is always the possession of a portion of power, or the removal of some constraint, which constitutes a certain portion of happiness. The exclamation, "O if I could!" comprehends the desire of accomplishing all our wishes; every wish would be gratified if we could effect it by willing it: all powerful, or what is the same thing, entire liberty, is inseparable from perfect happiness.

This remark conducts us farther, and explains to us why men have formed to themselves different ideas of liberty, according to their different ideas of happiness. They must always have attached the idea of liberty in an eminent degree, to the power of doing what they please, and of which satisfaction is the attribute. Montesquieu, in his second chapter, appears to be astonished that many people should entertain false ideas of liberty, making it consist in things foreign to their solid interests, or at least not essential thereto; but he should have first considered that men have often placed their happiness and satisfaction in the enjoyment of unimportant or even hurtful things: the first fault committed, the second follows as a consequence. A Russian in the time of Peter the great, placed his greatest interest in his long beard,* which was in fact of no use, or an incumbrance, or very ridiculous. The native of Poland was passionately attached to his *liberum veto*,† which was the great source of affliction to his country. Both Russians and Poles would have deemed themselves

---

* Peter the Great banned long beards from his court.

† The *liberum veto* was a parliamentary device existing in the Polish-Lithuanian Commonwealth during the seventeenth and eighteenth centuries. It allowed any member of the legislature to block legislation.

subjected to the greatest tyranny, if obliged to part with either; and their subjection was certainly great, when they were deprived thereof, for their strongest
desires were frustrated. Montesquieu answers himself by adding this remarkable phrase, "In fine, every one has called that government free, which was
most conformable to his inclinations;" which is unquestionably true, it could
not be otherwise, and each has so expressed himself reasonably, because every
one is truly free when all his wishes are gratified, and we cannot be free in any
other manner.

From this last observation flows many consequences; the first which presents itself is that a nation should be considered truly free as long as it continues satisfied with its government, even if in its nature the government should
be less conformable to the principles of liberty than another which displeases
him. It is often mentioned that *Solon* said, *"I have not given to the Athenians,
the best possible laws that they could receive,"* that is, the best they were worthy
of.* I do not believe that Solon said so; such contemptuous boasting would
have been very ill placed in the mouth of one who had adapted his laws so
injudiciously to the character of the nation, that they did not last his life time.
But I believe he did say, *"I have given them the best laws they would receive."*
This might have been true, and justifies him under the circumstances of his
want of success; and it necessarily must have been so, because as he did not
impose his laws by force, he was necessitated to give them as they would be
received; now the Athenians, in adopting such imperfect laws, were certainly
ill advised; but they were very free; while in modern times a great part of
France, in receiving their constitution of the year three (1795), however free
it might be in its form, were really slaves, since it was established in opposition to their will;† hence we may conclude, that institutions can be ameliorated only in proportion to the increase of information among the people at
large, and even those which are the best absolutely are not always so relatively;
for the better they are, the more they are opposed to false ideas, and if they
are disagreeable to too great a number, they cannot be maintained without
using forcible means, after which there could be no more liberty, no more happiness, no more security; this may serve as an apology for many institutions

---

* Solon (c. 630–c. 560 BC) is best remembered as an Athenian lawgiver.

† The French Constitution of Year III replaced the Jacobin Constitution of Year I.
Pushing back the claims of popular democracy, it gave the executive branch considerable powers (including restrictions on freedom of the press).

bad in themselves, which may have been at one period well adapted to the circumstances in which they existed, but furnishes no argument for our preserving them when they are found to be pernicious; and it may also serve to explain the causes of failure of many good institutions, and will not prevent us from adopting them at a more favorable time.

The second consequence of the observation which we have made above is, that the government under which the greatest liberty is enjoyed, whatever may be its form, is that which governs the best, for in it the greatest number of people are the happiest; and when we are as happy as we can be, our desires are accomplished as much as possible. If the most despotic prince should administer public affairs in a perfect manner, we should enjoy the greatest possible happiness under his rule, which is the same thing as *liberty*. It is not then the form of government in itself, that is so important; it would indeed be a very weak argument in its favor, that it was in form more agreeable to reason, because it is not mere speculation or theory, which constitute the happiness of mankind in society, but practical good and beneficial results; for it concerns individuals who possess the faculties of life, and are sensible of good and evil, not ideal or abstract beings. Those, who in the political convulsions of our times, said, "I do not care about being free, all I desire is to be happy," uttered a sentiment contradictory in itself, being both very sensible and very insignificant: sensible, in as much as happiness is the only object worthy of our attention; insignificant, in as much as happiness is really true liberty. For the same reason, those enthusiasts, who said that happiness is not to be taken into consideration, when liberty is in question, are guilty of the same absurdity; for if happiness could be separated from liberty, it should without hesitation be preferred: but we are not happy when we are not free, for certainly suffering is not doing as we wish. The only circumstance, therefore, which renders any one social organization preferable to another, is its being better adapted to render the members of society happy; and if in general it be desired, that the social constitution should leave to the people a great facility to make known their wishes, it is then more probable that under a government which secures this power, they are governed as they desire.

Let us examine, with Montesquieu, which are the principal conditions to be fulfilled in order to accomplish this end; and like him, let us only occupy ourselves on the question generally, without respect to any local or particular conjuncture.

This justly celebrated philosopher has remarked, in the first place, that public functions may be reduced to three principles: that of making laws; that of conducting internal and external affairs, according to the intention of the laws; and, that of passing judgment on private or civil differences, as well as on accusations of private and public offences: that is to say, in other words, that social action is comprised in *willing, executing,* and *judging.*

Then it may be easily perceived that these three great functions, or even two of them, could not be united in the same person or persons, without the greatest danger to the rest of the citizens; for if the same man, or body of men, were at the same time authorised to will and to execute, the single person or the body of men, would be too powerful for any to interpose or form a judgment, and consequently would be obliged to submit. If the one only who made the law also judged, it is probable that he would soon rule the one entrusted with the execution of the law; and in short, this last person who executes, being always the most to be feared, on account of the physical force entrusted to him; if he should be invested with the function of judging, there can be no doubt that he would soon so arrange the means of authority, that the legislating power must enact such laws only as he should please.

These dangers are too palpable to attach any merit to their discovery; the great difficulty appears to be, how to devise the means of avoiding them. Montesquieu spares himself the trouble of such an enquiry, by persuading himself that they are already found: he even blames Harrington for occupying himself with the subject. "We may say of him," says Montesquieu, "that he has only sought liberty, after stumbling upon it without knowing it; that he looked for Chalcedon with the coast of Byzantium in his view."* He is so well satisfied of the problem being solved, that he says in another place, "To discover political liberty in the constitution, does not require so much trouble, if we can possess it where it is; if we have found it, why seek it:" and he immediately presents the form of the English government, as he imagined it to exist in its administration. It is true, that at the period in which he wrote, England was a very flourishing and celebrated state; its government was, of those till then known, that which produced, or appeared to produce, the most flattering results in every respect. However, this superiority, partly real, partly apparent, but in a greater measure the effect of causes wholly foreign, should not have prepossessed so strong a mind as Montesquieu, or induced him to

---

* James Harrington (1611–77), author of *The Commonwealth of Oceana* (1656). The text was a description of a utopia designed to support the cause of republicanism.

suppress the errors of the theory, or to insinuate that it leaves nothing more to be desired.

This prepossession in favor of English institutions and ideas, led him in the first place to forget, that the legislative, executive, and judicial functions, are properly only delegated trusts, functions which may indeed confer power and credit, on the persons invested with them, but are not therefore self-existent in the persons who exercise them There is by *right,* only one power in society, and that is the will of the nation or society, from which all authority flows; and in fact there is not any other change, than that of the authority delegated to the man, or body of men, of the several functions by which they disburse the necessary expences, and exercise all the physical force of the society. Montesquieu does not deny this, he is only unmindful of it; he is entirely taken up with his triple powers, his legislative, executive, and judiciary, considering them as rivals, and as powers independent of each other; and that it is only necessary to reconcile or restrain them, each by the other, in order to make every thing go on well, without taking any notice, whatever, of the natural power from which they are derived, and upon which they depend.

By not perceiving that his executive power is the only real one in fact, and that it influences all the others, he concedes, without consideration or enquiry, this power to an individual, and even makes it hereditary in that individual's family, and for no other reason than because one man is better calculated for action than many: if this principle were well founded, it would have been yet worth enquiry, whether if an individual be so much better fitted for action, he would suffer any other free action to exist round him; and moreover, whether this individual, chosen at hazard, is so likely to be competent to the exercise of that wise deliberation which should precede every action.

He also approves of the legislative power, being confided to the legislators, freely elected by the people for a limited period, and from all parts of the nation; but what is still more extraordinary, he approves of the existence of the privileged hereditary body in the nation, and that this body should compose of itself, by right, a part of the legislative body, distinct and separate from that elected by the people, and that it should possess the right of a negative upon the resolves of the elected representatives! His reasons are curious; it is, he says, "because their prerogatives are *odious in themselves,* and they should be enabled to defend them;" it would seem a more natural conclusion, we should think, that being odious they should rather be abolished.

He also thinks, that this second section of the legislative body is very useful, because there can be placed therein, all that is really important in the judiciary authority, the passing of judgment on crimes against the state; so that, as he says, it becomes the *regulating power*, of which both the executive and legislative powers stand in need to mutually temper them. He does not look to facts in the history of England, nor perceive what it attests, that the house of lords is any thing else, rather than an independent and regulating power; that it is, in fact, only an appendage to the court, the advanced guard of the executive power, whose fortunes it has always followed; and that giving this irresponsible body a negative in legislation and a high judiciary function, is only investing the court with an additional force, and rendering the punishment of state criminals a matter of mere discretion with the executive, or rendering it impossible to punish whenever it is not the pleasure of the court.

Notwithstanding these advantages, and the great power which the executive has at its disposal, he does not think the right of a negative upon the laws necessary to the executive; nor that of convoking, nor of proroguing, nor of dissolving them; and he imagines that the popular representatives possess a sufficient defence, in their precautionary power of voting the supplies only for one year, as if they must not renew them every year, or witness a dissolution of the government; and that this power is further augmented by their having it in their discretion to prohibit or permit the raising of a military force, or the establishment of camps, barracks, or fortified places; as if they must not be forced into the establishment of either, whenever a necessity shall call for it, a necessity which the executive can at any time create.

Montesquieu terminates this long detail, by a sentence obscure and embarrassed: "This is the fundamental constitution of the government of which we speak; the legislative body being composed of two parts, each of them constrains the other, by their mutual preventative faculty; both are restrained by the executive, which will itself be restrained by the legislative:" and to this he adds this singular reflection: "These three powers should naturally form a state of repose or inaction; but as in the nature of things they must move, they are under the necessity of acting in concert." I must acknowledge, that I do not perceive the absolute necessity of this conclusion; on the contrary, it appears evident, that where every thing is constituted, so as to constrain or impede motion, nothing can be perfectly accomplished. If the king were not effectively master of the parliament, and if he did not consequently lead them, I can see nothing in this weak fabric of government that could prevent him; neither can I perceive any thing in favor of such an organization, which is in my opinion very imperfect, but a circumstance which belongs to it rather than forming a part of it, and which has not been noticed; that is, the constancy with which the nation wills that it should so subsist. But as at the same time, they are wisely attached to the maintenance of personal liberty and the freedom of the press, the power is always preserved of making the public opinion known; so that when the king abuses his power, of which he really possesses too much, he is subject to be opposed by a general movement in favor of those who resist his oppression; as has been twice exemplified in the seventeenth century,* and which is always very easy in an island, where there can be no motives, consistent with the principles of the government, for maintaining a large standing army. This is in fact the only effective *veto,* which is to be found under the English constitution, compared with which all the rest are nothing.

The great point in the English constitution is, that the nation six or seven times deposed its kings: but then it must be remarked, that this is not a constitutional expedient; it is rather an insurrection arising out of necessity, as it was formerly said to be according to the laws of Crete. Legislative deposition, to my great astonishment, Montesquieu praises in another part of his book, notwithstanding it is certain that this remedy is so cruel, that a sensible people would endure great evils, before they could resort to it; and though it may happen that they defer redress so long, that if the usurpation be conducted with address, the people may insensibly acquire the habit of slavery so inveterately, as no longer to feel the desire, or may cease to possess the capacity, of breaking their chains by any means.

What very much characterises the warmth of Montesquieu's imagination, is, that on the faith of three lines from Tacitus, which would require a copious commentary, he has persuaded himself, that he found among the savages of ancient Germany, the model and the spirit of the government, which he considers as a masterpiece of human reason; in the excess of his admiration, he thus exclaims, "This excellent system was discovered in the woods:" and a little after he adds, "It does not belong to me to examine whether the English actually enjoy liberty or not, it is sufficient to say, it is established by their laws."† Nevertheless, I am of opinion, that the first point was well worthy of examination, were it only to assure himself, that he had a just knowledge of the second; because if he had bestowed more attention on *their laws,* he would have discovered that among the English, there exists really no more than *two* powers instead of three; that these two powers exist only when

* A reference to the removal of both Charles I and James II.

† See the previous footnote on Tacitus, at the end of Book VI.

both are present, because one has all the real force and no public attachment, while the other possesses no force, but enjoys all the public confidence, until it manifests a disposition to overpower its rival, and sometimes even then: that these two powers, by uniting, are legally competent to the change of the public established laws, and even those which determine their relations and their existence, for no law obstructs them, and they have exercised this power on various occasions: so that, in fact, liberty is not truly established by their political laws; and if the English really enjoy liberty to a certain extent, it originates in the causes which I have explained, and has reference to certain received usages in their civil and criminal proceedings, rather than to positive laws; as, in fact, it is altogether without law established.

The great problem, therefore, of the distribution of the powers of society, so that neither of them may trespass on the authority of the other, or the limits assigned them by the general interests; and that it may always be easy to keep them within bounds, or to bring them back by peaceable and legal means, is not, I conceive, resolved in that country: I would rather claim this honor for the United States of America, the constitution of which determines what should be done when the executive, or when the legislative, or when both together, go beyond their legitimate powers, or are in opposition to each other; and when it becomes necessary to change the constitutional act of a state, or of the confederation itself. But it may be objected, that in case of such regulations, the great difficulty lies in their execution; that the Americans, when the authorities of a particular state are in question, are guaranteed by the force of the superior authority of the confederation; and that when it becomes a question of guarantee, it resolves itself into the union of the several confederated states, acting for one state; and that in this view of the facts, we have rather eluded than solved it, by the aid of the confederative system; and that it therefore remains to be explained, how the same end could be obtained, where the established government is an indivisible body or unity.

Such a subject requires to be treated of in the manner of a theory, rather than historically; I shall therefore endeavor to establish *à priori*, the principles of a truly free, legal, and peaceable constitution; for which purpose we must take a fair point of view, from ground a little more retired and elevated.

BOOK XI.

How Can the Proposed Problem Be Solved?

The problem can only be solved by never placing more power in the hands of a single man, than may be taken from him without violence; and by changing every thing with him.

SPIRIT OF LAWS, BOOK XI.

CHAP. II.

WE have said, that perfect power or perfect liberty, is perfect happiness: this perfect state is not assigned to man: it is incompatible with the weakness of all finite beings.

If it were possible for a man to live in a state of self-dependence and absolute independence, he would certainly not be constrained by the will of other men, but he would be the slave of all the powers of nature, so as not to be able to resist them sufficiently for his own preservation.

When men, therefore, unite in society, it is not true, as has been so often said, that they sacrifice a part of their liberties to enjoy the rest with security; on the contrary, every one of them acquires by association an encrease of power. This it is that so imperiously inclines men to unite, and is the reason why there is so much less evil in the most imperfect state of society, than in a state of separation; men are from time to time oppressed by society, but they are constantly receiving assistance therefrom. Suppose yourself placed in the desert of Lybia, proceed from thence into the territory of the emperor of Morocco, and you imagine yourself arrived in a hospitable country. For men to live together, every one should make some kind of arrangement, perfect or imperfect, with all the others; it is the manner of this arrangement in which consists what is called the constitution of society.

These social arrangements were made in the beginning of all societies, and without any principles to govern their formation; afterwards they were modi-

94

fied, ameliorated, and even rendered worse in many respects, according to circumstances; and hence originates the almost infinite number of social organizations among men, of which scarce one resembles any other, without our being able, in general, to say which is the worst. These rude arrangements necessarily subsist, as long as they do not become absolutely insupportable to the greatest part of those who are interested therein, for changing them generally costs very dear. But let us suppose a large and enlightened nation to become tired of their constitution, or rather conscious of not having duly digested and determined upon a good one, as is generally the case; let us examine what it should do to form one, according to the light of reason simply.

It appears evident to me, that it could only take one of the three following courses: either to change the authorities governing it, and to arrange among themselves reciprocally the limits of the several functions, and clearly to define their rights and duties; that is to say, the cases wherein they should be obeyed or might be resisted: or to nominate some enlightened person to draw up a complete plan of a new government: or to confide this important task to an assembly of deputies freely chosen for the purpose, and exercising no other function.

The first of these methods was pursued by the English in 1688, when they consented, at least tacitly, to their parliament dethroning James II. receiving William III. and making a convention with him called the bill of rights,* and which they in fact ratified by their obedience and even attachment. The second method was had recourse to by several ancient nations: and the third has been preferred by the Americans and French in modern times, when they shook off the yoke of their former monarchs. But the Americans have followed it exactly, excepting in the *first* instance; whereas the others have departed therefrom two different times, by leaving the power of governing and constituting in the same persons; each of these three courses has its advantages and disadvantages.

The first is the most simple, prompt, and easy in practice; but it amounts to only a kind of transaction between the different authorities, and the limits of their power taken together, will not be circumscribed with due exactness, nor will the means of reforming or entirely changing it, be provided for, nor will the rights of the nation, in respect to the rulers, be well known.

---

* The French text speaks of a constitution rather than of a bill of rights.

The second promises a more perfect renovation and more complete legislation; it even gives some reason to hope that a new system of government, originating with and formed by one person, will possess more uniformity and a better combination; but independently of the difficulty of finding a sage, worthy of placing so much confidence in, and the danger of granting it to an ambitious person, who would render it subservient to his own purposes, it is to be apprehended, that a plan the conception of any single man, and which had not been submitted to discussion, may not be sufficiently adapted to the national ideas, and would not, therefore, obtain the public sanction. It is even almost impossible, that it should obtain the general consent, unless its author, like most of the ancient legislators, should call in the divinity to his assistance, and persuade the people that he was only the interpreter of a supernatural power.

But this cannot be put in practice in our time; moreover, reason can never be well established, when it is founded on imposture: besides that there is this inconvenience, a constitution is always essentially bad, when it does not contain in itself a clear, legal, and peaceable means of modifying and changing it: when it is not so contrived, as to adapt itself to the progress of time and experience; or when it assumes a character of perpetuity and stability, inconsistent with any human institution; now it is very difficult to conceive, that all this should not be found in any government, which has been held forth as the work of a God.

Respecting the third manner of forming a constitution, when we reflect how much more unreasonable men are when united, than any of them taken separately; how much inferior the enlightened views of an assembly are to the best informed of its members; how much exposed its resolutions are to wavering and incoherency; we naturally conclude that its work cannot be the most perfect possible; and it may also be feared, that this assembly might assume to itself the sole power, and with a view not to be divested of that power, may very much retard the accomplishment of the purposes for which they were delegated, and by this or such means so lengthen out its authority, as to degenerate into a tyranny or anarchy.

The first of these objections is founded; but we must likewise consider, that this assembly, being composed of members approved of in different parts of the territory, and who are acquainted with the dispositions of the inhabitants, whatever it may determine upon will be very likely to be acceptable in practice, and received not only without effort but with pleasure.

Secondly: that the information of this assembly will always be superior to that of the people at large, and every thing being naturally and fully discussed by it, the motives of its determinations will be known and examined; and as it is itself formed upon a knowledge of public opinion, it will be in fact the opinion of the public; so that it will very much contribute to the rectification of general ideas, and to the progress of the social tie among the people: now these advantages are superior in effect to a greater perfection in the theory of the social organization which may be adopted.

The second inconvenience is more apparent than real, for a society should not undertake to form a new constitution, until it shall have united all the powers of society in such as are favorable to the undertaking; this is the thing previously necessary; it is in this that revolution and destruction properly consist; all the rest is only organization and reconstruction. Now this provisory authority which convokes an assembly charged with constituting a form of government, should invest it with that single function only, reserving to itself the superintendence of the social machine until completely renovated; for the transactions of society should suffer no interruption: there should always be an intermediary authority between the new and the old. The famous national convention of France,* which has perpetrated so much evil against humanity, and cast a temporary odium even upon reason itself; which, notwithstanding the great capacity and virtue of several of its members, permitted itself to be ruled by fanatics and hypocrites, villains and impostors, and thereby rendered useless, as if by anticipation, its best conceptions; this body became exposed to so many misfortunes, from the legislative body which preceded it, having devolved all their functions and powers upon it at the same time. The legislative body, after conceiving itself obliged to overturn the throne, after having proclaimed the national desire for a *republic* (as we have said according to Montesquieu's idea), that is to say, for the destruction of the hereditary executive power, should have called a convention, to realize these views only, and to organize society in a manner corresponding therewith; meantime they should have continued to watch over the interests of the moment, and reserved to themselves the care of conducting the national affairs. Then the national convention would infallibly have accomplished its legitimate purpose in a very short time and without commotion.

For the same reason, the first continental congress of America, and the first national assembly of France, having taken the power from the old authorities,

---

* A reference to the institution that eventually saw the rise of Robespierre to power and the inauguration of the Reign of Terror.

and being thereby the sole and exclusive governing powers, they should not have made themselves constituent authorities, but have convoked an assembly for that special purpose, and acted under their protection.[11] Notwithstanding this irregularity, experience has proved that they did not prolong their existence unnecessarily, and resigned their authority as soon as the public interests required, or rather permitted it: and even the French constituent assembly was so impatient to dissolve itself that it committed a great fault, in declaring its members incapable of being chosen for the legislative assembly, which was to follow it; depriving themselves also of every influence in ulterior transactions.

Of the three modes which a nation may adopt, that is desirous of altering its constitution, I believe the last is that which unites the most advantage and the least inconvenience; but whatever be that mode which is preferred, to choose it there should be an assemblage, and the assembly should be convoked by the authority actually existing.

If we desire to proceed with method, we should examine the first point: events never present themselves with the same regularity as they may be arranged by theory; but by a due attention to events, we may always find in the concatenation of causes which lead to their successive effects, a series of ideas which are nothing else than the data which constitute a good or an erroneous theory, the thread of which we should never lose sight of, if we mean not to go astray.

It is evident that the nation we speak of should be consulted for the object in question, that is, on the choice of the means which it desires to employ in reconstructing the edifice of society: it is no less true that all the members of a considerable society, cannot be assembled in one place for purposes of deliberation; the provisional authority which governs, should therefore convoke several assemblies in different parts of the territory, and regulate the mode in which their suffrages shall be collected; thus far there can be no doubt. But here a question presents itself, which will determine many others, for it will be met with in a thousand forms in all the subsequent details: should all the citizens be equally called to such assemblies, and vote in the same manner? I answer decidedly in the affirmative, and I will give my reasons.

11. It is thus, that the convention of 1787, which completed the federative constitution of America, was held; and which definitely fixed its form, eleven years and seventy-five days after the declaration of independence, and nine years and seventy days after the signature of the first act of confederation.

It is generally said, and Montesquieu has also said it, that "there are always in a state, people who are distinguished by birth, riches, or honors; that if they were confounded with the people, and had only a voice in common with the rest, to them liberty would become slavery, and they would have no interest in defending liberty so established, because the greatest preponderancy of public power would be against them. Their part in the legislation of the state, should be, therefore, proportioned to the other advantages which they possess; which would be accomplished by constituting them into a body, possessing the power of checking the enterprizes of the people, as the people would have a like right to check theirs."

I must acknowledge, that these arguments do not carry conviction to my judgment; indeed they appear to me, a mass of confusion, which it may be proper to extricate from disorder.

Beginning with birth, a man possessed of a name celebrated for great talents, or great public services, or only a name honored by a manner of living above the common, or by functions to which distinction is attached in society, possesses the advantages of being more generally known, rather than of rendering more various or more useful services to society; he may be generally presumed to have a better education, more enlarged ideas, and acquirements more extensive; he attracts more attention, and possibly more good will is borne towards him; his happiness may excite less envy, and his misfortunes inspire more interest. These are no doubt great advantages; but they cannot be lost, they exist in the nature of man and of society; no law can give, and no law can take them away; they stand in no need of special protection to assure their existence. But is it to be asserted, that these great advantages must also confer on the possessor, a positive right to more; to places of distinction, to powers, and prerogatives, of which his fellow citizens are deprived? Here the case is very different; such rights, if permitted to exist, can only be conferred by the society and granted for their use; and to society alone it belongs, to determine whether they are useful or pernicious; the individuals enjoying such advantages, should possess no particular power to defend them against the general interest.

The same principle holds good as to wealth: undoubtedly wealth in itself is a very great power; it has nearly the same advantages as birth, and others peculiarly its own. A great fortune gives to him who is the possessor a great superiority in every society, if he only knows how to use it, over those who are not wealthy; and on this account particularly, it is not necessary to add any power or privilege to wealth; for if this great fortune should happen to be a patrimonial right, it is guaranteed by the laws that relate to property and the protection of personal rights; if it consist of rewards conferred by the state, either as a recompense or a salary, there can be no reason for subjecting the state, in the distribution of its gifts, to any other consideration than those of public convenience and justice.

The same may be said, and with additional force, with respect to honors; if we understand by this word honor, the splendor and consideration which is attached to birth, fortune, or personal glory; no law can dispose thereof. If, on the contrary, by honor is to be understood, the distinctions and favors which government may have the right to grant, they should never be accompanied by any power capable of maintaining possession of them in opposition to the will of society.

It is therefore always useless or injurious that those who already possess great advantages in society, should also be invested with a superiority of power, which, under the pretext of defending themselves, would be the means of social oppression. It is certainly enough that those who do possess advantages which are not common to the society at large, are secured by the laws in the unmolested enjoyment of them. It is absurd to say that if they did not enjoy this increase of power, they would believe themselves oppressed, and would consider general liberty as slavery to them; it is as if men possessed of great bodily strength should declare themselves very much oppressed, in that they are not permitted so to use that strength for their particular benefit, because they are prevented from employing it against their fellow citizens and from forcing the weak to work for the profit of the strong against their own will.

This system of balancing, I consider as erroneous and indefensible: it originates in imperfect combinations, which confer powers of defence on particular personages, under the idea of protecting them against the general interest; by this means some of the public authorities can support themselves against other authorities, without having recourse to the general will; but this balancing is not securing peace, it is declaring war. We have seen above, that in this last case, notwithstanding the praises bestowed on the English government, nothing could be done, if, notwithstanding this pretended balance, there were not a really efficient power which put all in motion. It would be the same in the state which we are speaking of; society would be shackled or torn to pieces, if all the particular privileges were not really and practically destroyed, or tolerated by the general acquiescence of the nation.

I must add, that this pretension to a power independent of the people at large, and capable of contending against the people, is the cause of that constant warfare which is every where seen between the rich and the poor, and which, if it were abrogated in society, would render it no more difficult to enjoy a thousand ounces of gold than one ounce; for the laws cannot defend small possessions without equally defending the great; nor is that envy even to hatred cherished against the opulent, when they are not the source and means of insolence and oppression; and even if they could not escape the envy of those who are in poverty, the influence which naturally and necessarily arises out of wealth, more than counterbalances any danger that it could be supposed to be exposed to.

It may be also said with truth, that the wealth of men forming a contin-ued progression, from the humblest poverty to the most affluent fortune, and that even the fortunes of the same individuals, being subject to continual fluc-tuations, we should not be able to place the line of demarcation which exactly determines the rich and the poor. To constitute two opposite parties, if there were not already in society bodies of men formed and distinguished by favors, privileges, and powers, which the other members of society have not, would seem of itself preposterous; since it would be only forming a classification, in which each would be held up to the hatred or fear of the other, and holding forth incentives to intestine war, which could not exist without some motives; such discriminations are not, therefore, calculated to prevent them.

Another reason urged for giving those who have great advantages in soci-ety additional power is, that they generally unite with these advantages, that of information; and that consequently, taking it generally, it is better to be governed by men of intelligence, than by those who do not possess it in the same degree. This is true; but it may be avowed, that if superiority of knowl-edge, is really that which is desired to be rendered predominant, it must be perceived, that intellect or talent are not always united with other advantages; that superiority of understanding, is above all other advantages, that which can best defend itself and take its rank in society, when nothing else obstructs it, and that it is particularly essential to the free development of superior minds, and to give them more room for useful action, that no special protection should be granted to others. Talents will naturally prevail, whenever it is not contrary to the general interest; reason is perverted, by giving to it privileges for its sup-port, which may induce ideas, that its interests are directly hostile to those of society.

I therefore conclude, that all the citizens should be equally convoked, and vote in the same manner on those occasions where the means of giving a new organization of society is to be provided for by election: for all are alike interested, since all that every one possesses, all their interests, and their very existence, are there alike involved in a common fate. It is of little consequence that the existence of some on account of wealth or any other extrinsic circumstance, is apparently more important or precious than that of others; each person's existence is all his own, and the idea of all is not changed by the idea of more or less. Those individuals only should be excluded from elections, who, on account of their age, have not yet reached the years of discretion; those who are by legal judgments disqualified, or who have forfeited their rights by some public offence; perhaps those also, who having accepted some function, may be considered as having placed their suffrages at the will of another person.

It may be asked, should women be permitted to vote at these assemblies? Men whose authority is very respectable, have been of this opinion. I am not of this opinion. Women are sensible and rational beings, have undoubtedly the same rights, and nearly the same intelligence and capacity as men, but they appear not to be destined to maintain those rights and employ their capacities in the same manner. The interest of individuals in society is, that every thing should be well conducted; consequently, as we shall often see, when we enter into details, that it is not the interest of every one to take a direct part in all that is done; it is on the contrary their interest to be occupied with that to which they are properly adapted; now women are certainly destined for domestic duties, and men for public functions. It becomes them to advise the men as wives or mothers, but not to contend with them in public affairs. Men are the natural representatives and defenders of those they love; these should influence but not assume their place, nor contend with them. There is between beings of constitutions so different and so necessary to each other, a dissimilitude, but not an inequality. Besides, this question is more curious than useful; it has and always will be solved in practice, according to my opinion, excepting in some case where a long series of habitudes have perverted the intentions of nature and caused them to be lost sight of.

Every man then should be equally entitled to meet in the assembly we speak of, women should take no public concern therein. I also think that these assemblies should, in preference to all means of forming a constitution, prefer that of delegating the task of draughting it to an assembly elected freely from among the people, and who should be limited to the exercise of that function alone; for sake of perspicuity we shall call such an assembly, a *convention*. The members of this body, therefore, are to be nominated.

The first assembly may either itself elect these deputies, or choose electors for this purpose. This is the place to revert to the principles we have established in speaking of women. The interest of the members of society is, that every thing should be well conducted; therefore women should not take a direct part in all that is done, but confine themselves to what is best adapted to them; whence I conclude that those assemblies which contain the whole of the citizens, and which we may denominate primitive, because they are the foundation of the edifice, should confine their functions to the nomination of electors. This it may be said is rendering the influence of each citizen very indirect on the formation of laws. I agree, it is so; but it should be understood, that I here speak of a populous nation, spread over a vast territory, and which has not adopted the federative system, but exists in the state of indivisibility. Now the number of deputies to be elected must be necessarily too small for each original assembly to have one; either then the votes of all the assemblies should be collected, which is subject to a great many inconveniencies, or allow an intermediate proportion. Beside the citizens at large cannot be supposed to know generally all those who are properly qualified for such a purpose, and therefore not competent to make the very best choice from knowledge; in which circumstances it would be a good expedient to choose from among the members of the primitive assembly some person worthy of confidence and capable of making a proper selection for the purpose. It will generally happen that the men so chosen will be men of more information than the great mass of the people, better educated, of more comprehensive views, less subject to local prejudices, and will consequently fulfil this function better: this is what may be styled a good aristocracy. So that without being influenced by any example or authority, following the simple light of natural reason, we are now arrived at the formation of a body entrusted with establishing a constitution for society. Let us in like manner examine what this constitution should be, and upon what principles it should be founded.

We shall not here enter into details, which must always be in some degree governed by local circumstances, but enquire after those great principles, which are of an equal and general application. It has already been established, that the executive and legislative powers, should not be united in the same person or persons; let us now determine to whom each should be confided; we shall then enquire how the depositaries of each authority should be appointed or removed, commencing with the legislative power.

No country, I believe, has ever entrusted to a single individual, the exclusive function of making the laws;[12] that is to say, to will for society at large, without having any other function: the reason probably is, that when a nation has had sufficient confidence in an individual, to consent that his particular will should be considered as the expression of the general will, it has always allowed him at the same time, to assume sufficient power to carry this will into execution; in such a case he is invested with every power at the same time: this is very dangerous, as we have seen, and many nations have had reason to repent of their having adopted such a course; whereas the other, which appears so singular, would be without any inconvenience, as it respects liberty. Certainly a single man, whose functions consist only in forming laws, without having any power at his disposal, would not be formidable, he might at all times be removed from his place, if it should be deemed necessary; he could not even hope to keep possession of it, but inasmuch as his determinations should conduce to the general welfare. It would then be his interest to give wise decisions, to watch over their execution, to urge the punishment of infractions, as an evidence that the failure of success does not originate in the law, but from the law not being duly executed; for he would be obeyed only as a prudent friend, whose advice is followed as long as advantage is derived from it, not as a master, whose worst orders we are under the necessity of executing;[13] thus liberty would be at its height.

Two objections may be made against this idea; the one, that this sole legislator would not possess sufficient power, to cause the laws to be executed; the other, that he could not alone attend to all the immense duties of his station. To this I answer, in the first place, that a legislative body of three or four hundred persons, or of a thousand if you will, has no more real and physical power than a single person, it having only the power of opinion, which this individual may in like manner obtain, when invested with public confidence, and when it is determined, that he may be deprived thereof in certain cases, and according to certain forms; but as long as he is in office, his decision should be followed and executed. As to what respects the extent and multitude of his duties, I shall

12. It is to be understood of the ordinary laws, and not of constitutions; we have already noticed several of the latter kind.

13. This office would moreover have the advantage, that the ridiculous idea of rendering its functions hereditary, would never take place, the absurdity would then be too evident.

observe, that a well regulated state does not require new laws every day, and that even their multiplicity is a very great evil; beside the lawgiver may have assistants or agents under his direction, instructed in the different parts of his duty, who might explain subjects and facilitate his work. In fact, many monarchs are charged not only with making, but also with executing the law, and are found adequate to this double function.

I shall further add, that it is even much more easy to find a single man of talents, than two hundred, or a thousand; so that with a single lawgiver, it is probable that legislation would be conducted with more knowledge and talents than by an assembly of legislators; and it is certain there would be more connection and unity, which is an important advantage. In short, I believe that nothing solid can be said in favor of the contrary opinion, if it be not: *first,* that a legislative body composed of a great many members, each having influence in different parts of the territory, will more easily obtain the general confidence, and will more readily be obeyed; *secondly,* that its members cannot all leave it at the same time, the body may be renewed in parts without producing any interruption or change of system; whereas, when every thing depends on a single man, when he is changed every thing changes with him.

I must acknowledge the force of these two reasons, particularly the last; and besides, I shall not obstinately uphold an extraordinary opinion which may seem paradoxical; consequently I consent that the legislative power shall be confided to an assembly, on condition, however, that its members be appointed only for a short period of time, and all possess the same privileges. We might, if requisite, for the order and maturity of deliberation, divide the assembly into two or three sections, making some little difference in their functions, and the duration of their mission; but these sections in themselves, should be of the same nature, and particularly they should have no right of an absolute negative, against each other. The legislative body should be essentially one, and deliberate collectively, but not contend with itself. *All systems which assume the name of balances, are no more than tricks; unless it may be said that they constitute an established civil war.*

We are now arrived at the executive power, respecting which I must say, though it be held forth as absolutely indispensable, that it should not altogether be confided to a single person. The only reason which has ever been given in favor of the individuality of the executive, is that a single man is better calculated for action than several men united; a position utterly false. Unity is in willing, not in executing; the proof of which is, that we have but a single head and several members which obey it; and another more direct proof is, that there is no monarch who has not several ministers, and these are the persons who really execute, he only wills, and often does nothing whatever. This is so true, that in a country organized like England, the king is actually a non-entity, only where he has a share in the legislative power, and if this were but taken away from him, he would be completely useless; the legislative body and ministers would be really the government. As it is, the king in that government is only a superfluous wheel in the machine, augmenting its friction and its expence, answering no other purpose than to fill with the least possible inconvenience, a station fatal to public tranquillity, which every ambitious person would desire to take possession of, if not already occupied, because accustomed to see it exist; but if this habit were, or could be broken, it is evident, that the creation of such a place would not be thought of, since, notwithstanding its existence and vicious influence, whenever public affairs require it, the function of king is disregarded and set aside, since deliberations and decisions, war and peace, are arranged between the council of ministers and parliament, and when one or the other changes, every thing changes, though the king, who truly does nothing, remains the same.

All this is so constant and founded on human nature, that a nation never submitted itself to a monarch with the intention that the executive should be in one, but to be governed by a single will, which has been held prudent to avoid the inconvenience of discordant wills. Now the natural measure to be pursued, in taking this resolution up at a time when society has not yet arrived at perfection, is to give this will, to which it is desirous of submitting, the power of bringing all others to submission, and thence arises absolute monarchy. Such were monarchs when first voluntarily and inconsiderately created: afterwards, it was perceived, that the nation was oppressed or injuriously governed by them; a union was formed, not with the intention of restraining them by open force, because ignorant of the method of so doing, and much less with that of suppressing them, because unacquainted with the means of replacing them by proper substitutes; but being accustomed to entertain a certain respect for them, they entertained the desire of counselling and instructing them, of making fair representations, of pointing out the true interests of the good people, and of persuading them that their personal interests were the same.

This has been attended with more or less success, according to the times, countries, and circumstances, under which it has occurred. But a nation cannot be united for any length of time, nor make remonstrances, supplications, or complaints, without recollecting or perceiving that it has the incontestible and inherent right to give its orders and dictate its will. It has then claimed for itself, or at least for its deputies, the legislative power, and when it has resolved to exercise that power, the monarch was necessarily induced to let them take it, lest they should also demand the executive. Precisely at this point, the two powers which originally were vested in one person, were resumed and distributed among several persons, and the nation was easily persuaded that the executive power would be usefully and peaceably exercised, and might be delegated with safety to a single person, and even made hereditary in his family; the friends of the monarch never losing sight of exercising the power left, to regain what was from necessity relinquished. It is nearly in this way that the institutions of government have been conducted among the nations who have submitted to a monarchical authority; they in the course of time have obtained a national representation, somewhat regular, which consequently becomes a moderate government; and this is the reason, that under such governments the people are only half free, and are every moment in danger of becoming slaves.

However, it is not in the nature of the executive power to be better exercised by a single man, than by several united; nor can the execution of the laws have essentially more need of being confided to a single person than legislation; for the majority of a council of a few members produces an unity of action, the same as a single chief, and dispatch will be equal, if not superior: nor is it always to be desired, that action should be so sudden and rapid. But it may on the contrary be said, that the affairs of a great nation, directed in general by a legislative body, requires in its execution to be conducted in an uniform manner, and according to the same system; now this cannot be expected of a single man; for besides that he is more liable to change his views and principles than a council, when he is absent or changed, all is wanting or changed with him; whereas, the council is only renewed in part, its spirit is really unchangeable, and eternal as the political body. This consideration is certainly of greater importance than that which is so much upheld in favor of the contrary opinion: however, I do not consider it as peremptory.

In matters so complicated, where there are so many things to be considered, so many consequences to be foreseen; the foresight or reason of one cannot be truly decisive. Let us examine the subject a little more intimately, and endeavor to discover in farther details, the consequences resulting from a single chief being the depository of the executive power; we shall then be better enabled to judge of causes.

This single chief can be only hereditary or elective. If he be elected, it is for his life or for a certain period. Let us commence with the last supposition. If the same sagacity and discretion, which had limited the exercise of executive authority to a few years, also requires of him to follow certain forms, and to associate with him certain persons, against whose advice he must not act, and if efficient means be taken to prevent his breaking through these restraints, then without doubt this principal agent will not be inconvenient, his station would not be of such importance, as to render the something wanting always very troublesome; he would probably be chosen from among the men most capable and most respected; he would exercise the office only during that period of life, when the faculties of men are unfolded; he would not be so entirely separated from the other citizens, as to feel an interest distinct from those of the state; he might be changed without commotion, and without every thing's changing with him; nor would he be in reality a single chief, for he would not have the entire disposition of the national power; his authority, therefore, does not correspond with the idea of a *monarch;* he is only the first magistrate of a free people, which they may continue to be. The more we depart from this supposition, the more we shall see advantages diminish and inconveniencies encrease.

I shall even suppose this same single chief elected in a similar manner for a limited time, and no precaution taken respecting his disposing of the public money and troops, though always under the direction of the legislative power. This office becomes immediately too important to be disposed of without competition; factions are formed, and contentions follow; the avenue of ambition is laid open, and the period of election becomes a period of exasperation; the competitors will themselves become violent; individuals on both sides will endeavor to render themselves formidable, and the idea of election ceases when power alone operates. When a candidate fails to be elected himself, he will endeavor that the choice shall fall upon an old man, a child, or some silly person, and through that means obtain the disposition of every thing, and the attainment will be held worth the trouble. Capable men are then no more at the head of affairs, and if there should be such a person, it will be an ambitious man more dexterous than his competitors. He holds in his hands all the real power, and it will be employed exclusively for himself: he is too much elevated above his fellow citizens to have an interest in common with them; and he stands only in need of the opportunity to perpetuate his power: the people require tranquillity and happiness, his element is bustle, disorder, contention; war, which rendering his talents necessary, gives him more power; his measures may not be necessary to the interests of his country, as military renown cannot make them prosperous, and external advantages are not required by their internal possessions; conquest cannot give them quiet: but it becomes impossible now to change this chief for another. This effect is so easily produced in such circumstances, that no man possessed of such power, has ever failed to keep that power during his life; or he has been forced from it, at the expence of great public calamity.

We are now arrived at the second supposition, that of a single chief invested with the executive power for life: I have not much to say upon this; it will be perceived that all which I have urged on the preceding cases, is still more applicable to this. Arrived at this point, we must content ourselves to live in a state of convulsion and insecurity; and even to see society itself menaced with dissolution,* till the chief is suffered to become hereditary, as has been the case in Holland, and every where else; very fortunate if by chance or the reaction of opposing interests, the succession become constantly and clearly determined; that by being sufficiently moderate and reasonable, the society be not torn to pieces by civil conflicts, nor become a prey to some foreign power, which has so frequently happened. If it be impossible then that great power cannot be confided for a limited period to a single man, without danger of his soon attempting to possess it during his life, it is yet more impossible that several men successively, enjoying power for life, should not include one who was disposed to perpetuate it in his family; and this brings us to consider the effects of hereditary monarchy.

For men who do not reflect, and they are the greatest number, there is nothing worthy of particular attention but that which is rare; much of what is frequently seen has no power in exciting their curiosity or admiration; though in the natural as in the moral world, the phenomena most common are the most wonderful. He who should declare the functions of his coachman or his cook to be hereditary, would be treated as insane; the man who should solemnly determine that the confidence which he reposed in his lawyer, or his physician, should be perpetual in the family of this lawyer or physician; who should oblige himself and all those who were connected with him, to employ those only or their descendants in the order of primogeniture for ever, whether children, cripples, or idiots, wicked or weak, deranged or dishonored; a man who should do this, would be considered as a fit subject for an hospital of incurable maniacs: yet in obeying a monarch who derives power this way, nothing preposterous presents itself to the great mass of mankind; it is those only that think, who are confounded at human inconsistency.

* The French text here has "as was the case in Poland."

It is so very difficult to meet with a man capable of governing, who in the course of time is not seduced by power so as to become unworthy of possessing it; it is so much more probable that the children of a man invested with great power will be badly educated and the worst of their kind; it is so improbable, if any one of them should escape the evils of a vicious education, that it should be precisely the eldest; and if even this should happen, his youth, his inexperience, his passions, his indispositions, his old age, fill up so a great portion of his life, during which time it is dangerous to be subject to him; all these circumstances form such a disproportion of chances against a favorable fortune, that it is difficult to conceive how the idea could have originated of incurring so many risks, or become so generally adopted, or rather that it has not been universally discarded. It is necessary to pursue, as we have done, all the consequences of individual power, to perceive how nations have been led, nay forced, to play this disadvantageous and dangerous game of hazard. We must be very much infatuated with the persuasion that there is a necessity for the unity of power, in order to say, with a great mathematician, and a man of distinguished talents with whom I was acquainted, *"All things calculated, I prefer hereditary power, because it is the easiest method of solving the problem."* These words, however, though apparently unmeaning, are profound in the idea which they conceal, for they include the institution of absolute power, and all that can be said in its favor.

Notwithstanding, I would still adopt this conclusion, if hereditary power was subject to no other inconvenience than those which have been stated; but in my opinion, it has another which is insupportable, that of being in its nature unlimited and illimitable; or in other words, the impossibility of circumscribing it within just bounds constantly and peaceably; and it has this further inconvenience, not as a hereditary power, but as a power one and not divided; for the authority of a single person is, as we have seen, essentially progressive; when confined to a limited period of years, it advances to possession for life, and from thence to hereditary power; and even this last state is only the complete development of its active nature, which will not, after it has acquired full strength, be more easily retarded in its progress; inasmuch as being then in possession of ample means and unrestrained, it will be deemed yet necessary to its being, to overturn all states which may be supposed likely to oppose it. In truth, no hereditary power can be secure where the supremacy of the general will is recognized, for it is in the nature of hereditary succession to perpetuate itself, and that of the will to be temporary and revocable: it is consequently *essential to the security of an hereditary monarch, that the principle of national sovereignty be destroyed.* It is not merely in the passions of men, but in the nature of things, that this obligation exists, we may at a glance perceive the result, and that there will be an incessant warfare, violent or partial, indirect or open: it may be restrained by the moderation of the monarch, or deferred by his prudence, disguised by his dexterity, diverted by events, or suspended by adventitious circumstances; but it can terminate only in the slavery of the people or the destruction of the throne, pure monarchy or divided power. To hope for liberty and monarchy, is to expect two things each of which excludes the other; many monarchs, and even citizens, have been ignorant of this truth, but it is not less true, and it is now very well understood, particularly by monarchs.

We should no longer be surprized at what we have noticed, and what Montesquieu himself has remarked of the immorality and corruption of monarchical governments, of their tendency to produce luxury, disorder, vanity, war, conquest, mismanagement of the finances, the depravity of courtiers, and the degradation of the lower classes; their propensity to stifle information, particularly in moral philosophy, and to disseminate through the nation inconstancy, selfishness, and a want of reflection: all these effects must take place, since the hereditary power, having distinct interests from the general good, is obliged as a faction acts in a popular state, to divide and weaken the national power, in order to combat it; to array the nation in different classes, to overcome the one by the other, and to subject them all by illusions, and consequently to produce unhappiness and error in theory and in practice.

We may also perceive why the partisans of monarchy, when occupied with the social organization, could never devise any thing else than a system of balances, which, by continually arraying the powers of society against each other, really make enemies of them, always ready to overwhelm and destroy each other, instead of agreeing, as parts of the same whole, mutually co-operating in the means of common interest; it is because they admitted into society two irreconcilable elements, according to which mere compromises or temporary arrangements only could take place, but an intimate union and perfect utility never.

Probably they did not themselves perceive it; but when we see men of talents employed in attempting to solve a problem, and never going beyond an incomplete solution, which does not satisfy the understanding, we may take it for granted, that there is a previous error, which prevents their arriving at truth: it is too often imagined that the passions or the habits of men form their opinions when they are not conformable to reason; but a little more consideration will discover, they more frequently proceed from a want of sufficient reflection, and that a little resolution to think and examine, would bring them to the knowledge of principles which are true, and to the formation of opinions necessarily correct.

But whatever the cause may be, so much error and evil as exists, must necessarily originate in a single cause, *the confiding of national power to a single person*, and I conclude, as I have announced, that the executive power should be confided only to a council, composed of a small number of persons elected for a limited time, and partially renewing itself at fixed periods and numbers; that the legislative power should be entrusted to a more numerous assembly, likewise composed of members chosen for a limited period, and partially renewed every year.

Thus two bodies are established, the one authorised to express the national will, the other to act upon it in the name of the people. These bodies should not be placed parallel to each other, one being consistently preordinate, the other secondary, for this reason, that we will before we execute; they should not be considered as rivals and placed in opposition to each other, as the second necessarily depends on the first, and action succeeds the will. Their respective interests should not be stipulated, not even such as are usually allowed to gratify vanity, for they have no rights which properly belong to them exclusively; they are derived, being only invested with functions confided to them, and to be exercised for others. They should have no other concerns than the gratification arising from the discharge of their trust in the most effectual manner, and to the advantage and satisfaction of those who had delegated them. These ideas, incompatible with the language of courts, are the determinations of common sense. Now these few assertions of truth solve a great many difficulties, to which too much importance has been generally attached, and shews us at once how the members of this corps should be chosen, how they should be distinguished when there is occasion to do so, and how their differences may be terminated when they occur.

There can be no difficulty in the election of the members of the legislative body; they are numerous, and should be elected from all parts of the territory; they may be chosen by electoral bodies assembled in different districts; this method is well adapted to the choice of two or three of the persons of best qualifications and credit in a district. The punishment of their offences presents no difficulty; their functions are limited to speaking and writing, to suggesting their opinions, to explaining and supporting them with all the reasons they can devise; and they should possess the most unbounded liberty to do so, and in the manner which may appear to them most proper, and without any other responsibility than such as is essential to the maintenance of order in their proceedings. They are, therefore, not accountable for whatever they may say in the exercise of their functions. They are not liable to punishment for any thing, unless it be for acts not forming part of their duties, nor arising out of them, and be treated like all other citizens; and like them, they should in case of the commission of ordinary crimes, be proceeded against in the ordinary manner; always taking care, that accusations of such a nature, should not be feigned nor deprive the state of useful representatives, nor injure the public interests; but above all, they should not possess the power of excluding any of their own members, nor of interdicting them under any pretence from the exercise of the functions for which they were elected.

The same principles do not exactly apply to the executive corps; they are few in number; too few to afford to each of the electoral districts the power of electing one; besides these dispersed electoral bodies, who are well adapted to designate men for the legislature, may not be so competent to judge of the fitness of eight or ten men to conduct the affairs of a nation, which they may be entrusted with. Besides, it must be well considered, that those members of the executive are required to act, to give orders, to exercise effective power, to put the military force in motion, to disburse the public treasure, to create or to suppress offices. They must do all this conformably to the laws and in their spirit. But they may violate their duties or pervert them, and their culpability call for condign punishment. Yet the legislature should not be invested with the authority to inflict this punishment, nor of nominating their judges, nor of deposing them, nor of passing judgment upon them; for as we have said, they should depend on the legislature only as the action follows the will: nevertheless, it does not follow that their dependence should be so passive, as to execute what should not be legitimate. One of these authorities may charge the other, of having acted in an unauthorised manner, that is for not having conformed in its proceedings to the laws; but this last may in its turn accuse the other of having willed or legislated erroneously, that is of having made laws contrary to the constitution, which all the constituted bodies are bound alike to respect. Whence it follows, that these two bodies may contend upon points which neither have a right to determine, but for the peaceable and legal decision of which there should be some provision; without which, this constitution, like many others, would be incomplete, as no one would know the extent or limits of duty, and though it should not be publicly avowed, the force and violence would really be the paramount authority.

These last observations, connected with the preceding, prove that there is still something wanting to the political machine, in order that it may go regularly. It has already a body for willing, and a body for executing that will; it yet requires a preserving power, that is to facilitate and regulate the action of the other two; and in this conservative body, we shall find all that is requisite, to complete the organization of society.

The functions of this power will be: 1. To verify the election of the members of the legislative body, before they take their seats, and to judge of their validity. 2. To take part in the election of the members of the executive corps, either by receiving from the electoral body a list of candidates, from among whom they may choose; or, on the contrary, by sending them a list of those from among whom they may elect.

If the second method be preferred, the constitution may ordain, that when the electoral body shall not meet with a name on the list which they desire, they may demand that it be added thereto, and if a majority of the electoral bodies request it, the conservative body shall be obliged to insert it.*

3. To participate in the same manner, and nearly in the same forms, in the nomination of the supreme judges, whether a chief justice and judges of the supreme court, as in the United States of America, or as a member of the tribunal of cassation in France.

4. To pronounce the removal of a member of the executive body, or a vacancy, if any, on the request of the legislature.

5. To decide on cases of complaint against any of the executive body, and in such case to nominate some of its members, according to a pre-determined form, who shall compose a grand jury before the supreme court.

6. To pronounce the unconstitutionality, and consequently the nullity of the acts of the legislative body, or the executive body, on the accusation of either against the other, and their decision to be made absolute by the constitution.

7. To declare, on their application, or on that of the mass of the citizens, in form, and with intermediate time for consideration, when a revision of the constitution shall take place, and consequently to call a convention, *ad hoc;* all the established authorities remaining, in the mean time, in the same state.

These two last acts of the duty of the conservative body should, before being carried into execution, be submitted to the decision of the nation at

---

* In the French text this paragraph appears as a footnote.

large, which should decide thereon in their election districts, by *Ayes* and *Noes*; or in electoral bodies nominated for the special purpose.*

By the means of these functions vested in a conservative body, I can no longer see any obstacle to impede the operations of society, no difficulty which cannot be peaceably accommodated; I can discover no case where any citizen can be ignorant whom to obey; nor any circumstance in which there are not legal means to assure the enforcement of the public will, and to repress any resistance whatever, in as much as the power should be exercised, as it is intended, for the general good: while at the same time these functions appear to me so necessary, that in the government of every nation† in whose constitution a like conservative body has not been established, it seems manifest to me, that it is abandoned to constant hazard and violence.

This body should be composed of men to continue in the station for life, who could no longer fill any other station in society, and who have no other interest than that of maintaining the peace and happiness of the nation, and enjoying an honorable existence. It would become the retreat and recompense of those who have fulfilled great functions; and this is an advantage not to be despised; for the political department should be so arranged as to give no great temptations to ambition, neither should it be so ungrateful as to neglect great virtues or services, or to deny to talents opportunities of participating in public confidence and honors, without changing the fundamental laws or eluding them.

The members of the conservative body, should the first time be nominated by the convention which formed the constitution, and of which they would become the depositaries; but afterwards the vacancies should be filled by the electoral bodies, from lists of eligible persons, formed by the legislative and executive bodies.

I have been somewhat prolix on this subject of a conservative body, because this institution has had a very recent existence,[14] and because it appears to me of the greatest importance. It is in my opinion the keystone of the arch, without which the edifice of society has neither strength nor durability.

---

* This paragraph does not appear in the French edition.

† Here the French text speaks of a "one and indivisible government" rather than "the government of every nation."

14. Did the author know any thing of the old Pennsylvania constitution and its *council of censors?*

Two opposite objections may be made to it; the one, that this body by deciding on matters of difference between the other constituted powers, and presiding in judgment in the most important concerns of the state, would thereby acquire inordinate authority, and become very dangerous to public liberty. To which I answer, this body being composed of men satisfied with the station in which they are placed, have every thing to lose and nothing to gain by any disorder of the state; and having passed the age of the passions and great projects, and without any effective power at their command; they can scarcely do any thing more, than by their decisions afford an appeal to the nation, and give it time and means to manifest its will.

Other persons, on the contrary, will pretend that this body will be but an useless phantom, which every ambitious man may convert to his purposes; and the evidence produced to support this objection, will be, that in France it could not for a moment defend the trust confided to it. To this I answer, that this example proves nothing to the purpose, for it is always impossible to defend liberty in a nation so fatigued by its mighty efforts and misfortunes, that slavery would be preferable to the least exertion of resistance; and such was the disposition of the French at the period when their senate was established; so much so, that they suffered themselves to be deprived thereof without the least murmur, and almost with pleasure, at least as far as the liberty of the press and individual liberty. I have moreover often said, that nothing can prevent usurpation when once all the active force is invested in one man, as it was by the French constitution in 1799 (year *eight*), for the two other consuls were mere cyphers.* But if the French had placed their conservative body in their constitution of 1795 (year *three*), and in which the executive was really divided, it would have maintained itself with success, between the directory and the legislative body; it would have prevented the violent contests between them in 1797 (18 Fructidor, year *five*), and that nation would now enjoy liberty, which has always escaped from it, at the moment when on the point of attaining it.[15]

---

* This was the French constitution that saw the emergence of Napoleon Bonaparte as First Consul.

15. It must be moreover observed, that the manner of nominating and replacing the French senators, was very different from that which I have proposed. It was vicious in its principle, in their constitution of the year VIII. (1799), and afterwards rendered more so by new attributes and illegal dispositions of these same senators, which they call the constitution of their empire.

This I believe to be the means of solving the problem proposed. Not contemplating the exhibition of a complete plan of a constitution, but simply to describe the principles upon which it may be founded, I shall content myself with these principal points, and not enter into details which may vary without inconvenience, according to local necessities and circumstances. I do not assert, that the principles which I have explained, are practicable every where, and at all times; it may be that there are countries, where the authority of a chief, even the most unlimited, may be necessary; as even the establishment of monks may have been useful in certain circumstances, though bad and absurd taken in the abstract; but I believe, that when desirous of following the soundest dictates of reason and justice, it is nearly so that society would be organized, and that there never will be any secure and durable peace otherwise. I submit this system, if it may be called one, to the meditations of the man of reflection. He will easily perceive the happy consequences of which it is susceptible, and how powerfully it is supported by all that we have before said on the spirit and principle of different governments, and their effects on the riches, power, manners, sentiments, and information of the people. I shall only add: *the greatest advantage of moderate and limited authorities, being that of leaving the general will the possibility of forming and making itself known, and the manifestation of this will being the best means of resisting oppression; individual liberty and the liberty of the press, are the two things most indispensable for the happiness and good order of society, and without which all the combinations that can be made in order to establish the best distribution of power, are only vain speculations.* But this belongs to the subject of which we are to treat in the following book, and it is time to close this chapter, already too long.

BOOK XII.

Of Laws That Establish Political Liberty in Relation to the Citizens.

Political liberty cannot exist without individual liberty, and that of the press, nor this without trial by jury.

SPIRIT OR LAWS, BOOK XII.

THE book preceding, Montesquieu entitles, Of laws establishing political liberty in relation to the constitution. We have seen that, under this title, he treats of the effects which the laws forming the constitution of a state, produce on the liberty of man; that is to say, which regulate the distribution of political power. These laws, in effect, contain the principles of those which affect the general interests of society, and by combining them with those which regulate the public economy, that is those which govern the formation and distribution of wealth, we shall be in possession of the whole code by which the aggregate interests of the political body are regulated, and by which the happiness and liberty of each is influenced, and thence the happiness and liberty of the whole.

The question here is, what are the laws which directly concern each citizen in his private interests? It is no longer public and political liberty it attacks, or immediately protects, it is individual and particular liberty. It will be perceived, that this second species of liberty is very necessary to the first, and intimately connected with it; because every citizen should be secure against oppression in his person and goods, in order to be able to defend political liberty: and it is very evident that if any authority, for example, should be possessed of the right of inflicting imprisonment, banishment, or fines, it would be impracticable to restrain it within the bounds that may be prescribed to it by the constitution of the state, if it has a constitution very exact and formal. Montesquieu also says that under the consideration in question, *liberty* consists in *security*, and that the constitution may be free; that is, it may contain clauses favorable to liberty, while the citizens do not really enjoy liberty; and he adds, with much reason, that in most states, he might have said in all, individual liberty is more restrained, violated, and kept down, than the constitution authorises or requires. The reason is, that the functionaries, always desirous of going beyond the bounds of law, instead of regarding them, find it necessary to check and repress political liberty, in order to keep down individual liberty. As principles the constitutional laws, and in operation the administrative laws, influence general liberty, so criminal and civil laws dispose of civil liberty. The subject we are treating of belongs almost entirely to the sixth book, where Montesquieu proposed examining *the consequences and principles of different governments, in relation to the simplicity of criminal laws, the forms of judgment, and the infliction of punishment.* A better method of distribution and connexion of ideas, would have united that book with this, and even with the twenty-ninth, which treats of the manner of composing laws, and at the same time to appreciate their effects; but we must follow the order adopted by our author: any one so disposed, would do well to new model both his work and ours, and form for himself a connected and complete system of principles.

We have said at the opening of the sixth book, that notwithstanding the great and admirable views which it contains, we do not there meet with all the instruction we had a right to expect; we are obliged to say the same of this. Naturally it ought to comprehend an exposition and estimate of the principal institutions, most favorable or most adverse to the security of each citizen, and the free exercise of his natural, civil, and political rights. Now we do not meet with any of these topics. Montesquieu, according to custom, travels through all times and countries, and particularly through remote ages and countries not well known, in a multitude of small unconnected chapters. It is true, that he generally draws very exact inferences from all the facts he produces, but there was no necessity for so much enquiry or such a display of learning, to inform us that the accusations for exercising magic were absurd, that errors purely religious should be corrected by means purely religious, or that in monarchies the law against high treason has been often abused even to barbarity, and so far as to become ridiculous that it is tyrannical to punish for satirical writings, or indiscreet words, that judgments should not be sought by special commissions, nor by spies, nor by anonymous informers; all of which are odious, often atrocious: if he had been obliged to employ address, in daring to declare such truths, and if it was impossible for him to go beyond such a course, we should condole with him, but we should not stop there.

But even among all this, I meet with only one reflection of real importance, which is, that it is very dangerous in a republic to multiply punishments on account of the crime of high treason, or treason against the nation, under pretence of avenging the republic; for then, says Montesquieu, the tyranny of vengeance will be established: it is those who are dominated over, and not the dominator, that will be punished or destroyed. The ordinary course of government should be pursued in such cases, as well as in all others, and the laws which protect all, operate equally against all who transgress them. These sentiments are admirable, they are derived from facts in Grecian history, and cannot be invalidated. The exile, or the return from exile, of proscribed citizens, are always attended with commotion and a change in the constitution; and the history of modern times is not deficient of examples which might be cited to corroborate it, if it were necessary.

But accompanying these wise considerations, there is one principle admitted that is very dangerous, and contrary to the formal advice of Cicero;* which is, that there are occasions which may authorise a law to be made against a single man; and that there are cases *when a veil should for a moment be cast over liberty, as the statues of the Gods are sometimes concealed.* To what lengths has the prepossession for the government of England conducted this great man.

Whatever political liberty may be, for our author has not thought proper to penetrate further into the subject, we shall confine ourselves here to repeating that it cannot subsist without individual liberty and that of the press; and that for the preservation of this last, all arbitrary seizure and detention should be proscribed, and the use of trial by jury adopted, at least in criminal cases: referring the reader to what we have said on these subjects in the preceding books, particularly in the fourth, sixth, and eleventh, where we have shewn why these principles are favored or opposed by the nature and spirit of each kind of government.

* Cicero's argument against such laws is found in *De Legibus* (*On the Laws*).

A REVIEW.

Of the Twelve First Books of the Spirit of Laws.

WE have yet the greatest part of our task to accomplish: I cannot resist the desire of stopping where we are: for although Montesquieu's Spirit of Laws, be composed of thirty-one books, the twelve first contain all that directly and immediately concerns the social organization, and the distribution of its powers; in the others we only meet with economical, philosophical, and historical considerations, on the causes, effects, circumstances, and connexion, of the different conditions of society, in certain times and particular countries, and on the relations of all these with the social organization. The opinions there offered, the views there presented, will be found more or less exact, more or less perspicuous, more or less profound; but it will be obvious still, that this organization is only formed to produce good results, in as much as it is preferable to anarchy (understood by natural independence of the will), by the evils which it prevents, and the advantages it procures. We can only judge of its degree of perfection, by the effects it produces; it is therefore proper, before we go any farther, briefly to recall the principles we have extracted from the preceding discussions; we shall then perceive more distinctly, how they unite with different circumstances, and whether it is on account of having neglected or followed them, that the good or evil fortune of mankind has been produced.

Desirous of explaining the *spirit of laws*, that is to say, the *spirit* in which laws are or should be made, we have commenced by defining the word *law*, that its primitive and essential signification is *a rule prescribed for our actions by an authority invested with the right to do so.* This word is, therefore, necessarily relative to the social organization, and could have been formed in the infancy of society only; however, by an extension of the sense, it was afterwards denominated the *laws of nature,* in other words, they constitute the apparent rules which phenomena daily taking place before our eyes, appear to be governed by and to follow, considering them always so acting, as if an irresistible and unchangeable authority had ordered all beings to follow a certain order of action, in relation to each other. These laws, or rules of nature, are nothing else than the expression of the manner in which things inevitably present themselves to our senses; we cannot change this universal order of things, we must therefore submit to it, conforming our actions and our institutions also thereto. So that in entering upon the subject, we at once perceive, that *our positive laws should be consequent of the laws of our nature.*

But our different social organizations are not in all places alike conformable to this principle; they have not all an equal tendency to submit themselves thereto, and become conformable to the laws of nature; their forms are very much varied; it is therefore indispensable, to study these separately. In the second book, we shall perceive, that all governments may be classed under two heads, namely, *those which are founded on the general rights of man and those which are supposed to be founded on particular rights.*

Montesquieu has not adopted this distribution; he classes governments according to the accidental circumstances of the number of men invested with authority; and in the third book he enquires which are the moving, or rather conservative principles of each kind of government. *To despotism* he assigns the attribute of *fear;* to *monarchy, honor;* to a *republic, virtue.* These principles may be more or less subject to explanation or doubt; but without pretending absolutely to deny them, we believe it may be asserted, that from the discussion in which they have engaged us, it results that the *principle of government founded on the rights of men, is reason.* We shall confine ourselves to this conclusion, which all that follows will confirm.

The fourth book concerns *education:* Montesquieu determines that it should be accordant with the principles of the government, in order to secure its existence; this is reasonable, and from it I draw this consequence, that those governments which support themselves by false ideas, should not venture to give to their subjects a very solid education; that those which require to keep certain classes in a state of degradation and oppression, should not permit them to obtain instruction; and that those governments only which are founded on reason, can desire that education should be solid, profound, and generally diffused.

If precepts of education should be relative to the principles of government, there can be no doubt that the laws, strictly so called, should with still greater reason be so; for laws constitute the education of men: and this is what Montesquieu says in the fifth book, and in consequence there are none of the governments he speaks of, to which he does not propose some principles evidently contrary to distributive justice and to the natural sentiments of man. I do not deny that these miserable expedients are necessary for their support; but I have also shewn, that *governments founded on reason have only to leave nature to act and follow it without restraint.*

Montesquieu appropriates the sixth book to the examination of the consequences of the principles of different governments, applied to the simplicity of civil and criminal laws, and the forms of judgment. In treating of this subject with him, and profiting by what had been previously said, I have obtained more general and extensive results. I noticed that the human mind is as progressive in the social as in all other sciences, that democracy or despotism were the first governments imagined by men, and *mark the first degree of civilization*; that *aristocracy under one or more chiefs*, whatever name may be given to it, has every where taken the place of these in artificial governments, and *constitutes the second degree of civilization*; and that *representative democracy under one or several delegates*, is a new invention, which forms and constitutes *the third degree* of civilization. I added, that in the first state, it is ignorance which governs or force that dictates; in the second, opinions are formed, and religion has the greatest power; in the third, reason begins to prevail and philosophy has more influence. I also observed, that the principal motive of punishment in the first stage of civilization, is human vengeance; in the second, divine vengeance; and in the third, to prevent future evil. I shall not here lengthen out my observations on this topic, which must give way to considerations and objects of another kind.

The seventh book treats of the consequences of the different principles of the three governments of Montesquieu, as they relate to sumptuary laws, to luxury, and to the condition of women. The merit of sumptuary laws has been determined by what we have said of civil laws in general, in the fifth book; what relates to women, will be better placed with the subject of manners and climate; luxury consequently only remained to be examined, and the result of the discussion has been, that *in agreeing to the necessity that certain governments are subject to, of encouraging luxury in order to the security of their power, the effect of luxury is to employ labor in a useful* or an injurious manner.* Now labor, and the employment of our faculties, being all our own, and our only means of action, I am very much deceived if this truth is not the basis of all social science, and if it does not decide all questions on the subject of luxury; for

---

* In the French text, the word used is "useless."

that which checks or stifles the unfolding of our faculties, or renders them hurtful, or even useless, cannot be proper for us.

The eighth book has other objects in view, the corruption of the principles of the three governments distinguished by Montesquieu; and after having explained in what the corruption of these pretended principles consists, he lays it down, that each of them is relative to a certain extent of territory, and is lost if it be changed. This decision induced me to consider the subject under very different aspects, to point out the great consequences which would result from a state possessing certain limits instead of others; and to conclude generally, that the extent proper for a state, is to have a sufficient force with the best possible limits; and that the sea is the best boundary of all, for various reasons.

Montesquieu having advanced that such a government can only exist in a small territory, another in a larger territory, is obliged to assign to each a particular and exclusive manner of defending itself against the aggressions of strangers; and he pretends in the ninth book, that republics have no other means of safety, but in forming confederations. I made use of the occasion to discuss the principles and effects of confederative governments, and concluded that *confederation produces more strength than separation, but less strength than an intimate and complete union.*

In the tenth book, our author examines these same governments in relation to their offensive force; and this leads him into a discussion on the foundation of the rights of war, and the consequences and principles of the rights of war, and the right of conquest. I confess, that to me his doctrine does not appear enlightened, and that probably *the perfection of the right of war would be the confederation of nations, and so far the right of war originates in the right of natural defence, and that of conquest out of the right of war.*

After having, in his first ten books, considered the different kinds of government, under every aspect, Montesquieu devotes the eleventh book, entitled *of laws which establish political liberty with relation to the constitution,* to shew that the English constitution is the most perfect example of the social science, and that it is folly to seek the means of securing political liberty, since it is already secured.

Not feeling any conviction of the correctness of this opinion, I divided the book into two chapters; and in the first, proved that *the problem had not been yet solved,* and that *it could not be solved so long as too much power is vested in a single person;* and in the second chapter I have endeavored to explain how the problem might be solved, by never giving to a single man, any more power than can be taken from him without violence; and that when he is changed, all shall not change with him.

To conclude: Montesquieu in his twelfth book, treats *of laws establishing political liberty with relation to the citizens;* there being little new to be drawn from this book, I confined myself to the investigation which produced this result: *Political liberty cannot exist, without individual liberty, and that of the press; nor these, without trial by jury.*

This view of our first twelve books, is necessarily rapid; it would not afford a sufficient idea of them, to those who have not read them, and even presents imperfectly to those who have, what they may themselves have remarked; however, it condenses a series of ideas, which, taken together, form an important whole.

Man is but an atom in the immensity of beings; he is so constituted by nature as to possess *sensibility,* and consequently *will;* his happiness consists in the accomplishment of this will, and he has but little power to execute it. This is the power which he denominates *liberty;* and therefore, he has *very little* liberty; particularly, he has not that of being otherwise than he is, nor to cause all others to be so; he is subject to all the laws of nature, and principally that of his own nature; he cannot change them; he can benefit himself only by conforming to them.

Happily or unhappily, it is in his nature to combine the perceptions of his sensibility, and to analyse them sufficiently, and to clothe them with a diversity of characters, and to employ the means which he has devised for discriminating between them to multiply and express these perceptions; consequently he makes use of the faculties thus possessed and devised, to communicate with his kind, and to unite with them, so as to augment his *power,* or his *liberty*, by whichever name you may choose to call it.

In this state of society, men acquire laws to regulate their conduct with one another: these laws should be conformable to the unchangeable laws of human nature, and flow out of them; without which they can have no important effect, must be of short duration, and only productive of disorder. But men are not at first acquainted with these truths. They have not yet sufficiently examined their own nature, without which they cannot know the necessary laws. They can at first imagine no other means than submitting to the will of all, or to the will of one who has obtained their confidence; ignorance and force prevail with democracy and despotism; then it is that men resort to punishments to avenge themselves of the wrongs which they believe they have suffered, and this is the basis of their criminal code; it is the consequence of the natural right of self-defence; for the right of nations, and of one nation in relation to another, is an absolute nullity.

After some time, knowledge, mutual relations, and the concerns of society, become multiplied and complicated; neither the theory nor the links by which it is connected, are perceived; enquiry, speculation, and conjectures succeed; systems of various kinds and even religious systems, are created: opinions obtain respect; and even opinion itself is found to possess power: all these operations are found susceptible of use; arrangements take place by accident or particular circumstances, and remain so without any recurrence to principles, but subsisting solely on expediency. Hence originated different and incongruous orders of things; society itself assumed this discordant result of expediency in various modes, which always produced aristocracies of some kind under one or several chiefs, and in which religious opinions were made to perform a principal part. This was the period of partial knowledge and the power of opinion; then the idea of divine vengeance was subjoined to human vengeance, and became the foundation of the penal code; at this period also, some forms were established among nations, which, without meriting the honor of the denomination, were called laws of nations.

This period is of considerable duration; it exists yet: it exists over almost the whole earth. However, from time to time, the principles of nature, that is the eternal order of the universe in relation to us, has been observed, and some of its laws acknowledged. Controversy has discovered errors, and these errors have been discussed; and it was perceived, that if we do not comprehend every thing that is, we often know that which is not. Some men, more enlightened and enterprizing than others, or excited by some particular incident, have undertaken to regulate their conduct according to the discoveries which they have made; they have attempted, with various degrees of success, to give themselves a manner of being more conformable to nature, truth, and reason: behold the dawn of this last effort of the human mind, it is offences that are combated and not the offenders; if punishment takes place, it is only to prevent future evil. Such is the only principle of criminal laws, in the third epoch, which is now commencing.

The governments which have or may spring up under it, may be considered as having reason, for the principle of action and conservation.

Their first laws are declared to be formed for the governed, not the governed for them; consequently they only exist in virtue of the will of the majority of those governed, and should change when the will changes: and necessarily arising out of this state of things, at no time should any one be retained in their territory who does not wish to live under their laws.

It follows also, that no hereditary power can be established therein, nor can any class be constituted with exclusive privileges or honors, nor any class depressed or degraded to profit another.

The second principle of the laws is, that there should never be a power in society which cannot be changed without violence, nor any such that when it is changed all must change with it.

This principle prevents one man from being entrusted with the entire disposal of the power of a nation, and also guards against the investing of the same collective body which legislates, with the formation of the constitution, and from perverting these distinct functions; it tends carefully to preserve the separation of the executive and legislative powers, and the conservative, or that of passing judgment on political differences.

The third law of a rational government, is always to have in view the conservation of the independence of the nation, the liberty of its members, and such security for every individual as to supercede the idea of fear internal or external.

This principle implies the necessity of a proper extent of territory; but that the nation should not be composed of parts too much diversified, that its boundaries may be subject in the least possible degree to contention, and that its extent should require the smallest number of military forces; for the same reason, having obtained this end, an union might be formed by ties of confederation with the neighboring countries. The relations of independent nations should always approach as much as practicable to a state of confederation, for this is the perfection of the rights of nations, or in other words, *that in which violence gives way to the arbitration of justice,* and when what was called the laws of nations, first comes to merit the appellation of *law.*

It also follows from this law, that the government should never suffer any attempts upon the security of any citizen whatever, nor on their right of declaring their sentiments upon any subject whatever, nor interfere in any manner whatever with their religious opinions.

Such are nearly, I believe, the fundamental laws of all governments truly rational, and these alone are the real fundamental principles of government, inasmuch as they alone are unchangeable, and should always exist; for all others can and should be changed, when the members of the society will it; observing, however, the necessary forms: so that the laws we speak of are not properly positive laws, but those of our nature, the declaration of principles, the enunciation of eternal truth; they should be placed at the head of all constitutions, instead of those declarations of rights, which of late years have prefaced them; not because I censure this practice, for it is a great improvement in the social art, and will constitute an epoch in the history of human society;[16] it is very useful, for it dare not be followed by giving a nation a constitution, vicious in its principles, or in the manner in which it is established.

But it is no less true, that this precaution of introducing the political code of a nation with the exposition of the rights of citizens, is an effect of the long forgetfulness in which these rights have been left, and a consequence of the continual war, that every where existed between the governed and governing. It is a kind of manifesto and protest against oppression, in case it should again shew itself. Without these motives, there is no reason why people freely uniting, to regulate the mode of association, should commence by enumerating the rights they suppose themselves to be possessed of;[17] for they have them all, and they can do what they please; they are to render an account of their determination to no one but themselves; it is not, therefore, a declaration of rights, that should precede a constitution, but rather a declaration of principles on which it should be founded, and truths to which it should be conformable. Then I think, there need not be placed in it, more than two or three laws, of which we have just explained the nature, and which equally flow out of the experience of mankind and their discovery of truths and errors.

Whatever it may be, this is a succinct view of the truths we have unfolded by an examination of Montesquieu's twelve first books; it seems in some measure sufficient to complete all that concerns the organization of society, and the distribution of its power, and consequently all the primary and most

16. The first declaration of the rights of man, that has been proposed in Europe, was presented to the constituent assembly of France, by general Lafayette, on the 11th July, 1789. I think it is the best ever made, for it consists in the enunciation of a small number of principles perfectly sound. It is remarkable that the man who so powerfully contributed to establish the rights of man in the western hemisphere, was the first who proclaimed them in the old world. At that period it was a declaration of war against oppression.

17. It is this same spirit of timid precaution, that afterwards caused a declaration of duties, to be added to the declaration of rights, as if it were not the same thing to say, "I am possessed of this right, or respect in me this right;" this repetition is very silly.

important part of the spirit of laws, or the spirit in which laws should be made. It is at this point I was desirous of resting a while: our author will now present a multitude of subjects for our contemplation: taxes, climate, the nature of the soil, the state of intelligence and habits, commerce, money, population, religion, the successive revolutions of certain laws, civil and political, in particular nations, all of which it may be interesting to examine with him; but it will still be impracticable to form a judgment upon any of them, without constantly reverting to the interests and dispositions of the different kinds of government, as well as the interests to which they should properly be made to tend: so that what precedes really serves to measure what follows; and that which follows will aid us in forming a fair estimate of their several relations. I may even venture to say, that the manner in which we have considered society, its organization, and its progress, is a ray of light, thrown in the midst of these important objects, which will one day dissipate all their obscurity. Let us hasten to realize this hope, at least in part.

BOOK XIII.

Of the Relation Which Taxes, and the Amount of the Public Revenue, Have to Public Liberty.

Taxes are always an evil, they injure liberty and property in several modes; according to their mode of operation, they affect different classes of citizens in a different manner: to form a proper judgment of their effects, we must consider labor as the source of all our riches, that landed property is in no manner different from other property: and that a plantation may be considered as the machinery of an art or trade.

SPIRIT OF LAWS, BOOK XIII.

MONTESQUIEU here presents a great and important subject, which alone embraces all the departments of social science; but I may venture to say that he has not treated it satisfactorily; he has, however, perceived the great absurdity of supposing that enormous taxation could be good in itself, or that it could excite or encourage industry. It may appear strange that his *not* professing so great an error should be noticed; but so many well informed men have run into this error, so many writers of the sect of economists have held, that consumption is the source of wealth, and that the causes of public prosperity are of a quite different nature from that of individuals; we should be the better pleased with our author, who has misconceived so many other important points in the principles of social order, for not suffering himself to be seduced by their sophisms and embarrassed by the subtlety of their erroneous metaphysics.

Though he has not taken the trouble of refuting them, which would have been important, he expressly declares that the revenues of the state constitute a sum to make up which each citizen contributes a portion of his property, to be secured in the possession of the remainder; that this portion should be the smallest possible; that it is not requisite to take from men all they can spare, or all that can be taken from them, but only that which is indispensable for the wants of the state; and that under every circumstance, if resort should be had to all the means that can be produced from the sacrifices of the citizens, the demand should not be so excessive as not to leave enough for an annual reproduction.

In effect, society must very much abuse its faculties, if it remain only stationary, since there is in human nature a great capacity for multiplying and accumulating the means of its enjoyments, particularly when arrived at a certain degree of information.

Montesquieu, however, remarks, that the more liberty is enjoyed in any country, the more it may be taxed; and fiscal offences punished with more severity: either because liberty permits enterprize to act, and industry to augment its means, or because the more a government is loved, the more it can exact without risk. But he also remarks, that the governments of Europe have very much abused this advantage, as they likewise have abused the resources of credit; so that almost all betake themselves to such expedients, as a person whose affairs were embarrassed would be ashamed to resort to; and further, he asserts that all modern governments are running fast to destruction; which the custom of keeping numerous armies constantly on foot, accelerates.

All these are truths, but they are nearly all that this book contains: now these few truths, dispersed without explanation, among assertions, very many of which are doubtful, and more are false; intermixed with some vague declamations against farmers of the revenue,* are not sufficient to develop the spirit of laws in relation to taxation: it does not even suffice to fulfil the promise implied by the title of the book; for more facts are required, in order to discover the real influence of political liberty on the wants and means of a state; or to discover even what is the reaction of taxation, and the effects which the amount of the public revenue, produce on liberty also. I shall, therefore, venture to offer a few ideas, which I believe may be useful, nay necessary, to the proper understanding of the subject.

1. I shall explain why, and how, taxes are always an evil: this is the more proper, because Montesquieu himself, seems to have been ignorant of the most substantial reasons, which authorise the assertion; since in other places, he speaks of the excess of consumption, as a useful thing, and a source of wealth.

---

* A better translation would be "tax farmers."

2. I shall explain the peculiar inconvenience of each kind of tax.

3. I shall endeavor to point out those on whom the loss, which is the result of each tax, really and ultimately falls.

4. I shall enquire into the cause of the diversity of opinions on the last point, and unfold the prejudices which have concealed them, while their real characters are easily discernible and pointed out, by certain indications.

Every time society, under whatever form, demands any sacrifice from some of its members, it becomes a collection of means, taken from particulars, and of which government assumes the disposal. To judge what will be the result of the tax, it is only required to know what use government will make of the revenue which it yields; for if it be employed in a manner which may be called profitable, it is evident that taxes then become the cause of an encrease in the mass of national wealth; if employed unprofitably, the opposite conclusion necessarily follows.

In the seventh book, on the subject of luxury, we have offered some reflections on *production* and *consumption,* which solve this question; we have seen that the only treasure of man, is the employment of his faculties, that the happiness of human society consists in the proper application of those faculties; its unhappiness in their loss or misapplication; that the only labor which causes the encrease of prosperity, is that which produces more than is consumed by those engaged in it; and that on the contrary, all labor which is unproductive is a cause of impoverishment; for all consumption is the result of previous production, and it is lost when it produces no equivalent; upon this principle, let us examine what idea we should form of the expence of government.

In the first place, almost the whole of the expence, all that which is employed in paying soldiers, seamen, judges, the public administration, priests and ministers, but particularly what is expended in supporting the luxury of the possessors or favorites of power, is absolutely lost; for none of those people produce any thing, which replaces what they consume.

There are, it is true, in every state, some funds required to excite emulation, and reward useful discoveries and improvements in the arts, sciences, and different kinds of industry, all of which may be considered as augmenting the public wealth; but in general, they are weak, inefficient, and so ill applied, that it is doubtful whether, as they have been used, the desired effect would not have been produced more substantially by the mere consumption of those who are amateurs, or can convert the discoveries into practical use, who have a more direct interest in their success, and are in general the best judges thereof.

There is no wise or provident government, which does not appropriate funds, more or less considerable, for the construction of bridges, turnpike roads, canals, and other public works, which enhance the value of land, facilitate the transportation of goods, and encourage industry. It is certain, that expences of this kind, directly encrease the national riches, and are, therefore, in reality productive. Nevertheless, if, as it frequently happens, the government which defrays the expence of construction, profits therefrom by establishing tolls, which, besides the expence of repairs, produces the interest of its money, and thus nothing is done which individuals would not have done with the same conditions and the same funds, if they had been permitted to do so; it may be said, that these individuals would almost always have attained the same end, with less expence.

From which it results, that almost all public expenditures, should be ranged in the class of expences denominated *sterile and unproductive*; and that consequently, all that is paid to the state, either as tax or loan, originates in productive labor, and should be considered as almost entirely consumed and expended, the day it enters the national treasury. But it is not therefore, to be inferred, that sacrifices of this kind, are not necessary, nay indispensable; for it is obvious that we require to have laws, to have them executed, to be defended, judged, governed, and our affairs administered; and unquestionably, every citizen should deduct from the produce of his *actual* industry, or from the revenues of his capital, originating from anterior labor, what is necessary for the state, for the same reason that it is necessary for him to keep his house in repair, that he may live therein with security. But still he ought to know that it is a sacrifice, and that what he gives is expended, both as it respects the public and his own private wealth; in short, it is *laying out*, and not *storing up* money. No man should be so blind, as to believe that expences of any kind are an augmentation of his fortune. Every one should know, that an expensive administration is ruinous to political society as well as to all others, and that the most economical is the best.

I believe the conclusion cannot be denied, and that it is very evident the sums absorbed by state expences are a continual cause of impoverishment, in most nations, and that consequently, the extent of revenue necessary to meet these expences, is an evil, as it respects economy; but it is evident, that the extent of revenue is injurious to national wealth; and it is no less evident, that it is still more so to political liberty, because it places in the hands of government, great means of corruption and oppression; it is not, therefore, and it cannot be too constantly present to our view, because the English pay enormous taxes, that they are free and opulent; but because they are free to a certain extent, that they are rich; it is because they are rich, that they can pay great taxes: but it is also because they are not sufficiently free, that they pay taxes which are enormous; and because their taxes are excessive, they must necessarily and very soon be neither wealthy nor free.

After having examined the general effect of taxes, if we were desirous of enquiring into the particular effects of each of them, we should be obliged to enter into details, which our author has not touched. All possible taxes, and I believe they have all been devised by the very gracious sovereigns of Europe, may be divided into six principal kinds, namely:[18]

1. Taxes on land; the real tax or tax on land, the twentieth, and *contribution fonciere,* in France; and the land tax in England.

2. That on the rent of houses.

3. That on the funds or interest due by the state.

4. Capitation or tax on persons, sumptuary and personal contributions, patents, corporation charters, freedom of corporations, &c.

5. Taxes on civil acts or deeds, social transactions, as stamp acts, registering of muniments, fines of alienation, the hundredth penny, mortmain, and others; to which may be added, the tax or rent or compensation, given by one person to another, for there is no other means of knowing than by the public offices in which the acts constituting them are preserved.

6. The impost, or tax on merchandize, either by monopoly or exclusion, or even the forced sale, as formerly that of salt and tobacco in France, either at their formation, as the taxes on salt works and on mines, and part of those on wine in France and those on breweries in England; either at the time of consumption or in their passage from the manufacturer to the consumer, on an internal excise or an internal duty, tolls on roads, canals, postage, tolls at the entrance of cities, of bridges, &c. Each of these kinds of taxes has one or more means peculiar to itself of affecting distributive justice, and consequently liberty, or of injuring public prosperity.

At the first glance we may perceive, that taxes on land are subject to the inconvenience of a difficult and unequal assessment, and to produce a dislike to the possession of any land the rent of which does not exceed the tax, or

---

18. To give a proper account of their effects, I believe the best method is to class them.

exceeds it in too small an amount to induce any one to incur the inevitable risques of seasons and other contingencies, and to make the necessary advances for cultivation.

Taxes on rented houses have the tendency to diminish the income of building, and consequently to prevent the erection of new houses for hire, so that the citizens are obliged to reside in houses less commodious and healthy than might have been otherwise had at the same rent.[19]

A tax on the rent or interest due by the state, or a tax on its own debts, is a real bankruptcy; if levied on funds already established, it is a diminution of the interest promised for a capital already received; it is a breach of contract, and it is deceptious; because at the moment of making the contract for the capital, it would have been more reasonable to have offered a smaller interest, than a great one and then retain a part of what was previously engaged to be paid.

Personal taxes occasion very disagreeable enquiries, in order to the equal assessment upon each individual's fortune, and must always be very variable because depending on imperfect information, either when the objects are acquired riches or the means of acquiring them; in the last case, when assessed upon any useful occupation, the effect is to discourage it, because industry is thus deprived of part of its own production, the fruits of that industry are enhanced in value, and the effect is that they are retarded or abandoned altogether.

Taxes on deeds, and in general on all conveyances of property, shackle the sales, lessen their nominal value, and by rendering the transfer expensive, augment the expences of justice so much, that persons who are not wealthy, cannot

---

19. I cannot agree with some French economists, that taxes should not be levied on houses, or at least should only be in proportion to the net produce of the cultivation of the ground they occupy, all the rest, according to them, being only the interest of the capital employed in building which they say cannot be taxed.

This opinion is a consequence of that which assumes that the cultivation of land is the only productive labor, that taxes can be levied on land, only because there is in the product of the earth a part purely gratuitous and entirely due to nature. According to these writers, this is the only part which it is reasonable and lawful to subject to taxation.

I hope presently to prove that all this is incorrect, yet I shall not oppose this tax, nor any of those which follow, though they are reprobated in common upon the principles of this system.

defray the charges, nor assert their rights; they cause the transaction of legal acts to be troublesome and difficult, lead to litigation and vexations from the officers of the revenue; they furnish temptation to concealments, and to the introduction of deceptious clauses and false valuations, which open wide the doors of injustice, and become the causes of multitudes of contentions and misfortunes.

Respecting duties on merchandize, the inconveniencies are yet more numerous and complex; but no less certain and lamentable.

Monopoly or exclusive sale made by the state, is odious, tyrannical, contrary to the common natural rights which every man has, of buying and selling as he deems to his advantage, and renders a multitude of violent measures necessary. It is yet worse, when the sale is forced, that is to say, when individuals are obliged, as has sometimes happened, to purchase that which they do not want, under the pretext that they cannot do without it, and that if they do not buy, it is to be inferred they must be provided with that which is smuggled.

Duties levied at the moment of production, evidently require, on the part of the person by whom they are produced, an advance of funds, which being a long time unrepaid by the sale of the production, greatly diminishes the mass of reproduction.

It is no less evident, that duties exacted, either on consumption, or during transportation, impede or destroy some branch of industry or commerce, rendering goods that are useful or necessary, scarce or dear; interrupting social happiness, deranging the nature and order of simple transactions, and forming between the different wants, and means of satisfying them, proportions and relations, which did not exist before those constraints, which are necessarily variable, and which continually render the laudable undertakings and resources of the citizens, precarious.

In fine, all those imposts upon merchandize, whatever they may be, require a multitude of restraints, precautions, and formalities. They occasion a variety of ruinous interruptions in the pursuits of the active citizen, and are very much subject to be arbitrary; they cause actions indifferent in themselves, to be converted into crimes, which are often expiated by inhuman penalties. Their collection is expensive, requiring almost an army of officers, and producing a multitude of peculators, all of whom become lost to society, and maintain against it real civil war, and all the consequences fatal to social economy and public morals.

On examining each of these remarks on different taxes, with attention, we may perceive that they are every one of them founded on experience; and after having considered that each tax is a sacrifice, and that the revenue arising therefrom, is almost generally employed in an unproductive manner, and often a fatal one; we have shewn, that each tax has besides a particular manner of becoming injurious to the liberty of the citizens, and to the prosperity of society: even this is perceiving a great deal. However, these are only general observations; they shew that taxes are hurtful, and in several different ways; but we do not yet distinctly perceive upon whom the loss, which is the result, ultimately falls, and who it is that really and unavoidably suffers the whole loss. This last consideration, requires a more close investigation of the subject; the explanations which it requires, are curious and very important, on account of the number of consequences which arise out of the investigation: let us then examine it, without adopting any system, limiting ourselves scrupulously to facts.

It is evident, that when a tax is laid upon land, the owner really pays it, without having it in his power to transfer the burthen to any one else, for the tax does not furnish him with the means of augmenting his income, since they add nothing either to the demand of produce nor to the fertility of the soil; nor do they enable him to diminish his expences, for they do not alter the nature of those which he already incurs and pays, nor do they procure a greater facility in the manner of employing them; all will agree to this. But it has not been sufficiently remarked, that the proprietor of such lands is not really to be considered as deprived of his annual income, but as having lost a portion of his capital equal to the principal which this part of his income would produce at the current interest. A proof of this is, that if a landed property producing five thousand dollars clear income, and worth one hundred thousand dollars, should on the day after a perpetual tax of one fifth laid on it, be offered for sale, it would not bring more than eighty thousand dollars, all things else equal; and in like manner, it would only be considered worth eighty thousand dollars, compared with other property which had not been subjected to any charge. In effect, when the state declares that it will forever claim the fifth of the income of landed property, it is the same as if it declared itself the proprietor of the fifth part of the capital, for no possession is worth any thing but on account of the utility that may be derived therefrom. This is so true that if in consequence of new taxes, the state negotiates a loan, at an interest equal to such taxes, it has really pledged the capital it has claimed and made away with it all at once, instead of annually expending the income that might be derived from it. It is as if Mr. Pitt had all at once demanded of the land holders of

England the capital of the land tax they were charged with, and it had been delivered and he had made away with it at once.

From thence it follows, that land, on changing proprietors, from the commencement of the taxes thereon, the taxes are really no longer paid by any person, for those who have acquired it, have only obtained what was left, and consequently lose nothing; the heirs have taken possession of only what they have found, the surplus for them is as if their predecessors had expended or lost it, as indeed they have lost it.

It also follows, that when the state remits all or part of the land tax, which had been previously established as a perpetuity, it purely and simply makes a present to the actual proprietor of the capital of the taxes which it ceases to demand: it is, as respects them, a free gift, to which they have no more right than any other citizen, for this part of the capital was not taken into consideration in the transactions by which they became the proprietors.

It would not absolutely be the same, if the tax had been originally established only for a limited period of years, then there would really have been taken from the proprietors only a portion of the capital corresponding with an annuity for such a number of years; nor could the state borrow more than the amount of an annuity for the years named, from those to whom the taxes thereon might be assigned as a security for the loan; and the lands could be considered in transfers as lessened in value only to that amount. In the event of the tax ceasing, as if the loans corresponding thereto were terminated, then on both sides it is a debt extinguished; as to the rest, the principle is the same as in the case of a tax and sale in perpetuity.

It is, therefore, ever true, that when a tax is levied on land, a value equal to the capital of this tax is taken from the actual possessor, and that afterwards, it is no longer paid in reality by any one: this observation is singular and important.

It is absolutely the same, with respect to the taxes on the income of houses; those possessing them, suffer at the time the taxes are established, the entire loss, for they have no means of indemnifying themselves; for those who buy them afterwards, pay only in proportion to the charges they are encumbered with; those who inherit them, calculate only on the value that remains; and those who build afterwards, make their calculations upon things as they find them established; if a sufficient interest should not arise therefrom to render the undertaking advantageous, they would not attempt it, until through the encreased demand for houses, rents should encrease; as, on the contrary, if it were very profitable, there would soon be a sufficiency of funds employed therein, to render it not more advantageous than any other.

Hence we may conclude, that the proprietors on whom the taxes fall, lose the entire capital thereof, and when they are all either dead, or have transferred their property, such taxes are paid by persons who cannot complain thereof.

The same may be said of the taxes which a government lays on the interest of money it has borrowed: certainly the unfortunate creditor from whom the deduction is made, suffers all the loss, not being able to throw it on any one; but beside, he loses his capital in proportion to the deduction; the proof is, that if he sells his interest or stock, he obtains less for it, in proportion as it is more encumbered, if the general rate of interest on money has not varied; and it also follows, that subsequent possessors of this stock, really pay nothing; for they have received it in this condition, and for the value which remains, in virtue of a purchase freely made, or a succession voluntarily accepted.

The effect of taxes on individuals, is not the same: we cannot distinguish* between those which are levied on riches realized, and on the means of acquiring them, that is to say, on industry of any kind. In the first place, it is evidently the person taxed, that undergoes the loss resulting from it, for he cannot put it off on any one else; but as in relation to each individual, the tax ceases with his life, and that every one is successively subjected thereto, in proportion to his supposed riches; the first person taxed, loses only the sum he pays, and not the capital thereof, but without exonerating those who succeed him; so that at whatever time the tax ceases, it is not a gain to those who had been subject to it, but a heavy burden from which they have been relieved.

In respect to the personal tax on any object of industry, it is not less true, that the person who first pays it does not lose the capital thereof, nor exempt those who succeed him therefrom; but it occasions consequences of another nature. A person engaged on some new object of industry, at the moment it becomes encumbered with a new tax, such as the encrease of the fees on taking out a patent, corporations, and the like, such person has only two courses to pursue, either to renounce his industrious undertaking, or pay the tax, and suffer the loss occasioned by it, if, notwithstanding this tax, he thinks his undertaking advantageous.

* The French text here reads, "we must distinguish."

In the first case he certainly suffers, but he does not pay the tax: consequently, I shall not notice it. In the second, the burden certainly falls upon himself; for neither augmenting the demand, nor diminishing the expence, it presents him with no immediate means of encreasing his own income, nor of lessening his expences; but a tax sufficiently heavy to force all the persons who pursue a particular branch of industry to abandon it, is never levied at once, because all industrious professions being necessary for society, the extinction of a single one would tend to produce a general disorder among other branches connected with it; so that when a tax is levied on such objects, it is those who are sufficiently rich not to care for a trifling profit, or those whose success is so small, that nothing would remain after paying the tax, that would abandon the profession; the others would continue them, and these, as we have already said, would really pay the tax, at least until a certain number of their fraternity had ceased to do business, and afforded them by the cessation of competition, the opportunity of transferring the tax, by an addition to the selling price, from the manufacturer to the consumer.

This is the condition of those exercising a profession at the time of laying the tax; those who embrace the same kind of industry after the tax has been established, are not in the same situation; the law is already made; we may say they agree to the conditions, and that the tax is as to them rated among the expences incident to the business, the same as the necessity of renting such a stand, or buying such a machine: they only enter into the business because, notwithstanding the tax, they think it the best business they can follow, with the capital and industry they possess; so that though they really pay the tax it takes nothing from them. Those to whom the tax is a real burthen are the consumers, who, without this charge, could have procured at a less expence the kind of articles which they purchase, which are the best they can obtain in the existing state of the society; whence it follows that if the taxes be removed, these persons really reap an advantage from it upon which they did not before calculate. They perceive themselves gratuitously and fortuitously transported into a class of society more favored by fortune than that in which they were placed, while those who exercised it anterior to the tax, only return to their first state; we may perceive that personal taxes, founded on industry, have very different effects; but the general effect is to diminish the enjoyments of the consumers, since their tradesmen do not give them goods for that part of their money which goes into the public treasury.

I shall enter into no more details: but we cannot accustom ourselves too much, to examine the operation and effects of indirect taxes, and to follow them with attention through all their modifications. Let us pass to taxes on deeds, records, and other papers, muniments of social transactions.

This part of the subject requires some discrimination. The portion of the tax which augments the expence of justice and makes a part thereof, is undoubtedly paid by the persons on whom the forms of office makes these expences fall, and it is difficult to say to what class of society it is most injurious; however, it is evident that it affects those possessions most which are liable to contention; now when they relate to landed property, the establishment of such taxes certainly diminishes their value in transfers; and this consequence also follows, that those who have purchased lands subsequent to the establishment of such taxes, are somewhat compensated by the reduction of the price; and that those who before possessed them incurred the entire loss if they become parties in one action, and even undergo a loss without any action or paying the tax, for the value of their property is diminished; consequently if the tax ceases, it is only a restitution for the last, and again for the others, for they are placed in a better condition than they had calculated upon, and on which they had formed their speculations.

All these principles are still more applicable, and without qualification of the portion of the tax, on transactions which relate to purchase and sale, such as fines of alienation, the hundredth penny, and others: this portion of the tax is altogether paid by him who holds the property at the time it is thus encumbered, for the person who afterwards buys it from him takes this into consideration, and consequently pays nothing; all that can be said is this, that if this tax on deeds of sale of certain possessions, be accompanied by other duties or other acts which burden other possessions, or different means of investing capital, it will happen that such kinds of property are those alone which suffer a diminution of value; and that thus a part of the loss is indirectly prevented by the effects which are produced upon others, because the price of every kind of revenue is relative to some other kind; so that if all these losses could exactly be balanced, the total loss resulting from the operation of taxes, would be proportionably and very exactly distributed. This is all that can be expected, for it must necessarily exist, since taxes are always a sum of money taken from the governed, to be placed at the disposal of the government.

Duties on merchandize have yet more various and complicated effects; in order to give them an effective examination, let us first observe, that at the time merchandize is delivered to the consumer, it has a natural and necessary value. This value is composed of the value of all that was necessary for the subsistence of those who have produced, manufactured, and transported the merchandize, during the time which they were employed upon it. This price, I say, is natural, because it is founded on the nature of human concerns, independently of any convention; and it is necessary, because if the people so employed did not obtain subsistence by their labor, they would perish, or devote their faculties to something else, and such occupations would no longer be undertaken. But this natural and necessary price has almost nothing in common with the market price, that is to say with the price given for it at a sale free on both sides; for they have cost very little trouble, or if it required a great deal of labor it may have been found or stolen by the person who exposes it to sale; so that he may sell it at a very low price, without losing any thing; but it may at the same time be so useful to him, that he would not part therewith without a considerable sum; and if several persons desire to obtain it, he will get his price and make a great gain; on the contrary, a thing may have cost the person offering it for sale a great deal of trouble, and it not only becomes necessary, but want forces him to part with it; or if there be no person desirous of purchasing it, he will then be obliged to offer it for the smallest possible price, and will suffer a great loss. The natural price is, therefore, composed of anterior sacrifices made by the person who sells it, and the conventional price fixed by the offers of the buyers. These are two things in themselves foreign to each other, only that when the conventional price of labor is constantly below the natural one, people cease to occupy themselves with it; then the produce of such labor becoming scarce, more attempts are made to procure it, if still in demand, so that if any wise productive, the conventional price becomes equal to the natural one, which is essential to production. It is in this manner that all prices in society are formed.

From this it follows, that those who occupy themselves on work of which the conventional price is lower than the natural price, ruin themselves or have to relinquish it; that those who exercise an industrious employment, the conventional price of the products of which is strictly equal to the natural value, that is to say those of which the profit is almost equal to the expenditures required to procure absolute necessaries, obtain no more than a miserable existence; those in possession of talents, the conventional price of the productions whereof is superior to the demands of absolute necessity, enjoy life, prosper and multiply; for the fecundity of all living kind, even among vegetables, is such, that only a want of nourishment for the buds prevents the encrease of individuals. These are the causes of the retrograde, stationary, or progressive state of population among men. Temporary calamities, such as famine or pestilence, have little effect thereon. Unproductive labor, or productive to an insufficient degree, that is to say luxury, in which war should be comprised, and unskilfulness, by which should be understood ignorance of all kinds, are the poisons which deeply infect the sources of life, and continually destroy reproduction. This truth confirms what we have established in the seventh book, or rather is the same in different terms; the population* of savage countries, and the weak population of those that are civilized, where an enormous inequality of fortunes has introduced great luxury on one side, and consequently great misery on the other, are incontestible and eternal evidences of the principles.

It is now easy to apprehend that duties on merchandize affect the price in different modes and in different limits, according to the manner in which they are levied, and according to the nature of the goods they operate upon; for example, in the case of a monopoly or exclusive sale made by the state, it is evident that the tax is paid directly or immediately, and without remedy, by the consumer, and that it has the greatest possible extension. But this sale, if forced, cannot either as to the price or quality exceed a certain term, which is that of the possibility of paying it. It stops when it would be useless to exact it, or that it would cost more than it produces.

This is the point which the duty on salt in France had reached, and is the maximum of exaction.

If the sale be not forced, the duties varying according to the nature of the merchandize, and that not being necessary, as the price encreases the consumption decreases; for there is only a certain sum of money in society, destined to procure certain kinds of enjoyment; it might even happen, that by raising the price a little, the profit may be greatly diminished; for many people may renounce the article entirely, or even replace it by another; however, the duty is always effectively paid by those who continue to consume.

If, on the contrary, the state has the exclusive sale, although optional in the buyer of an article of merchandize of the first necessity, it is in effect a forced sale; for the consumption, it is true, diminishes as the price rises, that is to say, we suffer and die; but as it is necessary, the price is always as high as the means of purchase, and it is paid by those who consume it.

From those more than heroic stratagems, employed by governments to disencumber their subjects of their superfluous wealth, we shall pass to humbler

* The French text has "depopulation."

artifices, analogous it is true, but not so energetic. The most efficacious of these, are the duties imposed on merchandize at the time of their production; for no part escapes; not even what is consumed by the manufacturer himself, nor what is damaged or lost in the storehouses before removal for use; such is the duty on salt, at the salt pits of France; that on wine, at the time of the vintage, or before the wine is sold; that on beer in the English brew house, that of the excise under the English system;* we may range in the same class the duties on sugar, coffee, and the like goods, exacted at the time of their arrival from the country in which they were produced; for it is only then, that they begin to exist in relation to the country that cannot produce, and yet has to consume them.

This duty, if imposed at the time of production, on goods of no great absolute necessity, is limited according to the taste or demand for them; thus when desirous of making a considerable profit on the article of tobacco, in order to encrease a revenue for the king of France, means were taken by the ministers to render tobacco a necessary among the people; for society is well constituted to satisfy, with ease, the necessities which nature has given us, and which cannot be dispensed with; but governments, which should be formed with a view to the interests of the governed, seem as if destined to create wants in us, of which they refuse us the use of a part, and make us pay heavily for the other part; these are, in fact, *manufactories of privation,* instead of enjoyment. I know of no industry which requires to be more carefully looked after than this, yet this it is which pretends to superintend the others!

When this same duty, at the time of production, is imposed on goods more necessary, it is susceptible of greater extension; however, if such goods have cost a great deal of labor and expence to produce them, the extent of the duty is soon stopt, not from any diminution of desire to possess them, but from the want of means; for those who produce them, must obtain a price sufficient for their support; consequently, there remains less to furnish the taxes for the state.

Duties act with their full power, when the goods are very necessary, and their prime cost is very small; as for example, salt, which is all profit, except to the last consumers; salt has particularly attracted the attention of great financiers and great kings. Rich mines produce, likewise, the same effect, to

---

* The French text makes no reference to English brewhouses here.

a certain point; but in general, governments take these into their own possession[20] which simplifies the operation, and is equal to an exclusive sale. The air and water, if possession could have been taken of them, would also have been objects of very advantageous speculations, or at least, of very great deductions, but nature has diffused them rather too much.[21]

I do not doubt that in Arabia a regular government might derive a great revenue from water, if it were so regulated that no one could drink without the permission of government. As to the air, the tax upon windows is a very ingenious means of accomplishing it, and as the phrase is, *rendering it useful.**

Wine is not a free gift of nature, it costs much labor, care, and expense, and notwithstanding the demand and great desire of obtaining it, it is surprizing that it can support the enormous charges with which it is burdened at the time of production; but it must also be considered that a part of this burden falls directly on the vineyards, and only occasions a greater diminution in the prices of the leases of vineyards; thus it has only the effect of a land tax, which, as we have seen, takes away a part of the capital of the possessor, without influencing the price of goods or making any encroachments on the value of productions; so that the capitalist is impoverished, but nothing is deranged as to society.

Grain in general, like wine, might be the object of a very heavy duty imposed also at the time of production, independent even of the tithe or tenth

---

20. In favor of these possessions, learned writers have established the very delicate maxim, that when an individual takes possession of a tract of land by right of first occupancy, or through a legal title, his right to the ground does not exceed a certain depth! From this luminous principle it results, that the *interior of the earth belongs to the prince,* wherever it is worth more than the superficies!

21. Montesquieu gives credit to the emperor Anastatius, for having conceived the happy idea of taxing the air we breathe, *pre haustu aeris;* we must not, however, flatter this great politician too much, he does not appear to have succeeded better than any one else, in effectually rendering himself master of this merchandize; besides, that the air here appears rather as a motive, than a means; and *haustu aeris,* is to be taken in a metaphorical sense, *for the happiness of breathing and living under the empire of so great a prince,* which of course, can never be too well paid for, though capitation fulfils this object.

* A property tax based on the number of windows in a building. Established in England in 1696, it was introduced in France in 1798 (and only repealed in 1926).

with which they are charged in a great part of Europe; a part of the tax would in like manner diminish the income from land by affecting the value of its products; and consequently, without encreasing the price of such articles, fall on the owner. If governments have refrained from imposing such taxes, it is, I am persuaded, not through a superstitious respect for the principal aliment of the industrious, who are generally sufficiently burdened by other means, but on account of the difficulty of entering and superintending every barn, granary, and which is still a greater trouble, of entering every hut and cellar: as to the rest, the similitude is complete.

It should be observed that the imposition laid at the moment of production, on goods of an indispensable use, is in effect, a real capitation tax, and of all capitations it is the most cruel for those who are not rich; because the poor consume the greatest quantity of productions of the first necessity, and because they cannot be supplied by any thing as a substitute; these constitute almost all their expences, and they can provide only for their most pressing wants. So that an additional capitation is thus imposed, and distributed according to the proportions of wretchedness, and not of riches, in the direct ratio of wants, and the inverse ratio of means. Thus we may estimate duties of this kind; but they are very productive, and occasion little emotion in *good company*, which is saying what is very much in their favor.

Respecting duties imposed on different merchandize, either at the time of their consumption, or at their different stations, as on a public road, in a market, at the entrance of cities, on deposit in warehouses, and the like, their effects have been already indicated by those we have seen resulting from them, in the case of an exclusive sale, and the duties imposed at the time of production; these are of the same kind, only not so general, because various and seldom capable of embracing a great extent of country; indeed the greatest part of these impositions are local, a toll affects the goods which pass on the road or canal, where it is established at the entrance of towns it only affects the consumers within them; a duty levied in a market or shop, does not affect those who sell in the country, or at an extraordinary fair; so that they only render prices more irregular, and always derange them in the places which they affect; for when an article of merchandize is charged with the tax, either the person who is the producer or the consumer must lose the amount of what is drawn off by it.

It is here, that the consequences of two important conditions, proper to all merchandize, should be stated, in relation to the products and effects of taxation: one, their being of the first necessity, or only administering to our comforts or luxury; the other, that the conventional price should be higher than the natural price, or only equal to it; as to being less, we already know it is impossible.

If the article taxed, be of the first necessity, it cannot be dispensed with, and will always be bought, so long as there are means to dispose of for the purpose; and if its natural price be equal to that of convention, the producer cannot abate any thing, so that all the loss must fall on the consumer, who must suffer thereby. Old societies, occupying territory circumscribed for a long time, are only able to encroach upon other territories already occupied; and this is the condition of almost all merchandize, of the first necessity; for the effect of a long contention between the opposed interests of the producer and consumer, is that each infringes somewhat on the social economy and order, according to the force of his capacity: those possessed of skill sufficient to seek or exact more than what absolute necessity calls for, will betake themselves to such methods; those who cannot, are not qualified to succeed by such courses, and will occupy themselves with indispensable productions, because the frequency or constancy of demand will compensate their want of skill; but they are paid only for what is strictly necessary; and there are always a sufficiency of people, of this degree of capacity, who have no other resource but employment of this kind, and it is necessary and natural that it should be so; for the goods of the first necessity, are absolutely requisite for all, and particularly for the poorest of all the other classes, who consume without producing, being otherwise employed; so that these poor people can only subsist in proportion as these articles are easy to be procured. It is therefore in vain, that the dignity and utility of agriculture, or any other necessary profession, is so much extolled; the more indispensable it is, the more inevitably must those occupied therein, want other talents, and thereby be reduced to a strict necessity. There is no other direct means of ameliorating the condition of these men, the last in rank in society, because almost destitute of intellectual knowledge, but by permitting them to exercise the little knowledge they may have, wherever they may think it will be more productive; for which reason, expatriation should always be allowed in every country and to every man, for he is already sufficiently miserable who is reduced to this resource. Many other political measures might also indirectly concur in defending poverty against the iron yoke of necessity, but this is not the place to treat of them; taxes alone, are our present object; moreover, these men, whom with justice we pity, suffer yet less, even in an imperfect state of society, than they would in the savage state; without entering into any details, the proof is, that on the same extent of territory there live more animals of our kind, even those belonging to the soil, and I might even assert a greater number of slaves than savages, for men become extinct only through an excess of misery; the proportions of any thing should be taken into consideration, and nothing exaggerated, even in that which we disapprove, or which afflicts us. The vicinity of immense regions of fertile and uncultivated lands, is an excellent means of remedying these evils; this is the condition of the United States of America, and of Russia in Europe. The different means of profiting by these happy circumstances, shews the difference between the two governments, or rather, the two nations; one of which is not as capable of governing itself as the other, and will continue so for a long time.

If the articles taxed are not of the first necessity, and the conventional price be only equal to its natural price, it is a proof that the consumers do not care much for it, and when duties are levied thereon, the producer has no other resource but to renounce his occupation to obtain subsistence in some other profession, thus encreasing his misery by his own concurrence, and in which he labors under a disadvantage of not having been at first acquainted with his new pursuit. Thus they perish at least in great part; the consumer only loses an enjoyment to which he was not attached, probably because he had substituted some other for it, and thus the tax produces nothing.

If, on the contrary, goods or industry of little necessity are taxed, and bear a conventional price far superior to their natural value, and which is the case with all articles of luxury; there are *bounds* within which they are *confined* without reducing any one to misery: the same total sum is expended for this enjoyment, unless the taste which causes it to be sought after decreases: it is the producer that pays the whole of what the tax takes from his entire sum, but as he gains more than what is absolutely a good profit, he succeeds. But we can only say that this is a general truth, for in some trades supposed to be advantageous, there are individuals, who, through want of skill and reputation, or other circumstances, obtain only a scanty subsistence; these, on the imposition of taxes, are forced to abandon their profession, which is always very distressing, for men are not like mathematical points; such changes are not effected without collisions productive of disorder. It is thus that the direct effect of different and partial local duties imposed upon merchandize in their transportation from the producer to the consumer, may be estimated.

But, besides these direct effects, such duties have others that are indirect and of a different character from the first, or which mixing with them render them more complicated; thus a heavy duty on an important article levied at the entrance of a town; on the one side it lowers the rent of houses, by causing it to be a less desirable place of abode; on the other, it diminishes the rent of lands producing the article, by rendering the sale thereof less considerable, or less advantageous; here the capitalists, even though absent and no wise connected with it, are injured in their capital, the same as by a land tax, while it was only contemplated to affect the consumer or producer thereby; this is so true, that the proprietors, if it were proposed to them, would make sacrifices more or less great to pay off a part of the fund of the duty, or directly furnish a part of their annual produce: we have frequently seen it.

What is more than all these economical considerations, we should only consider as real consumers of an article, those who effectively consume it for their personal satisfaction, and employ it for their own use. These only we can speak of under the denomination of consumers; however, they are far from being the only buyers of such articles, often the greatest part of those purchases are made as primary articles of other *productions,* and as the raw material for their own industry; then the duty imposed on such articles, affects all those *productions,* and the industry dependent thereon; this is what particularly happens to articles of very general use, and of indispensable necessity; they constitute a part of the expences of many different productions.

We must likewise consider that the duties of which we are treating, never act altogether upon a single article, they are at the same time levied upon many kinds of goods, that is to say, upon many articles of production and consumption; upon each according to its nature, they operate some of the effects we have explained, so that all of the different effects reciprocally balance and resist each other; for the new duties with which an industrious occupation is burdened, prevent the embracing of it in preference to another which has just received a like injury. The burden which oppresses one kind of consumption, renders it unfit for a substitute to one we are desirous of renouncing; whence it follows, that if it were possible completely to prevent them from clashing, and to form a perfect equilibrium of all the weights, so that by placing them all at the same time in such a situation as that they would every where act with an equal pressure, no proportion would be changed by them. They would together have no other effect than what is common to all taxes: namely, that the producer acquires a less profit on his industry, and the consumer less enjoyment for his money. Taxes might be considered as good, if to these general and inevitable evils they did not join evils of another and a particular kind, which are too distressing.

Such are the principal considerations that I was desirous of finding in this part of the Spirit of Laws, which treats of the levying of taxes, and the extent of the public revenue as connected with liberty; for we cannot too often repeat, that *liberty is happiness.* Economical science forms a considerable part of the social science; it is even its principal end, for we desire society to be well organised in order that our enjoyments[22] may be more multiplied, more perfect, and more tranquil; and so long as this end is not well understood, we are liable to a number of errors, from which our celebrated author is not always exempt.

The question, by whom are taxes really paid, is particularly interesting, because it affects the whole mechanism of society, and its true springs are known or unknown, according as it is perfectly or imperfectly resolved. If it should be thought that I have already said too much on this subject, its importance will be my justification; much is yet required fully to explain it, to make all the applications, to develop all the consequences, to the right understanding of it: this I shall leave to the sagacity of the reader; and I am persuaded that the more he takes the trouble to investigate it, the more solid and fruitful he will perceive the principles to be which we have already established. But if they are true, as I believe them to be, and even so true that I think I may confine myself to the bare declaration of them, and leave them to their own strength without any other support than their own evidence, how comes it that contrary opinions have been so generally adopted? This is a point which I demand further permission to discuss, should it even be thought that I trespass beyond the bounds prescribed by a commentator, by causing discussion after discussion to rise out of the subject, with an insupportable perseverance.

The old French economists were enlightened and estimable men, who have rendered great services to mankind; but they were very indifferent metaphysicians, until the physiologists took a share in the subject.

In this we may say, that GREAT TALENTS BELONG ONLY TO OUR TIME.

And yet they are scarce; the philosophers exclusively called economists, have not then sufficiently studied the nature of man, and particularly his intellectual dispositions. They did not perceive, that in our faculties and in the manner in which our will employs them, all our treasure consists, and that this employment of nature constitutes the only wealth that in itself has a natural and necessary primitive value, which it communicates to all things upon

22. Moral enjoyments always to be understood; and for the most part, the result of a happy order of society is, that virtue becomes first an effect, and then a cause.

which it is employed, and which could have no other; consequently, they have imagined, that there might be some useful labor unproductive of any real value. Then more struck with this negative power of nature, which appears to form creations in favor of agriculture which set it in motion, than with the other physical powers through the means of which all our other works are performed; they persuaded themselves, that there was really a gratuitous gift on the part of the earth, and that the labor employed in cultivating it, alone deserved to be called productive; without perceiving that there is as great difference between a bundle of hemp and a shirt, as between a bundle of hempseed and a bundle of hemp; and that the difference is entirely of the same kind, consisting of the labor employed in performing the manufacture.*

This false idea of a sort of magical virtue attributed to the earth, has led these philosophers into several consequences yet more false; among which was the notion that there are no true citizens in a state but the proprietors of land, and that they alone constitute society; another pernicious consequence was their admiration of the feudal system, altogether founded on these pretended rights of an inanimate tract of land, which infeoffs and sub-infeoffs the different parts, which establishes a gradation of slavery from the last tenant, and even the persons attached to the soil, up to the first paramount lord, in respect to whom, living on the territory over which he presided, possessed no rights but such as it was his pleasure or displeasure to grant:† and in fine, that all things as they erroneously asserted, being derived only from the earth, the earth *only* should be subject to taxation, and that even when other taxes were levied beside that on land; but as it necessarily happens, from the nature of things, that taxes ultimately fall in the proportion of lands, and even with a heavier weight; and as these results, ever found not to be rigorously exact, several of the economists have rejected some of them,‡ but they have all agreed in that which engages our present attention, the doctrine relative to duties.

---

* A reference to the physiocrats, an influential school of eighteenth-century French economists who believed that land was the source of all wealth.

† This is a complicated sentence. "Infeoff" is an obsolete version of "enfeoff." The meaning is to invest (a person) with a freehold estate by feoffment. In addition, the French text speaks not of "a gradation of slavery" but of a "hierarchy."

‡ The French text speaks not of "economists" but of "members of the sect."

This prejudice in relation to gratuitous production by the earth, has so much perplexed and taken such deep root in the mind, that it is difficult entirely to eradicate it. That learned and judicious writer, Adam Smith, perceived very clearly, that the human faculties are the only treasure of man, and that all which composes the wealth of a particular society, is nothing more than the accumulated productions of industry which have not been consumed;* he has acknowledged that all labor which makes an addition to the mass of wealth more than the person performing that labor consumes, should be called productive, and that labor is unproductive only in the contrary case; and he has completely refuted those who give the attribute of productiveness only to the cultivation of the earth. Yet he imagines, that there is in the *rent of land* something else, which he calls *profits of capital.* He considers it as a production of nature, and expressly says, book II, chap. 5, that *it is the work of nature that remains, after the deduction or balance is made, of all that can be considered as the work of man.* He likewise calls a portion of the accumulated wealth, the *fixed capital* of a nation, and in this he comprises the amelioration of the soil; but he does not, as he should, comprise therein the soil itself, for the value it has in commerce. It is true, he says that *a farm ameliorated, may be considered in the same light as those useful machines, which facilitate labor;* but he has not ventured to say explicitly what nevertheless is true, a field is a tool in the hands of a workman, as much as any other tool, and that the rent paid for it, is the same as the hire given for the use of a machine, or the interest on a sum of money borrowed.

J. B. Say, formerly a member of the French institute, is undoubtedly the author of the best work on political economy, that has yet appeared;† he wrote a long time after Smith, and acknowledges with him, that the employment of our faculties is the source of all wealth, and it alone, is the cause of the *necessary value* of all things that possess any; because this value is only the representation of all that was necessary to satisfy the person who had formed any thing by his industry during the time he employed his *faculties* thereupon. He goes yet farther, and expressly says, that being incapable of creating even an atom of matter, we can never effect any thing but transmutation and trans-

---

* The text referred to here is of course Smith, *An Inquiry into the Nature and Causes of the Wealth of Nations* (1776).

† *Traité d'économie politique, ou simple exposition de la manière dont se forment, se distribuent, et se composent les richesses* (1803).

formation, and that what we call producing, is in every imaginable case, giving a greater utility as it respects us, to the elements we combine and operate on, with the assistance of the powers of nature which are put into action by us; as that which we call consuming, is always diminishing or destroying this utility by making use thereof. This luminous principle, is equally applicable to the farmer, manufacturer, and merchant; to cultivate, is by the means of a tool called a field, to convert seeds by means of the air, earth, water, and other principles, into an abundant harvest.[23] To manufacture, is, with the assistance of some instruments, to change hemp first into linen, and then into shirts. To traffic, is, with such machines as ships and waggons, to convey for the consumer useful commodities produced at a distance from him, adding thereto the expence of transportation; while to those whom we take these things from, we send other articles, that they are in want of, and which, in like manner, are not within their reach. On the contrary, to consume food, is to convert it into dung; to consume a suit of clothes, is to change them into rags; to consume water, is to drink, make it foul, or only return it to the river.

With so clear and distinct an idea of the subject, it was impossible not to see things as they are. Mr. Say likewise pronounces, without hesitation, book I, chap. 5, *that a tract of land is only a machine;* yet influenced by the authority of his predecessor, whom he has so often corrected and excelled, or perhaps only overcome by the power of habit, or by deceptive appearances, he permits himself to be dazzled by the illusions he has so completely destroyed. He persists in considering a tract of land, as a possession of a particular nature, its productive service as something else than a utility to be derived from a tool; and its rent as different from the interest given for a capital lent. In fine, book IV, chap. 16, he more formally than Smith, says, in discussing with him the same subject, that it is from the action of the earth the profit of its proprietor

---

23. Agriculture is particularly a chemical art: a farmer causes the grain of which he is in want, to grow, as a chemist makes the inflammable gas which he requires for his uses. The farmer ploughs, harrows, manures, sows, and if necessary, waters it, to arrange the elements which are to act in contact with each other, in a convenient manner. The chemist disposes his apparatus, his acid of manganese, and his sulphuric acid, with the same view. After which, both leave the different affinities to act, and both obtain their object: if that which they produce has more pecuniary value, it is an incontestible proof of its being more useful than what they employed and consumed during the operation.

arises. This single fault, accounts for the ambiguity that prevails on all that he says on capital, revenue, and taxes.

In fact, with such a prepossession, it is impossible to give any consistent account of the progress of society, and of the formation of our wealth; we are obliged, like Mr. Say, to acknowledge as constituent parts of the value of all things, which possess any: 1. Profit of labor or income. 2. Profit on capital; which appears to be a thing quite different from the first. 3. Profit on land, which also appears to be an element of another kind. We know not how to determine the natural and necessary value of each thing; there is always a portion of which we cannot perceive the cause, much less could we see the effects which taxes produce thereon, and the influence of all this on the life of man, the extent of population, and the power of states; all is perplexed and sophisticated by their principles; and on these subjects, arbitrary and incoherent opinions only, can be formed.

On the contrary, by renouncing this prejudice, and firmly persuading ourselves that what we call land, that is to say, a cube of earth and stone having one of its faces on the superficies of our globe, is a mass of matter as well as any other, with this difference, that it cannot as a body change its place. This difference, it is true, occasions its being defended and preserved with more difficulty by its proprietor, because it cannot be concealed nor taken with him like *movable* property: but if society be sufficiently enlightened to acknowledge, and sufficiently powerful to protect it, it is a possession similar to others. This property might be such that its possession would be good for nothing; in which case it has no price in any part of the world, it could neither be sold nor let; on the contrary it may be useful in many ways. It may serve for the foundation of a dwelling house, or store houses for merchandizes, or a work shop; fuel may be procured from it, materials necessary for manure to fertilize other lands; there may be springs thereon well adapted for irrigation; precious metals, diamonds, or other stones, and minerals of great value; it may be particularly adapted to receive grain, yielding great abundance. In all these cases its value is great. It may perhaps be said that the value of the ground has then no proportion to that of the labor of the first person who sought after, examined, and appropriated it to himself; this is true; but a person who should unexpectedly find a large diamond in any other place, would be a great gainer thereby, while the one who after long seeking, should only find a very small one, is very trivially recompensed; however this does not prevent the natural price of the diamond from being the labor of the man who has sought and found it, and its pecuniary price, that which the desire of possessing it offers.

This proves no more than that in all kinds of industry, there is labor very unproductive and very profitable. The same may be said as to land, its natural price is very small when not obliged to go far to meet with some which has no owner; it is greater when this requires labor and an expensive removal; its money price varies like all other things, and through the same causes. A very indifferent tract of land may sell very dear, when there are many persons desirous of purchasing it; on the contrary, the United States of America sell very fine land at a very low price in their western territories; and in certain parts of Russia the government grants it for nothing, and even give some provisions and domestic animals to those who accept it, on condition of settling themselves thereon and cultivating it. Whatever it may be, a piece of ground, like any other tool, is susceptible of many uses, as we have just seen. When good for nothing, its value is nothing; when of any use, it has a value; when it belongs to no one, it requires only the trouble of taking possession; when it belongs to any one, some other useful thing must be given in exchange for it. In all cases, to express myself like others, it exactly and without any difference is equivalent to the *capital* that can be procured by giving it up, and may, as most convenient, be given away, or lent, sold or rented,[24] or used immediately by its proprietor, but nothing else can ever be done with either one or the other, but to apply them in one or other of these five ways.

When once satisfied in our own minds, of the truth of these ideas, nothing in the world can be more evident, than that these are the true sources from which our wealth is derived; there is then, no more need of an hundred thousand superfluous distinctions, which serve no purpose but to promote confusion; there is nothing besides the exercise of the human faculties, which can procure subsistence for man, and without this there is nothing; but all useful things, which are at our disposal, must be considered as well the fruit of our

24. It is a very absurd mode of expression to say when we part with our money for a certain time in consideration of a certain benefit called *interest,* that we have *lent it;* for in this case we *hire* or *rent* it, and we only really lend it when we permit any one to have the benefit of it for a certain time without any recompense. There are between these two actions the same difference as between *giving* and *selling.* This inaccuracy of language has caused nonsense to be both spoken of and believed, where such nonsense has been caused by this inaccuracy of expression, for there is always an action and reaction; to form a science, is to form the language thereof; and to form the language of a science, is to form the science itself.

intellectual as our manual labor, of our knowledge as well as our industry, and the surplus wealth of society consists of what remains after all are adequately subsisted. It is this labor, and the necessary consumption of those who are occupied therein, which regulates the natural price of things. The market price is governed by the relative value of other useful things, which we are disposed to give for them; but those other useful things are also the products of labor; so that whoever possesses the fruit of accumulated labor, can command actual labor from others, or remunerate them for what they have already performed by giving them an equivalent of this fruit of accumulated labor, whatever it may be; either in perpetuity, which is called *selling;* or for a time, which is called renting or hiring. If that which he receives for a certain time of any kind of rent, be sufficient for his subsistence, during that period he is said to live upon his *income;* on the contrary, if it be insufficient, he must either sacrifice part of his capital, or follow some productive employment. But he who is occupied in useful works is often obliged to purchase or to rent other things; in this case, these expences constitute a part of the necessary price of these productions of labor. If this price should not be obtained for the articles when wrought and exposed to sale, he could not subsist, and it would be a proof that what he has destroyed was as useful, if not more so, than what he produced; on the other hand, whoever produces any thing which obtains a value beyond that of the labor and expence employed upon it, in order to give this value, evidently augments the quantity of things which have value, and consequently does good; for the amount or value of all the useful things we possess, or rather the sum of their utility, is the same as the sum of our means of providing for our wants, multiplying our enjoyments, and diminishing our sufferings; to which may be added, that the existence of men collectively having no other limitation than the possibility of maintaining them, their number will always encrease in proportion to this possibility: whence we may conclude, that the happiness and power of a society encreases at the same time and by the same means, and that the multiplication of useful productions by labor, is the means to render it as productive as possible, and to diminish, in like manner, superfluous consumption: the number of people who do nothing else but consume, are the drones of the hive.

I shall confine myself to this small number of principal ideas, which, in my opinion, are of the greatest importance, and which admit of many applications, and lead to many important results. It would, without doubt, have been better to have explained them with some method, and in an elementary manner, instead of presenting them as I have done, incidentally, and only in the manner of a refutation of errors; but I had it not in my power to choose; moreover, such as they are, I hope they will appear more clear than those of the economists; for which they are substituted, and which it will be perceived, render what we have said, more intelligible, besides adding to the light which we have endeavored to throw on the subjects of luxury, labor, price, wealth, population, production, consumption, and the effects of taxation. Why has not Montesquieu undertaken this examination? Is not the spirit of laws, what laws should be? To be acquainted therewith, should not the motives which ought to determine the legislator to be comprehensible, and pointed out distinctly? He has done much: a single man cannot accomplish all that he may wish to do.

BOOK XIV.

Of Laws in Relation to Climate.

BOOK XV *The manner in which the laws of civil slavery relate to the climate.*

BOOK XVI *How the laws of domestic slavery relate to the climate.*

BOOK XVII *How the laws of political servitude relate to the climate.*

Certain climates have different inconveniencies for man:
institutions and habits may remedy them to a certain point:
good laws are those which effect this end.

SPIRIT OF LAWS, BOOK XIV.

I HAVE united these four chapters, because they relate to the same subject, which will occupy very little time, for I cannot perceive much instruction to be derived from them, and the subject offers no important question for discussion; I shall, therefore, confine myself to a small number of reflections.

In the first place I shall observe, that to form a just idea of climate, we must understand by this word, the aggregate of all the circumstances which form the physical constitution of a country: now this is not what Montesquieu has done; he appears to consider nothing else than the degree of latitude and the degree of heat: but it is not in these facts alone, that the difference of climate consists.

In the next place I must remark, that if there be no doubt that the climate has a great influence over every living creature, even over our vegetables, and consequently on man, it is nevertheless true, that it has less effect on man than any other animal; the proof is, that man not only inhabits every climate, but can accommodate himself to them all, in all positions, and under all circumstances; the reason whereof is to be found in the extent of his intellectual faculties, which, by exciting in him other wants, render him less dependent on those purely physical, and in the multitude of arts by which he contrives to provide for these different necessities; to which must be added, that the more variously and actively his faculties are employed, the more are these arts multiplied and improved. In other words, the more man becomes civilized, the less is the influence of climate upon him. I believe, therefore, that Montesquieu has not perceived all the causes of the influence of climate, and that he has exaggerated its effects: I may even venture to say, that he has endeavored to prove it by many doubtful anecdotes, and false or frivolous narratives, some of which are even very ridiculous.

After these preliminaries, he considers the influence of climate, as a cause of the use of slaves, which he denominates *civil slavery;* and the slavery of women, he calls *domestic slavery;* and to the oppression of the citizens, he gives the title of *political servitude;* these are in effect, three particulars very important in considering the state of society.

But after having first very energetically represented the use of slaves, as an abominable, iniquitous, and atrocious thing, which corrupts the oppressor more than the oppressed, and for whom it is impossible to form any reasonable laws, he himself acknowledges that no climate requires, nor absolutely could require, such excess of deprivation; and that in fact slavery has existed in the frozen marshes of Germany, and may be dispensed with in the Torrid Zone:* it must not then be attributed to climate, but to the ferocity and stupidity of men.

Secondly, in respect to political servitude, we see people subjected to it in the extreme, in those nations of Italy, and Greece, and Africa, where the people were of old very free, or at least, very fond of freedom, though they knew not well of what it consisted, nor how to secure it; it is, therefore, more the state of society than the climate, which determines these things.

In respect to women, it is too true that the misfortune of being marriageable when almost in a state of childhood, and to be in a state of decline on the verge of youth, must prevent them in general, from having many good qualities of head and heart; and that consequently, they easily become the playthings and victims of man, and rarely their companions or friends. This is,

---

* A reference to areas of the earth on either side of the equator.

without doubt, a very great obstacle to true morality, and true civilization; for if man becomes corrupted when he oppresses his fellow creature, he yet more extremely perverts his nature, when he reduces the object of his most lively desires to a state of servitude. The passion for sensuality being destructive of maturity, by prematurely preventing beings from becoming perfect, and while it lasts, putting reason itself astray, are great evils, and it cannot be denied that they exist in certain countries; though we should be cautious in believing all that Montesquieu says on this last point. But every thing reduced to its proper weight, what is the result? That there are circumstances of inconvenience attached to certain climates: keeping always in view, that the effects which we often see produced thereby, are far from being inevitable; that institutions and habits may very much correct them, and that reason always is, and should in every situation be, our guide. From all this, then, there is no other conclusion to be drawn, but to repeat, with Montesquieu, *that bad legislators alone, favor the vices of climates, and the good seek every means to avert them.* Let us then, pursue another subject.

BOOK XVIII.

Of Laws in Relation to the Nature of the Soil.

The progress of wealth and civilization, multiplying the chances of inequality among men; inequality is the cause of servitude, and the source of all the evils and vices of human society.

SPIRIT OF LAWS, BOOK XVIII.

So unconnected are the nature of the soil, the long hair of Clodion, and the debauchery of Childeric, with each other,* that it is difficult to discover the chain of thought which could have conducted our author from one of these topics to the other: and it is yet more difficult to say precisely what is the subject of this book.

We, in the first instance, meet with a confirmation of the propriety of the reproach which I have ventured to utter against Montesquieu in the eleventh book, for not having clearly defined the sense of the word liberty. In this book, chap. 2, he expresses himself thus: *the liberty they enjoy, that is to say, the government they are under.* It must be acknowledged that it would be a very singular kind of liberty, if the government should be oppressive, as governments generally are.

Then he says, chap. 4, the sterility of the soil renders men courageous and fit for war, while fertility induces a certain love of life: and in chap. 1, to prove that this same sterility disposes the mind for independence, he says, the sterility of the soil of Attica established a popular government there, and the fertility of Lacedemon† an aristocratical government; for at that time in Greece the government of a single person would not be permitted. It follows

---

* Chapter 23 of Book XVIII of the *Spirit of the Laws* is entitled "On the long hair of the Frankish Kings," while the short Chapter 25 is devoted to Childeric.

† Sparta.

from these principles, and the reasonings by which they are upheld, that the Spartans were neither possessed of courage nor love of liberty: this is somewhat difficult to believe.

If then it be true, as Montesquieu says, that the government of a single person is oftener to be found in fertile countries, and the government of many in those which are not so, which is sometimes a compensation; these are his words; we must look for a better reason than the soil: I believe it is not difficult to be found.

Fertility of soil does not deprive man of either strength or courage, nor of the love of liberty; but it furnishes him with more means of providing for his wants. Men multiply, and being more numerous, are more easily enlightened, and more wealthy; thus far we see only advantages; but see the inconveniencies: having more means of acquiring knowledge and wealth, it is evident that some succeed less and others more, and that the greatest inequality of fortune and talents is established among them: now inequality, under whatever form it presents itself, is the great evil of mankind: inequality leads to the spirit of servility, to many other vices, and to a pernicious employment of accumulated riches, as we have seen in chap. 7, speaking of luxury.

This I believe is the true explanation of the general slavery, not of *rich* people, but of *people among whom there are great riches*. This distinction is very essential, for it may be remarked, that the people in general are more rich in nations called poor, than in those called rich; and when we are told of a nation enervated by luxury and riches, we must always understand that nine hundred and ninety-nine parts of the people of such a nation are languishing in penury and debased by misery: so that when mention is made of effeminacy and corruption, inequality is to be understood thereby; and thus the key will be had to all the consequences that follow.

These considerations do not explain why poor, ignorant, and agricultural nations are free; for they are really not so. We have seen in the eleventh book, that in order to establish true political liberty, and to secure it, information and means which these people are not possessed of are essential; and that perhaps it was even impossible firmly to establish liberty any where, before the invention of printing, which renders communication among the members of society easy: but it explains why such people are fond of liberty, why they seek it, and are possessed of the spirit of independence. The reason is, that these agricultural people having few means, and these the means of mediocrity equally distributed among them, they are not habituated to inequality. They are rather independent than free, so long as a greater foreign power does not subject them, which usually happens when there is any inducement to do so; or so long as superstition under the name of religion, which is a great cause of inequality in the hands of rogues and hypocrites, does not enslave them, which too often happens.

Such, in general, is the case of the inhabitants of mountainous countries, who are not more brave than others, notwithstanding preposterous accounts of them; nor do their mountains so well defend them, whatever writers little conversant in military affairs may say; but poverty is their characteristic generally.

In this is contained an explanation of the effects attributed with reason by Montesquieu to the use of money, which no doubt favors inequality, and facilitates the partial accumulation of riches; but there is no nation in any degree improved, in which money is not to be found in use, so that all those who have not money may be ranked among the very poor and most uncivilized nations.

As it respects the inhabitants of islands, we have sufficiently explained in the eighth book, the principal cause which favors their liberty and prevents their losing their attachment to it. It is of a different kind, and takes place in all the degrees of civilization, which is, the advantage of not being obliged to maintain a large military force in constant readiness.

The simplicity of laws, another advantage of a people whose industry is yet in an unimproved state, we have already noticed in the sixth book, and shall not therefore say any thing further upon it here; I shall in like manner, pay no attention to the rights of nations, such as the Tartars, to the Salic law,* the kings of the Franks, &c. There is little useful knowledge to be derived from the examination of such subjects.

Such are nearly all the topics of which Montesquieu has treated in this book; indeed it was not precisely of the fertility of the soil which he intended to speak, for that is not the sole source of wealth; industry and commerce at least contribute thereto as much; it is the effects of riches and civilization which our author treats of, without perhaps clearly conceiving it. By thus generalizing the question, it becomes better determined. From the observations they give rise to, the following principles may be considered as established relative to the spirit of laws. The more improved society becomes, the more the means

---

* The French text here also refers to "lois ripuaires." These were the laws of the Ripuarian Franks from the Rhineland.

of enjoyment and power encreases among men, but the chances of inequality are also more multiplied among them: and in all degrees of civilization the laws should tend to diminish inequality as much as possible; for it is fatal to liberty, and is the source of all our evils and vices: every evidence of experience and reasoning proves this great principle, and every thing has that tendency.

BOOK XIX.

Of Laws in Relation to the Principles Which Form the General Dispositions, Morals, and Manners of a Nation.

For the best laws the mind should be prepared: wherefore, the legislative power should be exercised by delegates freely chosen for a limited period, from all parts of the territory.

SPIRIT OF LAWS, BOOK XIX.

THERE is a great deal of wit in this book of Montesquieu; the French character is rendered very amusing; the English character is very well drawn; that is, to shew what it should be, and sometimes to produce a reason for what does not exist: but is not all this more dazzling than substantial, and mixed with assertions that are unfounded?

All errors should not be corrected: is this proposition questionable? Then mark why should they not. Why, for fear of committing errors still worse! But is it to be presumed, that *vanity is a good resource for the support of a government,* and that by rendering the mind frivolous, commerce will be augmented? Surely, the most commercial nations are not the greatest triflers. Should it be established as a general maxim, that vices against morals are not vices in politics? I may venture to say it should not, if politics be the science of human happiness: if it be an art to deprave, only with a view to oppress, then I have no objection to the assumption: but such political principles as these shall not occupy my attention.

Can it be very singular then, as the author says, that a people like the Chinese, enslaved even by their manners, and continually occupied by the rules of ceremony, should be such great cheats? To explain so simple a fact, could it be possible for any one to affirm, that in China deception is tolerated. I may venture to say that deception is to be found every where; but that the laws never authorise any; no, not even in Lacedemon, notwithstanding their alleged allowance of robbery.

I may also affirm, that it is not the detestable manner of writing in China, that has established emulation among them, any more than industry or esteem for learning; it has, without doubt, contributed to make them respect rites and ceremonies, by rendering them incapable of learning any thing else; or in other words, it has assisted in subjecting, by debasing them. But if it be in this way the Chinese government triumphs, as our author says, it did not become him to extol this triumph; a philosopher should bestow his applause with more discrimination.

There is also a little want of reflexion in praising Rhadamanthus without some qualification,* for deciding all disputes with celerity, by only taking the oath on each head. I believe we know very little, notwithstanding the authority of Plato, about the acts of Rhadamanthus; but we very well know, and we have seen in the sixth book, that laws are more likely to be simple in proportion as society is less improved, and interests less complicated. We are also assured, that the more incapable a people are of writing, the more requisite it becomes, to make use of testimonial proof, and affirmation on oath: ignorance then, should not always be taken for innocence, nor rusticity for virtue.

Another singular assertion is, that a free nation may have a deliverer; an enslaved one, can have only another oppressor. It must follow, that a nation once oppressed, can never cease to be so; and it is yet more difficult to comprehend what is meant by a deliverer of a nation which is already free!

These absurdities do not prevent our author from discovering what is very true, when he says, that it is bad policy to attempt to change by laws, what should be changed by manners; and it is for this reason, that in the sixth book, where he holds a contrary opinion, I have disapproved of sumptuary laws. See also the seventh book.

Respecting the celebrated saying of Solon, to which the apologists of such institutions confessedly have always had recourse, I have said in the eleventh book to what value it ought to be reduced, and what ought to be thought of it; I have even explained how such institutions as are fundamentally bad, may possess some relative good; and why on the contrary, good laws have in

---

* Rhadamanthus was a king of Crete, and later an important figure in Greek mythology. His laws are briefly described in Book I of Plato's *Laws*. Montesquieu refers to him in Chapter 22 of Book XIX.

certain cases been inadmissible; so that in this opinion I entirely agree with our author, that for the best laws it is necessary that the mind should be first prepared by cultivation. This principle appears to me excellent, and the only good one that is to be met with in this book; but I draw this conclusion from it, that it is necessary that the legislative power should be exercised by delegates freely elected for a limited term, and from all parts of the territory of a nation; for this is the best way of being assured that the laws are well accommodated to the general disposition of the nation.

BOOK XX.

Of Laws in Relation to Commerce, Considered in Its Nature and Different Forms.

BOOK XXI *Of laws in relation to commerce, considered with reference to the revolutions it has undergone.*

Merchants are the agents of certain exchanges; money is the instrument employed to effect it; but this is not commerce, which really consists in simple exchanges. Commerce is society itself; it is an attribute of man; it is the source of all human good; its principal use is in stimulating industry; it is thus it has civilized the world: it weakens the spirit of devastation. The pretended balance of commerce is illusive and trifling.

In the same way that I have combined my view of the four books on climate, I here unite these two on commerce; but I must confess, that I scarcely know how to begin the discussion of subjects, which are not treated of in the books before me, but suddenly broken off: neither can I discover their connection in themselves, nor can I discover in one the elements of the other, which would have been the case had they been well explained and connected. This calls to my mind the expressions of a man of fine understanding, who said, my father, my eldest brother, and myself, have three different ways of working; my father breaks the threads and easily ties them again; my brother breaks them also, but he does not tie them again; I endeavor not to break them, for I should never be certain of being able to tie them well.

I take Montesquieu to be like the father, who though he breaks them, never loses the thread of his ideas, although the connection is not always seen; but I, in order not to be like the elder brother, must endeavor to act like the second:

I shall therefore advance sufficiently into the subject, to discover some point from whence to start, and to which I may refer every thing that arises as I proceed.

A very erroneous idea is generally formed of commerce, because it is too much circumscribed by the limits assigned to it. It is nearly subjected to the same misconceptions as what are called figures of rhetoric; we notice them only when we hear an oration or a studied discourse, so that on those occasions they appear to be great and peculiar inventions, and we never perceive that they are so natural to us, that we constantly employ them in the most ordinary discourse, without being even conscious that we do so. In like manner, we perceive commerce only in transactions with merchants, who make a sort of occult science and a particular trade of it; and even then we only see the operations of the money produced by or employed in it, but which really is not its true object; we do not appear conscious of continually and incessantly conducting a traffic ourselves; nor that the whole concerns of commerce are susceptible of being carried on without not only money, but without merchants; for merchants by profession are no more than the agents of a particular commerce, and money the instrument with which the agency is conducted. But these transactions do not properly constitute commerce, which essentially consists in *exchange;* all exchanges are acts of commerce, and the whole of human life is occupied by a series of exchanges and reciprocal services. We should all be very unhappy if it were otherwise, for we should in such a case be each reduced to our individual powers, without being able to derive benefit from the aid of others. By considering commerce in this point of view, which is the true one, we shall perceive therein what we never before observed; we shall discover that it is not only the foundation and basis of society, but that it is in effect the fabric itself; for society is nothing more than a continual exchange of mutual succours, which occasion the concurrence of the powers of all for the more effectual gratification of the wants of each.

It is therefore ridiculous to doubt of commerce being a good, and yet more ridiculous to believe that it can ever be an absolute evil, or only be useful to one of the parties concerned in it. To man, it must be at all times useful, to be enabled to procure that which he is in want of, by the means of some other thing; this faculty can never be an evil in itself; and when two men reciprocally and freely part with a thing which they esteem less, to receive another thing which they esteem more, since they desire it, and prefer it, it is possible that both may find their advantage in the exchange; and in this commerce consists. It is true, that one of them may make what we call a bad bargain, and the other a good bargain; that is to say, that the one does not receive for what he parts with, as much as he wishes to procure, and that the other receives more than he expected. It may also happen, that one or both of them, are wrong in desiring the things they have procured; but such cases are rare, and do not constitute the essence of commerce; they are accidents caused by certain circumstances, which we shall examine in the sequel, and of which we shall notice the effects. It is no less true, that in every transaction of commerce, that is, every free exchange, both the contracting parties have been satisfied; without which they would not have contracted, and consequently, this exchange, in itself, is beneficial to both.

If I do not mistake, Smith was the first who remarked, that *man alone exchanges,* in the manner *properly so termed.*[25] This is true, for we perceive certain animals performing labor which tends to a common use, and which appears to be to a certain extent, a work of concert; we perceive them contend, nay fight with each other, for the possession of what they desire, and fawn to obtain it; but they never exchange. The reason is, I believe, that they have no idea of property, sufficiently exact to believe that they can have any right to that which they do not actually possess, nor a language sufficiently formed to be enabled to make engagements; and these two inconveniencies, originate from their incapacity to sufficiently abstract their ideas, to generalize or express them, separately or in detail, under the form of a proposition; whence it results, that the ideas of which they are susceptible, are all particular, confounded with their attributes, and manifest themselves simultaneously, and as it were, by interrogatories, which can explain nothing explicitly. Man, on the contrary, endowed with all those means of which they are destitute, is naturally disposed to make use thereof, to make conventions with his fellow men. But whatever may be the cause, it is certain that he exchanges, and other animals do not, and therefore they cannot constitute society, for commerce is society itself, as labor is wealth.

It is Smith, likewise, who has perceived this second truth, that our faculties were our only original property. The employment of our faculties, is our only primitive wealth. It leads him to a third truth, which is also very important;

---

25. See the admirable chapter 2, of the first book of the treatise of wealth. I regret, in remarking this fact, that he has not more exactly examined the cause. The author of the theory of moral sentiments, should not have considered as useless, a scrutiny of the operations of intelligence: his success and his faults, should alike contribute to make him think the contrary.

namely, that this wealth is augmented incalculably, *by means of the division of labor.* That is to say, as each one of us applies more particularly to a single kind of industry, it is performed with more speed, becomes more perfect and productive, in a word it encreases the means of our enjoyment to a very great extent.

Thus, when we are on a good, well made, even road, we travel with more celerity and ease at the same time. But Smith has gone yet farther, he has observed that the distribution of labor, so very desirable and important, only becomes possible by exchanges, and in proportion to their number and facility; for as long as each individual cannot profit by the labors of others, he must himself provide for all his wants, and consequently exercise all trades. When exchanges afterwards commence, a single trade will not suffice for the maintenance of a man; he is still obliged to exercise several; this is the case with many descriptions of workmen, remote from cities; but when at length commerce becomes more perfect and more active, not only a single trade, but frequently the least part of a trade, is sufficient to occupy a man altogether, because he can always dispose of the products of his work, though very considerable and of a single kind. Sufficient attention has never been paid to this last observation of Smith; it is nevertheless admirable; and he has therein discovered the principal utility of commerce, which should never be lost sight of, and which should always and in all cases be considered as its most essential property and greatest advantage. Let us for a moment occupy ourselves therewith, and since commerce is the subject which at present engages our attention, let us remark, that at the moment exchange commences society also begins, and with it the probability that each one will exclusively devote himself to the kind of occupation in which he thinks he may be most likely to succeed, and that this will be as much the effect of natural disposition, as of the circumstances in which he is placed.

In the beginning commerce is carried on directly, that is the exchange is made between two persons without the mediation of a third; every man who desires to buy any thing is obliged to look for a person who has it to sell; and in a word, whoever has any thing to exchange, must himself take the trouble of finding a person with whom he can make it. But it is very soon discovered that by the *division of labor* which commerce so powerfully promotes, a class of men is formed, whose only business is to save this trouble to those who have exchanges to make, and thus facilitating such dealings. These men are known under the general name of traders. They soon divide themselves into merchants, factors, agents, dealers, retailers, commission brokers, and other auxiliaries of commerce, who all co-operate to a common end, by fulfilling different functions. Let us consider them all in one view, which will be sufficient for our purpose.

Traders are always ready to buy, when any one is desirous of selling; and to sell, when any one is desirous of buying: they send into one place the goods of another, and reciprocally, so that by their care each one has within reach all that he desires, and what he could not often procure but with great trouble and time. Their labor is then useful; since it is useful, it should procure them an adequate recompense, which it easily does: we should rather sell cheaper at home, than be obliged to sell at a distance: we prefer buying near us, to going very far for what we want. Merchants then, buy cheap and sell dear, which is their mode of assuring a recompense: their profits may be less, according as communications are secure or easy, their expences and risks less; when there are few merchants, they demand a greater profit; when there are many, they content themselves with less, in order to obtain a preference from purchasers: in this, they act like all other persons, engaged in industrious pursuits; whatever their profit may be, it is certainly taken from those who buy: but to pay this profit, is to the buyers of less importance than the trouble which it spares him, or the time which he saves; so that in general, even buyers gain by this kind of sacrifice: the proof of this fact is, that they always prefer making use of the services of the sellers; their existence is, therefore, useful to society.

In explaining the usefulness of traders, I am led to explain the usefulness of money: for it serves commerce as an instrument, precisely as the traders serve it as agents. Commerce may be carried on, without this instrument, and without these agents; but they very much facilitate its operations. Money, or the metal of which it is made, is an article of merchandize, as well as any other, proper for different purposes; having, like all the rest, its natural or intrinsic value, which is the value of the labor necessary to extract it from the earth, and form it; and its pecuniary value, which is that of the things offered to procure it, as we have explained in our observations on the thirteenth book: but this merchandize, has the peculiar quality that it is invariable in its physical and artificial properties, so that it may be preserved without fear of loss or damage: that it is all of the same quality when pure; so that it may always be compared with itself without any uncertainty as to its value; that it is susceptible of very multiplied, just, and uniform divisions; so that it is easily accommodated to the divisions of all other articles, from the most precious to the most trivial; from the smallest to the greatest quantity. These are the advantages to be obtained by adopting it as a common term of comparison of all values; it has consequently been adopted: when once adopted, it cannot frequently fluctuate or change its value, as other merchandize do, by being too much sought for at one time, and not at all at another. It can only change its value by small degrees, and with time, according as it is a little more or less scarce. This is also another very great advantage gained thereby, so that a person possessed of a thing which he does not want to retain, is no longer obliged to wait until he meets with the thing he desires to barter it for; if he can get money for it, he will take it, because he is sure, with this money, to procure all that he desires, particularly when there are merchants who have every thing to sell. Besides, money does not constitute the whole of our riches, nor such dealings the whole of our exchanges; the one is no more than a tool, and the others are workmen, who facilitate the business of commerce, but are not themselves to be mistaken for commerce. Only such a number of these tools and workmen is required as may be necessary for conducting commercial transactions. When there is more money in a country, than is requisite for circulation, it should be expended or converted into useful utensils: when there are too many merchants for the business that can be done, they should either expatriate themselves, or turn to some productive occupation.

The properties of commerce being well understood, as well as the functions of merchants, it is easy to perceive, that if traders are not indispensable, because commerce can take place to a certain extent without them, yet they are very useful since they very much facilitate it; but it does not at first appear so easy to decide whether their work is really *productive,* or if they merit being placed among the productive class; for some writers, who have acknowledged no other real *production,* than the labor which procured the first materials, and who in consequence have refused the character of *producers* to those who employ the rude materials, that is mechanics, have also refused the title to those who transport them, that is merchants: this, however, is an error, altogether arising from a misconception of the meaning of the word *productive.*

Mr. Say, as we have already stated, has dissipated all disputes about these words by a single and very just observation, that we can never create even a single atom of matter, that we only produce changes; and that what we call producing, is only giving a greater degree of utility as respects us to what already exists: it may be also said, and with as much truth, of our mental productions, that they are only transformations of impressions which we receive by our senses, that they compose all the knowledge that exists, of which we form all our ideas, and upon which we regulate our actions, deduce all the truths which we perceive, and form all the combinations we imagine.

In effect not to leave the physical path, men who obtain from the earth and waters by the labors of hunting, fishing, mining, quarrying, and cultivating all the raw materials which we make use of only by their labor, are indebted to commerce for rendering the animals, minerals, vegetables, useful to us. The metal is of more value than the mining, a rich harvest is of more value than the seed and manure producing it; an animal taken or killed is more likely to be of use to us than one which flies away, and a tame animal more than a wild one; these first workmen, therefore, have been useful, they have been productive of utility, and this is the only manner of being productive.

After them come other workmen, the mechanics, who form various articles out of these materials; if the metal be worth more than the mining, an axe or a spade is worth more than the metal of which they are made; if flax be worth more than the seed from which it has been produced, the linen into which it is converted is more valuable than the flax, and the cloth more than the fleece, flour more than the wheat, and bread more than the flour. These new workmen then are producers, as well as the others, and in the same manner. This is so true that they frequently cannot be distinguished from each other. I should like to know whether the person who from salt-water produces salt, is a farmer or an artisan; or why the man who kills deer should rather belong to the agricultural class, than he who dresses the skin and makes gloves of it; as well as to know what is produced by the ploughman, the sower of the seed, the reaper, or one of those laborers who has made ditches necessary to render the field productive.

But it is not sufficient that the materials have received their last form; for me to be enabled to make use of them, they must be near me. It is of little consequence to me that there is sugar in the West Indies, porcelain in China, coffee in Arabia; it requires to be brought to me; and this is the business of the merchants. They are also producers of utility, and this utility is so great, that without it the others would vanish. This is so evident, that in places where a thing is very abundant it has no value, but it soon acquires a great value when transported to those places where there is no commodity of that kind. We must then either acknowledge that we do not understand what we have here said, or confess that the merchants are producers as well as others, and acknowledge, *that all labor is productive which produces property greater in value than the amount of the expences employed in procuring it.* This is the only rational manner of understanding the word production. See book XIII.

It is true, that by the operations of the industry, inaccurately called *agricultural,* the materials oftener change their *nature;* manufacturing industry generally changing only the *form;* yet this is not true of chemical arts, they almost all change the nature of the materials more or less; commercial industry only changes their *place.* But what is it if this last be as useful as the first? If it be a last *form* given to it by art, and necessary to give value to all the others, and if this last form be so fruitful that it produces an encrease of value far superior to its first cost.

It may be said that this encrease of value, does not always take place, and that the merchandize is frequently lost or spoiled, or arrives in a wrong season; and that then the labors of commerce produce nothing: but it is the same with agriculture and manufactures, when not well conducted or injured by accident. It may also be said, that commerce often furnishes us with useless objects of consumption, which it would have been happy for us not to have known; that we take a liking to them; that we ruin ourselves to procure them; and that it impoverishes instead of enriching us: but it is the same also, of agriculture and the arts: if I convert a large field into a garden of roses, if I employ a great many men in cultivating and gathering them, and a great many men also in distilling them; and that from this there results only the temporary gratification of some females, who perfume themselves therewith, and expend considerable sums by means of which works of great utility and permanence might have been performed, there is certainly a great loss of wealth; but the loss is not in the production, but in the consumption: if this essence of roses had been exported, many things of the first necessity might have been had in return. In all cases, there is a complete similitude between the labor of the trader, and that of the farmer or the manufacturer: the one is not more or less *essentially productive* than the other; all through want of success are subject to loss; all by success, produce encrease of enjoyment if we consume, and encrease of wealth if we do not. It is of little consequence what name is given to the traders, provided that such a name does not lead to false conclusions, and that the nature of commerce be well understood, of which traders are only the agents. I believe we have explained the subject with sufficient precision to be enabled to establish some certain principles, and determine on the different questions which may arise from such general and constant views. Let us return to our author, and examine some of his opinions.

Montesquieu, who has spared himself the trouble we have taken, can perceive in commerce only the relations of nations among themselves, and their manner of influencing one another. He does not say a word of the commerce that is carried on in the interior of a country; and he appears to suppose, that it would be useless and of no effect, nor meriting any consideration, if it did not furnish the means of making profit on strangers. In this particular, he thinks like many other writers, and like many persons of consideration, too much admired in the world: however, even in this narrow view, internal commerce demands all our attention; and is in all cases, and at all times, by much the most important, particularly for a great nation; in effect, so long as there is no exchange among the persons of the same district, they are all strangers to each other, and are always miserable; whereas, by mutual traffic, they very much augment their power and their enjoyments. So likewise, in a large country, if each of its sub-divisions becomes insulated and without intercourse with the others adjoining, they are all in a state of privation and forced inaction; whereas, by forming connexions among them, each one profits by the industry of all; each finds employment, and discovers his own resources. Let us take some very large, well known country, for example, France: suppose the French nation alone existing in the world, or surrounded by impassable deserts. Some parts of its territory are very productive in grain; other parts more humid, are better adapted to pasturage; others, formed of dry declivities are proper only for the cultivation of the vine; others again, more mountainous, are productive of timber only. If each of these parts should be reduced to depend on itself alone, what would be the result? It is evident that the part productive of grain, may support a great many people; for at least it possesses wherewith to satisfy the first want, nourishment; but this is not the only want, clothes and lodging are also required. These people would then be obliged to sacrifice a great deal of this good land, to producing timber, to pasture, to raise bad grapes; and of which land, a smaller quantity would have been sufficient to procure, by means of exchange, that which they wanted, and the remaining part would have nourished a great many other men. Consequently, these people would not, under such circumstances, be so numerous, as if they had commerce; and after all, they would still be in want of many other things. This is still more applicable to those who inhabit the districts adapted to the cultivation of the vine: these, if possessed of industry, would only make wine for their own use, having no place whereat to sell it; they would exhaust themselves in unproductive labor, in order to raise some inferior grain along detached parts of their dry hills, not knowing where to buy any, and they would be in want of every thing else: the population, though composed of cultivators, would be miserable and few in number. In marshy meadow districts, too wet for wheat or barley, too cold for rice, their condition would be still worse: tillage must necessarily be renounced, and pasturage alone attended to; nor must they raise more animals than they themselves can consume. The only means of subsisting in woodland is hunting, in proportion and inasmuch as wild animals are to be met with, without even thinking of preserving the skins, for of what use would they be? This would be the state of such a country as France if all communication between its different parts were cut off: one part would become savage, and the other badly provided for.

Suppose this communication, instead of being thus restrained, to be active and easy, but still without any intercourse with foreign nations, then the productions proper for each district would no longer be circumscribed for want of vent; the necessity of attending to unproductive local concerns, would cease with the opportunities of exchange; and the necessity of providing, whether well or ill, for all our own wants, would no longer operate as a loss of half the value of time. The district of rich land will produce more grain than is wanted, and will be enabled to send some to the part planted with vineyards, which will produce a sufficiency of wine to sell; both will supply the country adapted to pasture, where the cattle will multiply in proportion to the demand, and the men in proportion to the subsistence which this demand procures for them; and these three districts united, will transport subsistence to the inhabitants of the most rugged mountains, who will furnish them with wood and metals. Flax and hemp will multiply in the north, and yield linen to furnish the south, which will encrease the manufactures of silk and oil to pay them in return: the local advantages will be turned to profit, a district covered with flints will furnish flint stones to all the rest who do not possess them and are in want of them, and its inhabitants will subsist by this exchange: another rocky district will furnish grindstones for several countries; a small sandy district will produce madder for all the dye-houses: some fields of earth of a certain argillaceous quality will supply clay for all the potteries: the inhabitants of the sea coast need not set bounds to their fisheries, since they can salt their fish and find purchasers in all the contiguous countries; it will be the same with sea salt, and the alkali of marine plants: gums and resins from the trees that produce them, will be in demand; new and active industry will every where be perceived, not only for the exchange of goods, but also by the communication of information; for if no country produces all, no country can invent all; when what is known in one place is communicated, it soon becomes general; it is more easy to learn, or even to improve or perfect, than to invent; besides it is commerce that inspires the desire of invention; *it is even its great extent which renders industrious occupations necessary and possible.*

However, these new arts engage a number of men, who do no more than live by their labor, because the labor of their neighbor is become more productive, and enables him to pay for them. Apply this to the country of France, which we have been just exhibiting in subdivided circumstances; and behold it now covered with a numerous population, well provided for, and consequently become happy and rich, without having derived any profit from strangers. All this is due to the best employment of those advantages which are peculiar to each district, and of the faculties of each individual. It should be observed also, that whether the country be rich or poor in gold or silver, or if it possess none, yet these effects will be produced without them; or if there should be money and the precious metals are scarce, then a very small quantity will be sufficient to pay for a great deal of merchandize; but if there be much of the metals, then a greater quantity will be required for articles of the same quality, and this is all the difference; in both cases circulation will go on in the same manner; such are the principles of internal commerce.

It is acknowledged, that I have taken for my example a country very extensive, and much favored by nature; but the same causes produce the same effects in all countries, in proportion to their extent and natural advantages; excepting however such as are absolutely incapable of producing articles of the first necessity in sufficient quantity: for these unquestionably foreign commerce is indispensable, in order to render it habitable, since by foreign commerce alone it can be furnished with subsistence: they are in the same predicament as the mountaineers, or inhabitants of the marshy parts of France, whom we have just spoken of, indebted for their population to the intercourse with districts that are fertile; but to all other countries foreign commerce is only accessory.

I do not, however, undertake to deny the utility of foreign commerce; what we have said shews us even that it is of the greatest advantage: indeed since it appears that interior commerce produces so much good by animating industry; and that industry is excited only by the possibility which commerce holds forth for the disposal of the products of labor, or as we have before observed, because it enlarges the *extent of the market* for the productions of every part of the country, so it is certain that external commerce very much enlarges the market and augments industry and production. Even France, though perhaps more capable than any other country on the European continent,* taken altogether, of dispensing with foreign commerce, would be deprived of many enjoyments if it did not obtain goods from the four sections of the globe; and

* The French text does not include "on the European continent."

many of its manufactures at present, even the most necessary, indispensably require raw materials which are imported from the extremities of the earth. It may be even said that certain provinces, though constituting a part of the same body politic, have often less facility of communication among themselves than with certain foreign countries; so that it is more easy to send the Bordeaux wines to England, the cloths of Languedoc to Turkey, those of Sedan to Germany, than to many parts of France, and reciprocally: many things may be had with more facility from foreign countries than from our own; it would then be very foolish to deprive ourselves of foreign commerce since it also promotes and rewards industry: what we have just said of internal commerce, points out to us how estimable its property of exciting industry is. What must we then think of those who do not take this advantage into consideration, and *who pay no attention to internal commerce, the most profitable and useful of all;* and who only perceive in external commerce a means of fleecing foreign nations of a few dollars? We may say without hesitation, that they have not the least idea of the manner in which the riches of nations are formed and distributed: it must be acknowledged that this is the condition of Montesquieu notwithstanding all his information.

After a few vague sentences on the moral effects of commerce, which we shall notice farther on, he immediately divides commerce into two kinds; the commerce of luxury and of economy; and faithful to his system of deducing every thing from three or four forms of government which he has judged proper to distinguish, he says that one of these kinds of commerce is more suitable for monarchies, the other for republics; and he perceives a great deal of reason for its being so. The truth is, that there never was, and never will be, a commerce of luxury. Whoever speaks of luxury, expresses the idea of consumption, and even consumption to excess. Commerce, commercial industry, constitute parts of the means of production. These two things have nothing in common, if by commerce of luxury is understood, that some expend what others gain. To gain is one thing, to eat is another quite different.[26]

If the commerce of luxury implies the commerce of objects of luxury, nothing can prevent the Dutch from importing porcelain from China, shawls from Cashmire, diamonds from Golconda, though French or German court-

---

26. We have already said, book VII, that there is no luxury on the part of a Jeweller who expends a great deal in precious stones; it is on those who ornament themselves with these trinkets, that the luxury falls.

iers may be foolish enough to buy them. In all cases, Mr. Say is very right when he asserts, *all this signifies absolutely nothing.* The same may be said of the reasoning by which Montesquieu undertakes to prove that *a commerce always disadvantageous, may be useful,* or that *the power granted to merchants to do what they please, would be the destruction of commerce;* or that the *acquisition of nobility for money, very much encourages merchants;* or that the *mines of Germany and Hungary encrease the cultivation of land, while those of Mexico and Peru destroy it;* and other paradoxes of the same nature. From all this, we must again conclude, with Mr. Say, that when an author, speaking of these things, forms to himself so indistinct an idea of their true nature, if by chance he should stumble on an useful truth, or if he should happen to give good advice, it is very lucky. Let us then, endeavor to complete the explanation of the effects of external commerce: thus far it has never been sufficiently done; and if we succeed, it will not be by chance, but by deductions the most rigorous: this knowledge conducts us to many useful truths, too little known.

We have seen, that as commerce between man and man alone constitutes society, and is the first cause of all industry and convenience, so that of one district with another, province with province, in the interior of the same country, gives new life to their industry, and produces an encrease of comfort, population, and means: and that external commerce augments all the advantages that internal commerce gives rise to, and contributes to set a value on all the gifts of nature, by rendering the labor of man more fruitful and productive.[27] This is the greatest advantage of external commerce, and though truly incalculable, it may, however, be represented by numbers giving an approximate idea thereof. Let us imagine twenty men working separately, without assisting each other: they will perform the labor of *twenty,* and if we suppose them all equal in capacity, their enjoyment will be as *one;* if they unite and assist one another, they will perform the work of *forty,* and perhaps of *eighty,* and consequently their enjoyments will be as *four;* if they profit by this advantage, of the leisure it procures them, of the intelligence it enables them to acquire, for discovering new resources, and inventing new means for

---

27. Let it not be forgotten, that *productive labor,* is that of which the value is greater than the things consumed by those occupied in the labor. The labor of soldiers, governors, lawyers, physicians, may be called useful, but not productive, because they produce nothing, since there remains nothing. That of a farmer or manufacturer, who expends ten thousand dollars, and produces only five thousand, is likewise not productive, and would not be useful, unless by way of experiment.

procuring new raw materials, they may produce as *one hundred and sixty,* or as *three hundred and twenty;* and enjoy as *eight* or *sixteen;* and their industry will indefinitely become more perfect, for it is impossible to set any limits to it: they may, if very intelligent, or very much favored by nature, go so far as to produce in the proportion of *a thousand,* or even *two thousand,* and consequently each to enjoy as *fifty* or an *hundred,* if the fruits of their labor be equally distributed; or to support one hundred or two hundred, where there were only twenty, and yet to enjoy as *ten* instead of *one;* and all this without having gained any thing from foreigners.

These estimates are not exaggerated, they are even short of the truth: there is more than this difference between the self dependence of the savage state, and society formed and improved by the invention of exchange; particularly if this society be well organized to prevent inequality, or at least that inequality should take place as little as possible; and that a surplus of means above immediate wants, do not become useless or injurious. (See the subject of luxury, book VII.) The greatest advantage of external commerce, we cannot too often repeat, is certainly to contribute to this happy phenomenon, which has scarcely ever occupied our attention, and which we have been always ready to sacrifice to temporary and sordid gain, or the appearance of the least profit to be made by foreigners. I say the appearance, not thereby intending to intimate that this profit is always deceitful; into this we shall look; I only maintain, that it is improperly the sole object of most politicians, and which is nothing in comparison with the advantages which commerce affords in creating society, and exciting industry; advantages which particularly belong to internal commerce, and to which external commerce contributes, and that in my opinion constitutes its greatest merit. Besides, a very extravagant importance has been attached to the direct profits which a nation may make on foreign nations, by means of its commerce with them; it is proper to examine this profit more clearly and in detail, in order to discover in what it consists, and how far it may be ascertained.

External commerce may be profitable, or rather the merchants engaged therein may directly augment the mass of national riches by the profits they make on foreigners with whom they traffic, and this effect they may produce in several different ways.

In the first place, they may be only the transporters and agents of foreigners; under this supposition they are rather artisans than merchants: in this quality they receive a compensation; they live on this compensation even if their country produces nothing; it is so much riches they import; if they consume it for their subsistence, it simply maintains in the country a certain portion of population which would not have existed there without it: if they do not use the whole of it, and if they practise some economy, so much as this economy yields is added to the permanent mass of national wealth.

Secondly, they may buy in a foreign country, goods that are there cheap, and sell them in another, where they are dear: the difference is sufficient to pay the subsistence of those they employ, and their own; in a word, all their expences, and leaving them a profit; this profit either in money or goods, and even all the parts of their expences gained from another nation, is a collection of means which they have added to those of their country, since it is all paid by foreigners. If this mass of means be not altogether consumed annually, what remains is so much added to the stock of national riches: this second case is the *carrying trade*.

Thirdly, merchants take such of their goods as are low priced in all the great markets of Europe, and all civilized nations, and send them to a great distance, bringing back into their country other goods which have a great value among all those nations. The difference in this case, more than covers the expence; from this expence, if paid to foreigners, a benefit results: this is done, when glass beads and other toys, are exchanged with savages for gold dust, ivory, furs, and other valuable things: certainly the mass of the wealth of society, which the merchants belong to, has been augmented. It is not necessary to be sure of this, that the goods imported be consumed in society, or re-exported, wasted, or a profit made thereon; this is another question, it is that of consumption, and opposite to that of production. These riches may again be lost, but they have been acquired, and this is all that is necessary in this place to be considered.

Fourthly, merchants may import from foreign parts, raw materials, cause them to be manufactured in their own country, and return them with profit to the same country in which the materials were produced, or to others; this is what the French merchants do, when they import hides from Spain, which they return tanned, and wool, which they return in cloth. The profits which they obtain, and the expences of all their agents, is an advantage to their country; for the sole object of the commerce being to furnish foreigners, all the industry that is put in motion by them, is exclusively paid by them: the artists* they employ, are actually in the pay of those foreigners; and so are the waggoners

---

* This is almost certainly a printing error: it should be "artisans."

and seamen who are employed in transporting the goods. This kind of commerce is what most enriches a nation, but it must be remarked, that this effect is produced less by the merchant, than by the industry he stimulates and sets in motion; for the public prosperity is at all times, under whatever forms, and in all respects, that which is most useful to a society of men.

Finally, the fifth kind of external commerce, is that which consists in exporting all the produce and merchandize for which there is no consumption nor demand in the country, and which without this commerce there would have been no advantage in producing, and which certainly would not have been produced; and to import all such things as are absolutely wanted, and which cannot be procured at home but at a much dearer rate; this is the commerce that takes place most generally among nations; the others of which we have been speaking are only particular cases; and the external commerce of almost all nations is of this kind; it is this which powerfully succors internal commerce, by extending the market, and which aids it in attaining the important end of augmenting the means of industry, unfolding the faculties of the people, and exciting their activity; and it procures for them all the enjoyments which industry looks to for its compensation. This object is so great, and this interest so superior, that it absorbs all others; while among the advantages of this commerce, the profit of the merchants who act only as agents, cannot be taken into the account, it is relatively insignificant.

This profit must, however, be obtained, to invite merchants to undergo the trouble, and if it were not obtained, it would be a proof that their services were neither useful nor agreeable, and that their operations being without an object, would consequently cease. This profit then, is acquired, but in the first place, it is necessarily taken from those of the nation, and it is impossible to determine the part they contribute to the sacrifice which the agents of exchange require from those who exchange. It is indeed necessarily shared by the foreign merchants with whom those of the country correspond, and it is very probable, that in general, each respectively gain what the buyers and sellers of their several countries sacrifice. We must again observe, that this profit is trifling, compared with the other advantages of such transactions, and the immense mass of riches which they put in motion, or collect; and I may affirm, contrary to the common opinion, that such profit merits no attention, on the part of the political enquirer. This commerce therefore, should not be considered as more useful, or the most considerable among those which *directly* augment the accumulation of national wealth, precisely because it is that which augments it most *indirectly*.

These are, I believe, the principal kinds of foreign commerce: the classification is not very rigorous, nor should too much importance be attached to such a circumstance; it has the inconvenience of every classification, that rational beings can with difficulty adapt themselves to the general and abstract manner of considering them. There is not, perhaps, a single commercial operation really and effectively existing, that strictly can be ranged in one of these five classes exclusively, or which in some of its parts does not belong to others. However, this analysis of the most remarkable effects of foreign commerce, throws some light upon its nature and opens the way to the enquiry concerning *the balance of trade.*

It will be admitted that these terms *balance of trade,* have not always a very clear *meaning;* and perhaps if those who make use of them, would examine the subject with attention, they may discover that they have *no meaning.* However, without examining deeply into the cause of the fact, or the manner in which it takes place, or the possibility of its taking place; when we think a nation sends more value to a foreign country than it receives therefrom, it is generally said that the balance is against it; and in the contrary case, it is said to be in its favor: this is what is understood by that balance of commerce, which we are desirous of having on our side.

But in the first place, it is evident, that in order to render the idea of a balance not wholly chimerical, the word value, should not be confined to the mere representation of money, or even precious metals; for gold and silver are far from being our only riches, or even the principal part of our riches; and it is very plain, that when I give five hundred dollars in money, and receive six hundred in merchandize, that I gain an hundred dollars; which shews that a nation may gain a great deal from another, to which it sends more money than it receives from it. This reason alone, if there were not many others, would suffice to prove, that the course of exchange, from which so many rash calculations are drawn, is a very insignificant index of the state of the balance; for at most, it can only indicate that more money is sent in one direction than another; and yet it does this, in a very uncertain manner: now to decide on this appearance, is to judge the whole by a part, and a part not well known.

Secondly: it is no less evident, even admitting the double supposition, that a civilized nation can receive from another more or less value than it delivers in return, and that it can be known; to judge of the balance for or against the first nation, at least all the branches of its external commerce should be taken into consideration, and no decision passed upon the mere examination of a part; for it may be that this nation loses with one only to gain more considerably with another; a dear piece of goods is bought in one place only to sell at another for a higher price, in order to procure other articles that are cheap; it is therefore the aggregate of the trade, and that only by which we can judge, if an accurate judgment can possibly be formed.

But to judge of any thing we must know what it is, and we cannot know what this balance is nearly, or even distantly: let us then at first take the *quantity* of merchandize, which is the easiest circumstance to ascertain. How rigorous so ever the regulations of the custom houses in many countries may be, there is no government that can flatter itself with knowing exactly by those it employs, the quantity of all the merchandize that passes into or out of the country: the products of contraband are always considerable and impossible to be ascertained: the invoices of merchandize which pass in a more lawful manner, are never strictly true: those which pay no duty on import or export, and these generally amount to a great deal, if recorded at all, are recorded negligently; so that we are yet far from our object, even in respect to the quantity, which is nevertheless the object least difficult to be ascertained.

The *quality* of merchandize is yet more difficult to be discovered, although its influence on the question of the *value* is of greater moment than quantity or number. Our riches are so multiplied and diversified, there is so much variety in the productions of nature and art, that the difference is often as one to an hundred, or one to a thousand, between the value of things nearly of the same kind, which go into the composition of merchandize imported or exported, and pass under the same general denomination; add to which that it is always the most precious articles that are thus disguised or totally concealed; because generally their bulk is not so great as articles of less value: it is therefore impossible to obtain even an approximation of the real value of merchandize, either imported or exported by commerce, and it is absolutely improper to place any dependance on general estimates or extracts from official records, which are unavoidably imperfect and incomplete.

But this is not all: when the quantity, quality, and consequently the value, of the merchandize imported and exported in the course of a year, is exactly known, we shall yet have to learn how much has been expended by all the merchants in the country during the same year, in effecting these transactions; that is to say, what they have expended in clerks, agents, ships, their naval equipments, provisions, stores, pay of seamen, and waggoners; in short all the expences incurred from the first purchase, to the arrival at the place of destination, and the expences there: in a word the whole amount of their expenditures should be known.

These expences, it will be perceived, are all sums paid for labor, and with which those who obtain it, may pay for the production of useful things, and thereby augment the sum of national wealth. These sums should then be deducted from the value of imported wealth also. Now these last particulars are still more difficult to ascertain than the others; there are no means, no elements upon which a probable estimate can be made; for even those who are most interested seldom know it themselves, or when they do, are not able to tell whether the expences should be placed to the account of the exports or the imports; which properly rests to the credit of his own country, which to the foreign nation; they are absorbed in the general circulation: here then is another important discovery.

We might also except with reason, to the valuations affixed to merchandize at the custom houses: it is not here they were bought, nor is it here they will be sold or consumed; yet those are the only places at which their *real* value can be known or proved. Many articles have been or may be damaged before or even after the custom house price is fixed; others acquire value when they reach their place of destination, or only by the effect of time, which by improving their quality renders them more desirable: here are new sources of uncertainty.

If under such deficiencies of accurate knowledge, any one can persuade himself, that he knows something about this celebrated *balance of trade,* he must be some conceited calculator. But there is yet a great deal more, if we only knew it: if we only suppose, that it can be ascertained with accuracy, that in the course of one or several years, there has been in reality imported an amount of value superior to that which has been sent out of the country, to what would it tend? In the first place, this difference could not be considerable, for it can only definitely consist in the gain of the merchants of the country, employed in foreign commerce. Now, this is very small in almost every country, compared with the total mass; it can be an important object in small states only, where the greatest part of the population subsists by the carrying trade: secondly, nothing can be inferred as to the encrease or diminution of national riches, for if this nation, supposed to have imported more than it exports during a certain time, consume all that it has imported, it is really impoverished to the value of all it has exported, of which there remains nothing, although it has gained in exchange; and if, on the contrary, a great quantity has been stored up, or what amounts to the same thing, if it has constructed great useful and durable works, it may have encreased the sum of its means; that is to say, it may, as by a canal, or road, have augmented its funds and enriched itself, though at the same time, it may have suffered some external losses.

Let us then conclude with Smith, that there is no true balance, but that between production and consumption of all kinds; this is the true measure of subsistence and amelioration; it is this, that by a slow progress too often crossed, has gradually conducted the different tribes of men from their primitive misery to a more happy condition; this it is, thanks to the activity and intelligence of men and the energy of their faculties, which would every where and at all times favor the interests and happiness of society, if those who govern societies did not put them astray and continually misdirect them. The state of this balance is, therefore, not easy to determine by direct estimates; the accounts of a nation should be drawn up at two given periods, and we should be enabled to place therein not only its wealth and debts, but also the truths and errors by which it is influenced, the good or bad sentiments which prevail and characterize it, the beneficial or pernicious habits to which it is addicted, and the good or bad institutions it has formed within itself. We already perceive, that it is impossible to draw up such an account. Yet the effects of such a statement duly weighed, would give a balance which must be evident to the accurate and rational observer; and after all, this is the only real balance, whatever it may be; that of commerce is deceptive, or a mere trifle, fit enough for some subaltern deceiver or deceived, to figure in the eyes of some ignorant or prejudiced superior, or to impose upon the too general mass of uninformed men.

There is, however, a precious and certain result to be obtained, even from very imperfect statements of importation and exportation. First, we must allow ourselves to be convinced that the one is nearly equal to the other; and that the small difference which may accidentally exist between them, supposing we could ascertain it, is of little importance: but afterwards, when we perceive that both are very considerable, in relation to the number of men of which the nation is composed, it is evident that this nation is possessed of great resources and great riches, and consequently each of its members is possessed of a great deal of enjoyment, if the wealth be well distributed among them; for they have devised the means of procuring all that they have exported; and all that they have imported, is so much the means of enjoyment, which they may indulge without impoverishing themselves, provided they do not give their capital away in exchange. So that when we perceive the value of those exportations and importations gradually and constantly encreasing in a country, during a certain number of years, it may with certainty be concluded, either that the number of its inhabitants is augmented, or that each of them has become very wealthy, if too great an inequality has not been produced by artificial means among them; or that the two progressions of wealth and population have existed at the same time, which is generally their natural course. In the opposite case, contrary results must take place: we can perceive that in the accumulation of the circulating wealth which I have spoken of, we are not to comprehend those simple transportations which are only set in motion by means of commerce, as they no more than indicate the extent of such commerce, and not the amount of production. With this precaution our conclusions are sure, as well as the consequences that may be drawn from them. This is nearly all that the accounts of the custom houses can inform us; but this fact is important, and they point it out to us with sufficient accuracy, without rendering it necessary for us to examine them very minutely.

Such are the principal reflections which have been suggested to me by the two books of the Spirit of Laws, upon which we have been occupied. It would perhaps be proper here to make a few remarks on the moral effects of commerce; but it is too extensive a subject, should we enter into the details; and if we only consider the leading points, it is easy to perceive that commerce, that is exchange, being in truth society itself, it is the only bond among men; the source of all their moral sentiments; and the first and most powerful cause of the improvement of their mutual sensibility and reciprocal benevolence: we owe to it all that we are possessed of, good or amiable; it commences by uniting all the men of the same tribe; it afterwards unites those societies with each other, and finishes by connecting all parts of the universe: it excites, extends, and propagates information, as well as reciprocal intercourse: it is the author of all social good: undoubtedly war arises out of it, as do also lawsuits, and for which we must thank the false views of pretended adepts, who are its most pernicious enemies: but it is no less true, that the more the spirit of commerce encreases, the more that of devastation diminishes, and that the least quarrelsome are those who are possessed of the peaceable means of accomplishing lawful pursuits, and who are possessed of wealth liable to be lost. The pretended avidity with which commerce, properly so called, is said to inspire those who are engaged in it, is a vague reproach, which may be considered as belonging to the most insipid and insignificant declamation. Avidity consists in taking the goods of others by force or deceit, as in the two noble trades of conquerors and courtiers; but merchants, like all other industrious persons, seek only for reward in their talents, by means of free agreements entered into with good faith and guaranteed by the laws. Application, probity, moderation, are necessary, for them to succeed; and consequently they contract the best moral habits. If the continual occupation of gain, renders them at times a little too eager for their interests, it may be said, we wish they had something more liberal and tender in their disposition; but perfection cannot be expected of men, taken collectively: a people modelled in general on such as those we have just mentioned, would be the most virtuous of all others. The want of a well regulated social order, is the most fatal enemy of man; wherever there is order, there is happiness. I love and admire those who do good; for if every one were only to avoid doing evil, we should soon see a change in the human condition: the industrious man is degraded by fatal customs; yet he does more good to humanity, often even without knowing it, than the most humane idler, with all his zeal. I shall say no more on this part of the subject, the chapter is already too long.

May it be permitted me to add, that if internal commerce be always a benefit, external commerce in itself, and left to itself, never can be an evil. Undoubtedly, if, with an intention to furnish an article of consumption more abundantly to foreign merchants who demand them, a government should limit or prohibit the production of another article useful or necessary for the well being of the inhabitants, which has taken place in Russia and elsewhere, it would then be better to have no foreign intercourse. But we must not confound the errors of policy with commerce, this is not the error of commerce but of the government. In Poland, where a small number of men are the only proprietors, not merely of all the land, but of all the persons cultivating it, when the proprietors collect the grain these persons have exhausted themselves in producing, to sell it to foreigners and receive in return objects of luxury which they consume, the whole people are thereby necessarily rendered miserable. It would be better for the cultivator if the *magnates* could not sell their grain. They would perhaps endeavor to nourish men therewith, whom they would by little and little seek to have instructed in fabricating at least a part of the things they require; but even this cannot be attributed to commerce; indeed it may be urged in this case, that by the slow and inevitable effect of impoverishing the prodigal by offering them enjoyments, and of enlightening the miserable people, by causing men more civilized to go among them, it necessarily tends to bring about an order of things less detestable: the same remarks may be applied to the absurd and ruinous wars too often carried on to preserve the dominion and exclusive monopoly of distant colonies.

But even this is not to be attributed to commerce, but to the fondness of men for dominion, and the madness of avidity; or as the celebrated Mirabeau* has said of forced paper money, and may be said of many other things, *it is one of the orgies of deleterious authority.*

This is, I think, a part of what our author should have said with all that eloquence and profoundness of views, of which he was so much a master, instead of urging so many and such erroneous and insignificant things, which he has suffered to escape from him, among many other things which are admirable. But let us follow him to other objects.

---

* A reference to Honoré Gabriel Riqueti, comte de Mirabeau, who played a leading role in the early stages of the French Revolution. The quotation comes from a letter to Joseph Cerutti, dated January 1789.

BOOK XXII.

Of Laws in Relation to the Use of Money.

Silver has a natural value, for which reason it is the measure of other values; which paper could not be, as it is only the sign of value. When silver has an impression stampt upon it, attesting the quantity and quality, it is then money; but two metals cannot both be the fundamental money.

The possessor of money, may consume or keep it, give or lend it, in the same way as other riches.

The business of exchange and banks, consists in converting one kind of money into another, by discounting notes or bills of exchange not yet due.

The large companies which are formed for this purpose, are always dangerous, or their success of little importance.

Public debts encrease the interest of money.

SPIRIT OF LAWS, BOOK XXII.

MONEY is a very profound subject in the eyes of certain people, who imagine themselves to be men of talents, and who think that fine things may be said upon its use, its circulation, or the means of facilitating its currency, or even supplying its place. I cannot discover any thing mysterious or occult in it, and am persuaded that in this, as in all other things, whatever partakes of subtlety leads us farther from direct reason. I shall, then, confine myself to a small number of observations, in as much as I think I have in the preceding chapter on commerce, noticed what is most essential in the actual possession and the operations of money.

Society essentially consists in commerce, and commerce is exchange: all merchandize, as we have seen, has a natural value;* that of the labor required

* Here the French text speaks of "a natural and necessary" value.

in producing it, and a pecuniary value, that of other merchandize given in exchange for it: all these different values, are successively measured by each other; but they are liable to fluctuation and destruction; and consequently difficult to measure, to fix, and to preserve: among these goods having a value, there is one unmixed, unalterable, divisible, and easily transported; it naturally becomes the measure of all others: this is silver. To specify the quantity and quality with great exactness; that is, the weight and name, the public authority has stamped a mark thereon, and it becomes money. This is the whole system of money.

This short explanation of the nature of money, shews in the first instance, that there can be only one metal which is really money; that is to say, to the value of which all other values may be referred; for in all calculations there can only be an unit for a standard of measure or quality. This metal is silver, because it can be formed into the greatest number of subdivisions we require for the uses of exchange. Gold comes to its aid, for the payment of larger sums; but it is as an auxiliary, the value of the gold being found only by a comparison with that of silver. The proportion in Europe is nearly fifteen or sixteen to one; but it is subject to variation like all other proportions of value, according to the demand. In China, it is generally only as twelve or thirteen for one, which is the reason that there is a profit in carrying silver to that country, for twelve ounces of silver will there procure one of gold, which in Europe is worth fifteen of silver: you consequently have gained three ounces of silver by the exchange. The political authorities may, however, stamp money of gold, and fix its proportion with silver; that is to say, they may declare by law, that whenever there is no stipulation to the contrary, we shall indifferently receive one ounce of gold, or fifteen or sixteen of silver. It will then be the same, in legal acceptance, as when there are sums due to one party from another, in which no stipulation of interest has been made, the law allows an interest of so much per cent. But they cannot, at least should not, prevent individuals from regulating among themselves, how much gold they are willing to give or receive for a certain quantity of silver; nor do more than determine the rate of interest of a sum lent or borrowed. Nay, in despite of all laws, these exchanges subject to variation, are always performed in commerce, because without it business could not be carried on. When there is copper money, it is not a true money, but a spurious one; if it contained a sufficient quantity of copper to be equal in value to the silver with which its nominal proportions correspond, it would be five or six times more weighty than it usually is, which would render it very incommodious; yet this proportion varies daily, like gold; nay, more: consequently copper money is only worth the quantity of silver agreed to be given for it in exchange, and therefore, should be made use of for articles of small value only, in which this excess of value is of little consequence; but when authorised, as has sometimes happened, to pay large sums of money in copper, it is an actual robbery; because the one who receives it, can never fairly get the sums realized in silver for their nominal value, but only for their intrinsic value, which is five or six times less.

Secondly: we see that when silver was formed into money the first time, it was very useless to invent names of an arbitrary kind: such as pound, livre, dollar, &c.; it would have been much more clear and significant, to have said a part of an ounce, dram, or grain, than as in France, a piece of three livres, or of twenty four, twelve, or fifteen sols: we should then have known what weight of money was required for each article; but when once these arbitrary denominations are admitted, and use has been made of them in all contracts and sales, care should be taken to guard against loss by the difference of intrinsic value between the several denominations of coin. For still supposing myself in France, if I should have received thirty thousand livres, and have promised to return them at such a time, if, meanwhile, the government should order the quantity of silver called three livres, to be called six ounces, which is the same thing as if it should make crowns of livres, which do not contain more than these three, I who pay with these new crowns, pay really only half the silver I had received; this would be robbery; and yet this is what governments have done to baffle their creditors, so often and with so much boldness, and so little compunction, that what is at present in France called *a livre,* was really, formerly, a pound of silver, and is at present scarcely the hundredth part, or one hundred and eighth part of a pound. Thus, at different times, they have defrauded their creditors, ninety-nine in an hundred, or one hundred and seven out of one hundred and eight; so that if a perpetual annuity of one livre had been formed in those remote times, for twenty livres received, it would at the present time be paid with the one hundredth and eighth part of what was promised in the original contract. It is true, that when a government has diminished one half of the real value of its money, and are the next day desirous of buying merchandize; to pay for it they must give double the nominal value which was given before the reduction, which will in fact, be only the same real value as before; while the same nominal quantity of taxes being paid, yields only half the actual value of what was before paid. So that taxes are in fact one half reduced; but this affords new causes to encrease taxes, till they at length actually reduce the denomination to the half value. Operations of this kind, are called *financiering;* but such injustice is rarely attempted in modern times, though what is equivalent thereto is frequent, as when paper is forced upon us as money, as is now the custom of all European governments.

We have said that money is only the means of determining the value of other things, inasmuch as it has one intrinsic value: it is evident that it is a great mistake to call it the sign of money, when in fact it is only a substitute; this mistake leads to another; that is, the notion that paper may, by public authority, be rendered an equivalent with silver. Paper really has no other intrinsic value, than the price of its fabrication, nor other pecuniary value than what it would bring at a trunk maker's shop. If I am in possession of a note, or any other obligation of a responsible person, to pay to me at sight an hundred ounces of silver, this is only a sign that I shall probably receive an hundred ounces of silver when I shall choose to call for it: if the sign or certificate of public security be satisfactory to me, that is, if I give it full credit, and do not immediately want the silver, I am not in haste to take it up; I may even without this trouble, pass the sign freely to another, who may place the same credit in it as I do myself, and who on account of the convenience, may even prefer it to the silver, which is more cumbersome and not so easily transported; but none of us who have held the paper, have really possessed any value, though we may be as certain of being put in possession of value whenever we require it, as we are of obtaining a dinner for money. But if a government should say, here is a piece of paper, on which is written, *good for an hundred ounces of silver,* it is commanded that it be taken for its value, and all persons are forbidden from attempting to realize the value in silver: it is evident that I am then only in possession of a piece of paper, which is not to me a sign that I shall receive the value it declares, nay it offers a possibility that I never shall receive it; that I shall never find any person willing to take it for that value; that it is only the apprehension of the legal penalties on a refusal which forces me to take it, and that in all free transactions, which can escape the notice of a government capable of such oppression, this paper will either be considered of no value, or of much the smallest possible value that is implied by the possibility that at some future day it may obtain the value it declares. So that, though no one will dare to tell me, " your hundred ounces of silver is mere paper, and as a remote insurance only worth one ounce," yet ten thousand *written ounces* will be asked me for an article that I could purchase for one hundred ounces in *solid silver.* This is the inevitable fate of all forced paper money; for if it be good, it is not necessary to resort to force to give it currency; if it be bad, to force the circulation is still to depreciate and deprive it of credit.

Since money, then, has a value peculiar to itself, as all useful things have, and since it constitutes a property vested in the owner like all other possessions, it follows that the possessor being the proprietor may dispose of it like any other chattel; that he has the right of consuming or keeping it, of bestowing or lending it, letting or selling it in any such manner as he pleases, as we have said in the thirteenth book; to sell it is to make use of it in buying something else; to let or hire it is to give up the use of it for a time, in consideration of a recompense called *interest.* There is no more reason for obliging the possessor of money, to let it for a compensation less than he can freely obtain for it, than to force him to give for another article of merchandize, more than it has been proffered to him for, or than to force the owner of the merchandize to sell it for less money than has been offered him. Every time a government makes an attack of this kind upon property, the social obligations are broken and disordered; rigorous means will be required to enforce it, which renders the government odious, while it is evaded by subterfuge, concealment, and every artifice which favors roguery and wounds honesty. We must have been born without faculties for reason, or like certain religious sects who prohibit the use of reason, not to perceive this.[28]

As to *exchange,* which consists in converting the money of one country into that of another, all that is required, is to know that the quantity of money which a person demands will contain exactly the quantity of silver which he gives, and to pay the commission for performing the service: as for bankers and brokers, it is requisite for them to know the equation, in order to introduce some inequality for their profit, as they by this inequality augment their own income. There is besides this circumstance, that at certain times a great many inhabitants of a town, may have debts to pay to the inhabitants of another town: they come in crowds to the bankers, and bring their money to

28. It were to be wished, that those rectors of certain religious communities, who would command me to hire my money to his tenant for half the price he offers me, was obliged to rent the lands of his benefice to the same tenant as a farm, for the half of the price he is willing to give; for the comparison is perfectly equal: his farm is a capital, the same as money, with which he may buy my money; as with my money I may buy his farm; and it is of very little consequence to the farmer whether it is the field or the money he rents for one half.

obtain drafts or notes payable at the other town; this might be somewhat inconvenient for the bankers, if they did not possess sufficient funds at that place; as otherwise, they must either not transact the business, or send money to the place to meet the drafts: this transport of money is liable to some risk and expence; whence it follows, that those who make the deposits of money, are satisfied to receive for every hundred ounces of silver, bills for only ninety-eight ounces, or even ninety-seven ounces; so that they lose two or three per cent. by the transaction. On the contrary, the same kind of operation takes place at the other town, upon which the drafts are drawn: if ninety-eight or ninety-seven ounces of silver are deposited with them, they may give bills payable for one hundred ounces in the first town, and without losing any thing; but they always arrange matters so as to make individual dealings sustain more than the loss, and not to let them profit by their advantages. The same bankers or brokers also at times advance money on good notes or bills of exchange not yet due, deducting from the same the interest for the time that is to elapse before it becomes due; this is called discounting.

Several persons of this description, sometimes unite and form large companies, in order to be possessed of more ample funds to transact one or both branches of business. This may be useful, inasmuch as by doing more business they may be content with less profit on each transaction, thereby obliging their rivals to reduce theirs also, in order that they may be enabled to compete with them, and thus diminish the general rate of the expences of exchange and discount, and in the end, the interest of money itself, which is a great benefit. It is also the practice of such companies, having extensive credit, to issue bills or notes payable on demand for considerable sums; and as they are known to be very good, they are taken as ready money, while the bankers at the same time employ their money also to the best advantage. This encreases the quantity of the circulating medium in the country, which in many respects is a great advantage, though I believe not so considerable as is generally assumed; for whether there be little or much money in a country, circulation goes on in the same manner in both cases; the only difference is, that the same quantity of silver represents more or less merchandize in one case than the other: whatever it may be, this is the nature of the operation of the banks; but in order to produce the good effects we have noticed, they should neither be protected nor privileged more than any other merchants; that competition should be open and free; but that they should always be peremptorily obliged to pay their notes with silver at sight; for without these conditions, instead of diminishing the price of their services, they would augment them very speedily, by means of monopoly; and they would next fix a time more distant at which to pay their notes that were originally payable on demand, which would be a real bankruptcy; and what is still worse, establish in society a forced paper currency. But even if these banks are well conducted, which is very rare, and never has been seen for any great length of time in any country, they are still less entitled to the credit usually given them.

To produce, to manufacture, to transport from the place of production to the place of sale; that is to say, to cultivate and collect the raw materials with intelligence, to form them with skill, and exchange them with judgment, or in other words, to perform the greatest quantity of useful labor, and dispose of the product in the most advantageous manner, these are the great sources of the riches of nations. All the little profit that can be made by exchange, discount, interest, or any other imaginary sum, and other occupations partaking of the nature of privilege or exclusion, are very trifling to society: they may make the fortunes of a few individuals, which is the reason that they have been so much extolled; but they are of little account in comparison with the fruits of useful industry, acquired by men whose daily occupation is production, and very indifferent to the true prosperity of a country; to attach great importance to them, is a great deception. This, I believe, is all that is essential and true, that can be said on money.

Since Montesquieu has thought proper to speak of public debts in this book, it should be observed, that they have not only the inconvenience of requiring taxes to pay the interest, and with this interest, of supporting a number of people in idleness who otherwise would have been obliged to put their capital to some useful purpose, but also as they have not the advantage of diminishing the current rate of the interest of money, as our author has advanced in the sixth chapter; but on the contrary, has the effect of augmenting the interest of money; for a government whose policy is loans, cannot force any one to lend; it is therefore necessary it should offer an interest sufficient to satisfy the lender, and consequently an interest equal to what men of good credit will give, or the employment of money will produce: now all the loans made to government, would have been made to others; that is, the money would have circulated in active hands; consequently the demand for loans encrease; or which is the same, the means of satisfying demands are diminished, and in the end, higher premiums are offered for a preference, and thus the rate of interest is augmented; whence it happens frequently, that speculations in agriculture, manufactures, and commerce, which would prosper if money could be had at a low interest, are rendered impracticable, or are devoured by excessive interest: this is a grievous obstacle to the prosperity of a country, and to production in general.

The interest of money borrowed, occasions in all undertakings, the effects produced by land taxes on cultivation; as both encrease, there is always some land, or some industrious enterprize, which cannot be attended to in consequence thereof.

BOOK XXIII.

Of Laws in Relation to Population.

Population is stopt among savages, by want of the abundant
means of subsistence; among civilized people, by a pernicious
distribution of the means possessed. In every place where there is
sufficiency, liberty, equality, and correct information, population
encreases: still it is not the encrease of mankind that is so desirable
as their happiness.

SPIRIT OF LAWS, BOOK XXIII.

IF we are astonished on seeing a chapter of politics commencing with a translation, and even one that cannot be considered the best, of a part of Lucretius,*
we are still more surprised on a perusal of the matter of which the book is
composed; the book is cited without discussion, and even without approbation, on the means of augmenting or diminishing the number of citizens in a
state, on the rights of fathers over the lives of their children, and over their
marriage, of the interference of government in all these concerns, &c. It is
impossible to follow ideas so promiscuous as these, with minuteness; we shall,
therefore, commence with some ideas more general, and then endeavor to
investigate more closely, the nature of the human character; because it is in
relation to man that the social art should at all times regulate and model its
conceptions and institutions. Every animated being is inclined to re-produce
itself by the most irresistible of all inclinations. A man and woman, arrived at
the age of maturity, well formed, and possessed of all the means of providing
for their subsistence, may, during the time that they are constitutionally

---

* Book XXIII of *The Spirit of the Laws* begins with fourteen lines of poetry from
The Nature of Things by Lucretius.

tempered for propagation, have more than two, more than four, even more than six children; so that when we suppose, that according to the course of nature, the half, or even two thirds of these children, perish before they are enabled to propagate their species; suppositions certainly much exaggerated; the man and woman in question, will then, before their death, have a posterity more than sufficient to replace them, and the population must always encrease. But if we see population stationary, and this among savage people, and almost stationary among more numerous but ancient and civilized nations, we should enquire into the cause. Among savages, without doubt, the reason is, that great scarcity, unforeseen accidents, intemperance, and epidemics, often destroy a part of the adults, and alter the sources of production for the remainder; and that privations, want, and the impossibility of assuring necessary care in particular circumstances, the want of intelligence, and of affection, occasion the greatest part of the children who are born to die in infancy.

In respect to civilized nations, though the improvement of industry, the encrease of means, the multiplication of resources, have permitted population to encrease more rapidly; the progress is checked as soon as the advantages of civilization are unequally distributed. A small number of men in those ancient nations, who form a portion of the privileged classes, make away with the subsistence of a great multitude. However they are enervated by excess, by indolence, by intellectual labor, by the passions; whether the effect be produced by physical or moral causes, or their nature changes under their circumstances, they do not proportionably multiply. In the mean time, the men and women of the poor classes, from whom a considerable part of the fruits of their daily labor is taken, are weakened by excessive fatigue, they languish in penury, and become prematurely old; yet they have a great many children, but they are feeble, and they cannot know how to take care of them when in health, nor succor them in sickness; a prodigious number of them perishes; as these unfortunate people are the most numerous in all old nations, their distress considerably increases the bills of mortality; and I am persuaded that this is the phenomenon which has occasioned the discovery to be made in Europe, that about one half of the number of children die before the age of seven years; whatever it may be, certain it is that among savage people there exists as many men as their unimproved state can defend against all the chances of death, and that is but little. Civilized people, on the contrary, have more powerful means; they are more numerous on a like extent of territory; but not as numerous as they might be: among them men exist only in proportion as the government, the grandees or nobility, the rich, and in general all the idle, leave means of subsistence to the laborious and poor classes, who produce more than they consume. When government becomes more mild and less rapacious, as soon as it reforms some abuses, as soon as it prevents some oppressions; in short, as soon as the idle classes are under the necessity of paying the industrious a reasonable recompence for their labor, we immediately see population encrease almost suddenly. This is so true, that in the United States of America, where we have the advantages of civilization without its inconveniencies; where the people are intelligent and their faculties untrammelled by absurd institutions or establishments, their labor is very productive, and they enjoy the fruits of it; they are neither burthened with tithes nor glebe rents, for generally the ground that is cultivated is the property of the cultivator; neither have they burdensome taxes, nor the still greater burthen of idleness and ignorance, the usual attendants and consequences of social misery and oppressive institutions or usages; therefore the population doubles in every twenty years, and whatever may be said of emigration, the addition is too small to be taken into any account of the proportion of encrease: we may even on the contrary observe, that whatever the cause may be, we have very few old men, few remarkable examples of longevity, so that the mean duration of the life of man is shorter among us than in Europe, if in Europe the prodigious number of children who perish did not diminish the mean rate. It is very certain that when we shall have no more cultivated lands to settle, men will then incommode each other a little more, and this progression may diminish; but so long as every man exercises his faculties with equal freedom and intelligence, and reaps the fruit of his own usefulness, there can scarcely be a family that will not leave after it more children than are necessary to replace it. In general it may be said, that in our species, natural fecundity being very great, it encreases as individuals better their condition; and there will always exist men in a country, in proportion to their knowledge of the means and power of procuring subsistence. Yet though this maxim be strictly true, we should not understand by means of subsistence, provisions or food alone, but all the knowledge, all the resources, and all the succors by which we may preserve ourselves against the miseries and misfortunes which our nature is liable to. So much for what concerns the possibility of population. By this manner of considering the subject, we already clearly perceive the means by which it may be augmented, that these principally consist of sufficient subsistence, liberty, equality, and liberal information: and all the regulations of an Augustus,* or a Louis XIV.† on marriages, are miserable and ridiculous expedients.

We shall now consider this subject under another point of view. Is the encrease of men so much to be desired in a country, as that of rabbits in a warren? None of our politicians have imagined that there can be any doubt thereof, and no despot has hesitated to give an answer. One of the ablest men that reigned, Frederick the second, has sullied one of his letters to Voltaire, with the following sentence: *"I look upon* (men) *as a horde of stags in the park of a great lord, who have no other functions to fulfil than to stock the enclosure."*[29] It is true, Voltaire severely reproached him for so barbarous an idea, and answered him by quoting another maxim from Milton: *"amongst unequals there's no society,"*[30] a terrible truth for oppressors.‡ Yet such were the sentiments of a king still young, who had passed his early years in adversity, and had not been longer than a year on the throne; and this king was one of the best that ever existed: we may judge of the rest by comparison. Upon this principle, the necessity of multiplying the *game in the park* is perceived; for the greater the number is, the more may be killed, and the more that may be killed, the more will be to be eaten! As for us, who have in view only the happiness of these poor animals, and not the true or false gratifications of royal or noble masters, it appears evident to us, that the principal object should be to render them happy, and not to encrease their numbers to an excess. We have seen, in

* Emperor Augustus introduced laws to penalize sexual indulgence, promote child bearing, and restore the family. Montesquieu discusses these in Chapter 21 of Book XXIII.

† Louis XIV introduced pensions for those who had ten children. Montesquieu cites this in Chapter 27 of Book XXIII.

29. Letter 24 August, 1741.

30. It is, in a word, placing out of the pale of law, all those who pretend to be above the common rule. The miserable, says Voltaire, and often the best men, flatter the powerful. It is true, that to encourage powerful men, Voltaire has often praised to excess the good they have done; but he has never applauded their bad actions nor their wicked sentiments; nor even their bad maxims: but he has frequently censured them very severely: could any of his vile slanderers justly boast of having done as much?

‡ The correct quotation from Milton's *Paradise Lost* is, "Among unequals, what society can sort, what harmony, or true delight."

speaking of commerce, that when twenty men labor without art or implements, they procure enjoyment as twenty, and each enjoys as one; and that when by working with some intelligence, they render it more productive, they may attain to procuring an hundred times more enjoyment, and each to enjoy an hundred times more, if they continue to be of the same number; but they will enjoy only each as ten, if during that period, they have become ten times more numerous. This is a simple calculation: it is however true, that when ten times more numerous, they perform ten times more labor, and that so their encrease is not detrimental to their means; or at least, their means are not more decreased than the amount of the sum employed in the education of their children, who compose the encreased number; and this is not an evil, but a provision for future production and protection, unless when men have become so numerous as to incommode each other, and obstruct the exercise of each others faculties, in pursuits in which, with a less numerous population, they might employ themselves beneficially: nevertheless, it is certain, that the augmentation of the number of individuals, is a consequence of their happiness, which is the true end of society, and that their encrease is sometimes only a concomitant, and in unpropitious circumstances not to be desired. Moreover, if it should be made the principal object, the means we have indicated would yet be the only efficacious ones to produce this encrease, so much coveted and frustrated. All that is contrary to nature, which injures natural liberty, which chills or freezes up the feelings of the heart, which takes from every individual either the partial or the total use of his free dispositions and of his personal faculties, all those in a word, which require the violent exertion of power, in order to obtain an authority which no one would be willing to give to another over himself, cannot attain the object. For men are not passive machines, but sensible beings, and those feelings which are the cause of their sentiments, are the great springs of their lives, particularly those which are intimately constitutional. When I say that it is to be desired that the number of men should not encrease beyond a certain point, we must not conclude that a power can be given to any one to abridge the number of those in existence: no animated being once born, and capable of enjoyment and suffering, is, or ought to be, the property of any one; neither of his father nor of the state; he belongs to himself alone: by his existence, he has the right of self preservation: to deprive him of his life, is a crime authorised by many legislators, against whom the theologians of those countries have not protested. On the other hand, to take measures in advance, to prevent animated beings from being born, when they could only have been unhappy and rendered their species so, is an act of prudence which some theologians have considered a crime; and barbarous legislators have been sufficiently ignorant to support their decisions, by the fear of punishments. Thus it is, that the affairs of the world are too frequently conducted: but this leads us naturally, to the subject of Montesquieu's two following books.

BOOK XXIV.

Of Laws in Relation to a Religious Establishment, Its Practical Operation, and Doctrines.

BOOK XXV *Of laws in relation to a religious establishment, and its effects on external policy.*

The less power religious ideas possess in the political concerns of a country, the more virtuous, happy, free, and peaceable the people will be.

RELIGION is not a very difficult subject to treat of, in relation to the social art: the spirit of laws on this subject, should be neither to disturb nor constrain the religious opinions of any citizen, to give none a legal adoption, and to prevent any of them from obtaining the least influence in civil affairs. Without doubt, there are some religions more injurious than others, through the usages which they establish, and the pernicious maxims they propagate; by the celibacy of their priests, by means of seduction, by intolerance, by their dependance on a foreign authority, and particularly, by their aversion more or less extravagant to rational information of all kind; but none of those sects or their doctrinal tenets belong in any manner to the social organization; it is an immediate particular relation which they bear to the author of all things; it does not appertain to those things that man should or could have in common with his associates and fellow citizens. We can never pledge ourselves to think in the same manner as another person, nor the contrary, for the will is involuntary, we are not masters of our own opinions, nor can we even force ourselves always to hold the same opinion on any subject. All religions consist simply of speculative opinions called dogmas; under this view, they are the systems of a philosophy more or less rash, more or less contrary to the wise reserve of a sound logic. All sects join to their dogmas, some precepts of conduct called discipline: if some of these precepts be contrary to true social morals, these principles are bad; and this always is the case, because those religions have been formed in times of ignorance, and morals can only be preserved in an enlightened age, and are not yet completely perfect.[31] If, what is utterly impossible, the rules of conduct adopted by a sect, were altogether irreprehensible, they would yet possess the disadvantage of being founded on hazardous opinions, instead of being established on reason and solid motives: for every sect must, in relation to all other sects, be but a few. This then, is the place to say with yet more reason, what *Omar* said of the *Koran*: if all these books contain only the same thing as the Koran, they are useless; if they contain any thing contrary thereto, they are pernicious. Government, therefore, should never suffer any system of religion to be taught by authority, but the best moral doctrine, that the most enlightened persons of the time are acquainted with should be inculcated. Moreover, religious opinions have this in particular, that they give an unlimited power to those who promulge them, over those who believe them to be the depositaries and interpreters of the divine will. Their promises are immense for the next world, no temporal powers can balance them; whence it follows, that priests in all nations, are ever dangerous to the civil authority; or if supported by the government, they are always found prepared to extol its abuses, and to persuade man that it is his duty to sacrifice all his rights: so that as long as they hold a powerful influence, neither liberty, nor even peaceable oppression is possible. So that all governments desirous of establishing a tyranny, attach the priesthood to themselves, and render the priesthood sufficiently powerful to accomplish the service assigned to them: a government desirous of liberty and happiness, endeavors to promote the progress of information. This is what the spirit of laws may be reduced to on this point. It appears sufficiently useless to examine what the author of a religious sect should do to make it spread. I may venture to say that no more new sects will be formed, at least among polished and civilized nations.

31. Religion is too constantly employed for political purposes, or as a particular kind of merchandize. In all such cases it should have another denomination: otherwise, religion and morals will be considered as distinct things: this renders it necessary to repress the unceasing efforts to subject civil society to the tenets of some one sect, for we have not yet heard of a sect that was not desirous of ruling or restraining others. We have heard of too many who tormented and destroyed their fellow men, for only holding an opinion which they could not avoid holding.

BOOK XXVI.

Of Laws in Relation to the Nature of Things Upon Which They Decide.

UNDER a title sufficiently enigmatical, all this book is reduced to a single point; that we should not decide on a question by the same motives which induced the determination of another question of quite a different nature. This is too evident for any one to attempt to deny it. I shall not occupy myself therewith, inasmuch as all decisions on numerous objects, which are made upon the authority of precedents or examples, are in fact prejudgments; or judgments given upon evidence that has nothing to do with the subject: at least this is my manner of seeing things, conformable to the principles already established, in treating of the different articles to which these objects relate. If I were to discuss them again, it would be a useless repetition; and when principles are established, it is not necessary to examine one after another every particular case. Having therefore no new instruction to draw from this book, I shall pass to another.

BOOK XXVII.

Of the Origin and Revolutions of the Roman Laws on Succession.

BOOK XXVIII *Of the origin and revolutions of civil law among the Franks.*

These two books being purely historical, I shall not examine them.

It not being my object in this commentary to defend Montesquieu's erudition, and yet less to join those who reproach him of not having well understood the spirit of the laws of those remote periods, the obscurity of which he has endeavored to penetrate; it being my view only to establish some principles of the social science; now as these two books are entirely historical, and nothing can be drawn from them for the theory of the formation and distribution of power, nor for the formation and distribution of wealth, I shall say nothing more on these chapters.

BOOK XXIX.

Of the Manner in Which Laws Should Be Composed.

[There is nothing instructive here, excepting what arises out of the manner in which Condorcet has criticised this book, or rather new modeled it.]

THIS title, alike vague, requires some explanation to be well understood, as well as several others on which we have already made the same remark. The author, in this book proposes to prove that the laws should be clear and precise, worded with dignity and simplicity; not couched in the style and manner of dissertation; and particularly when motives are assigned for their enactment, that they should not support themselves by ridiculous reasons; laws too frequently contain clauses that are calculated to produce effects directly contrary to the intentions of the legislator; that they should be in harmony with each other; that several laws often mutually correct and support each other, and that to appreciate their effects correctly, they should be judged collectively, and not each one particularly and separately; that the legislator should not lose sight of the nature of the object they enact on one side, nor decide by motives contrary thereto on the other. In this much the book is comprised; the subject is already treated of in the twenty-seventh, and in other respects it approaches the sixth and eleventh books.

The author also shews that to form a proper estimate of a law, the circumstances in which it was enacted are to be taken into view; this has been already said and proved elsewhere. He also recommends that the laws should always be enacted in a general manner, and not given as prescriptions for particular facts. In a word he recommends it to legislators to divest themselves of their prejudices. No one will be inclined to differ from him on all these points. Indeed we might not be well satisfied with the divers examples nor with some of the reasons which he employs to prove things to be evident; some of them may deserve to be subjected to criticism; but as no information of any importance would result therefrom, I shall say nothing. It is not sufficient to be in the right when not opposed to great men, but when we undertake to contradict them it is always necessary not to be in the wrong.

I am in possession of a criticism on this book of the Spirit of Laws, written by the greatest philosopher in modern times, Condorcet;[32] it has never been published, and probably never was intended for publication. I shall venture to insert it here, and we shall see with what strength Montesquieu is refuted, and with what a superiority of views he retouches his work; it may be also perceived, that if my capacity be inferior, the severity of my investigation is at least equal.

32. See page 214, of this volume.

BOOK XXX.

Theory of the Feudal Laws among the Franks, Relative to the Establishment of Monarchy.

BOOK XXXI *Theory of feudal laws, relative to the revolutions of monarchy.*

These two books are also purely historical. Notwithstanding all its faults, the Spirit of Laws, when it appeared, merited the attacks of all the enemies of information and humanity, and the support of all their friends.

THE reasons which induced me to pass over the twenty-seventh and twenty-eighth books, will lead me to act in the same manner with this: I very much respect these enquiries; they have, without doubt, their utility, but they have but a very remote connexion with the subject which occupies me; consequently, I shall not examine them. I shall only observe, without entering far into the discussion, that every sensible man is sorry to see Montesquieu (chap. 25, book XXX) give as a strong reason against the Abbé Dubos,* that *it would be injurious* to the great families of France, and for the three races of their kings, to allege that at the commencement of the monarchy there was only one order of citizens; that there were none with exclusive privileges; because upon that supposition, there must have been a time *when they were common families!* We are no less disgusted at the emphasis with which he parts from this famous nobility, which he uniformly represents as *constantly covered with*

---

* Jean-Baptiste Dubos (1672–1742), author of *Critique de l'établissement de la monarchie française dans les Gaules* (1734). Montesquieu makes extensive reference to Dubos, largely to criticize him.

dust, blood, and sweat, and that at the close he has rendered himself ridiculous by being so much infatuated with this pompous trash. There is also some other foolery which even contradicts these; as for example, when he says that *at the time of Gontram* the French armies were no longer dreadful but to their own country;* and when he exclaims, *a singular thing, it* (monarchy) *was in its decline in the time of the grandson of Clovis.* It would have been much better, in my opinion, to have said it was a still born child, or at least very ill formed; but I shall leave all this for the reflections of the reader; consequently my task is finished.

It would perhaps be proper in this place, to hazard a general judgment on the work of which we have just discussed the different parts. I shall, however, avoid it. I shall content myself with remarking that when the Spirit of Laws appeared, it was scarce ever attacked, but by men of a very despicable party and of evil dispositions; and that, notwithstanding its numerous faults, known, acknowledged, and avowed, it was always and constantly defended by all the true friends of information and humanity, even by those who had just personal motives of complaint against the author. At their head, Voltaire may be placed; who, on this occasion, as on all others of a similar nature, manifested his noble and generous character, as superior to the triflings of vanity, as his mind was to that of prejudice.†

---

* Guntram (Gontram) was king of the Kingdom of Orleans from AD 561 to 592. By all accounts he was ineffective.

† The text here excludes the latter part of the sentence found in the French edition. It should continue, "by making the most complete and exaggerated eulogy of *The Spirit of the Laws*: 'The human race had lost its way: Montesquieu found it again and led them back to the right path.'"

Appendix
❧

Observations

ON THE TWENTY-NINTH BOOK OF THE SPIRIT OF LAWS.

by M. Condorcet*

BOOK XXIX.

Of the Manner of Forming Laws.

CHAP. I *Of the spirit of the legislator.*

CHAP. II *Continuation of the same subject.*

I DO not understand what is contained in this first chapter; but I know that the spirit of a legislator should be justice. A faithful regard to the laws of nature is all that is properly law. In the regulation of the forms of proceeding, or in particular decisions, he should seek the best method of rendering them conformable to the laws and to truth. It is not by the spirit of moderation, but by the spirit of justice, that criminal laws should be mild, that civil laws should tend to equality, and the laws of the municipal administration to liberty and prosperity.

The two examples quoted are ill chosen. The simplicity of forms is not repugnant to security, whether personal or of property, for the preservation of which only all forms are established. M. Montesquieu seems to believe it, but

---

* It is not clear why Destutt de Tracy chose to end his text by citing Condorcet at length, except that, as we have seen, Destutt de Tracy has little to say about Book XXIX. However, it was a reading of Condorcet's that led to the largely critical account of Montesquieu's text. Crucially, Condorcet rejected Montesquieu's thesis that government and laws varied according to circumstances, geography, and climate: see, for example, his comment below that "reason, justice, the rights of man, the interests of property, of liberty, of security, are in all places the same."

he no where proves it; and the injustice caused by complicated forms, renders the contrary opinion at least probable.

The second example is preposterous: what is it to the science of composing laws, that Cecilius or Aulus Gellius uttered an absurdity?

By the spirit of moderation, does not M. Montesquieu understand that spirit of uncertainty which alters by a hundred little irrelative motives, the principles of justice, which are in themselves invariable. See chap. 18.

CHAP. III *That laws which appear to deviate from the intentions of the legislator, are often conformable thereto.*

THE first duty of a legislator is to be just and reasonable. It is unjust to punish a man for not having sided with a party, for he may be either ignorant which party is most actuated by justice, or he may think them both culpable. It is contrary to reason to punish with infamy by positive law, since *opinion* only can adjudge this punishment; if the laws be in unison with the opinion, it is useless; and if it be contrary to opinion it becomes ridiculous.

Does not Montesquieu mistake the intention of Solon? It would appear to be rather intended to oblige the body of the nation, to take part in the quarrels which might arise between a tyrant, an oppressive senate, or iniquitous magistrates, and the defenders of liberty; in order to secure to these last the support of well disposed citizens, whom fear might have deterred from declaring their sentiments; it was in fact a means by which every particular insurrection would become a civil war; but the motive was consonant with the spirit of the Greek republics.

CHAP. IV *Of laws which clash with the views of the legislator.*

A BENEFICE being a public function, conferring a recompense for the discharge of the duties appertaining to it, should be given in the name of the state, and it should be known to whom the state gives it; an action at law for a benefice is therefore ridiculous.

If, on the contrary, a benefice be looked upon as a real estate, and the right of giving it another kind of real estate, then the law quoted is evidently unjust.

Why has not Montesquieu in the Spirit of Laws spoken of the justice or the injustice of the laws he quotes, and the motives which he attributes to the laws? Why has he not laid down some principles which would enable us to discriminate among the laws flowing from a legitimate power, those which are unjust, and those which are conformable to justice? Why in the Spirit of Laws is there no notice taken of the nature of the rights of possession, of their consequences, extent, and limits?

CHAP. V *Continuation of the same subject.*

I DO not know why Montesquieu has given the name of a law, to an oath which was equally inconsiderate and barbarous; a law which commanded a town to be destroyed because its inhabitants had destroyed another town, may be very unjust; but it would be no more contrary to the views of the legislator, than the law which determines the punishment of death against assassins, with the intention of preventing murder.

There are so many important laws nearer home, which are contrary to the intentions of the legislator in establishing them, that it is strange the author of the Spirit of Laws should choose these two examples.

This observation often presents itself, and the reason may be assigned. See chap. 16.

CHAP. VI *Laws which appear to be the same have not uniformly the same effect.*

THE law of Caesar was unjust and absurd: what, then, would the tyranny of this man have been, though so clement, if he had arrogated to himself the right of searching the houses of citizens, and of taking away their money; and if he did not intend to employ such means, of what use were his laws? Besides, it would only have augmented debts, and could have been useful to the debtor only, by diminishing the interest of money: now the freedom of commerce is the only means of producing this effect; all other laws are only calculated to raise interest above its natural rate. The law of Caesar was probably a robbery, which for law, is abominable. See Dio. Cassius, book 49.

CHAP. VII *Continuation of the same subject. The necessity of composing laws in a proper manner.*

THE ostracism was an injustice: we are not criminal for possessing credit, wealth, great talents: it was moreover the means of depriving the republic of its best citizens, who never returned, unless on account of a foreign war or a sedition.

But how is this necessity of composing laws properly, and what would be the consequence, shewn; and how are the principles determined upon which they should be composed, by the example of the two bad laws that had been established in two Greek cities?

It is requisite to give men such laws as are most conformable to justice, to nature, and to reason; and such laws should be composed, so that they may be properly executed and not liable to abuse. The author of the Spirit of Laws extols a law of the Athenians, which was an extremely absurd law.

We no where find an example illustrated, never any discussion, nor any precise principles; but always one or two quotations which generally prove no more than that nothing is more common than bad laws.

CHAP. VIII *Laws which appear the same have not always been established on the same motives.*

THE principle of the law of entails originates in the Roman laws, as well as in ours, from the assumption that the right of possession extends to the disposal of our goods after our death. This principle is generally established, because in almost every place those in actual possession have made the laws. If the Romans were desirous of perpetuating certain sacrifices, as we are of making certain titles hereditary, it is very probable that vanity was equally the motive: it was in all cases choosing a future representative.

CHAP. IX *The Greek and Roman laws punished suicide from different motives.*

IN what country of Greece was suicide punished, and what was the punishment? Montesquieu does not inform us. Nor does Plato in his dialogues, speak of any such laws established. He says, for example, that a slave who should kill a free man in defending himself, should be punished with death. As respects suicide, Plato advises the relations to bury those who die by their own hands, without any ceremony, without any inscription, and finally to consult the priests upon the form of the expiatory sacrifice.

Indeed, the expression *shall be punished*, is not to be found in Plato: and this is the manner in which Montesquieu quotes Plato, and shews that suicide was punished in Greece.

In Rome, if a person deprived himself of life, before being condemned, he avoided the confiscation of his goods and a denial of the right of sepulture. The emperors afterwards decreed, that the accused, who should deprive themselves of life to prevent condemnation, should be treated as if they had been condemned. The laws which authorised confiscation after condemnation, were unjust; those which deprived the condemned of burial, might be barbarous, but in all this there was no punishment of suicide.

In England an exception is granted from certain punishments, to those who can read. Suppose that a law had been made to deprive those of this privilege, who had learned to read during the trial: could it be said that in England these punishments were enacted against those who had learned to read?

CHAP. X *Laws which appear contradictory, sometimes originate in the same spirit.*

IN order that the example should correspond with the title, the intent and effect of the French laws should be to assure a due respect for the asylum of a citizen.

And for the title to correspond with the example, it should be stated, that the consequences of the same principles are more or less understood in different countries. But then, the title would not have been so profound.

Montesquieu might have observed, that from the same principle of respect for the life of a man, may be deduced laws either very mild, or cruelly severe: and he should have concluded thence, that a principle very different from that of justice, may lead to false consequences.

CHAP. XI *How shall we be able to compare and judge between two laws.*

FOR the principle asserted in this chapter to be true, a system of laws must be selected, in which there are some good and some bad; otherwise, it is more natural to judge of every law separately, to examine and discover whether it contains any thing repugnant to justice or to natural rights: if contrary thereto, it should be rejected; and in any case where it might have a local utility, it should be superceded by another law, calculated to produce the same utility, without violating justice.

In the example quoted, we should discover first, false testimony considered in itself as a crime, and false testimony considered only as an attempt against the life and honor of a citizen, and prove that it is only under this point of view that it is a crime: secondly, if I should be shewn that the law of France is not only not necessary, but that it is bad; not that it punishes as a capital crime and with death, the person who by false testimony has caused the death of an innocent person; but because it authorises the prosecution of any one, as a false witness, who, after an examination, should retract that to which he had sworn, or whose false evidence should be discovered, so that consequently it is only a greater obstacle in the way of justification to an innocent person: thirdly, because it is difficult in England, to cause the death of an innocent person by false testimony; it does not follow, that we should not consider it as a capital crime, whenever it is committed.

So that not only the principle explained in this chapter is very uncertain, but the facts cited as illustrations, do not apply.

We cannot help being a little surprised that the disparity of fortune, the unjust and tyrannical refusal to admit justificatory facts in evidence, and the equivocal and perhaps too rigorous laws against false witnesses, should be held forth by Montesquieu, as forming a system of legislation, of which we should examine the whole: if this be intended as ridicule, it is not sufficiently pointed.

CHAP. XII *Laws which appear the same, are sometimes really different.*

This chapter contains nothing but what is right, but the title seems to announce something extraordinary, which the chapter does not contain. The proposition that the receiver of stolen goods, should be punished in the same manner as the thief, is not a law, but a general maxim, true or false; if it be true, the laws of France and the Romans, are equally good or bad; either when they operate against the thief or the receiver; if it be false, both are necessarily bad as respects one of them.

CHAP. XIII *We should not separate the laws from the purposes for which they were established: of the Roman laws against theft.*

The distinction between open robbery and robbery that is not open, requires no illustration from a law of Lacedemon. The difference of punishment could have no other motive than the certainty of the one kind of robbery, and the difficulty of proving the other; and as the second was only punished by a fine, this distinction is not unreasonable, because a receiver, an imprudent purchaser, or a person of bad character, may be, without injustice, condemned to this double fine. These are cases in which our tribunals do not take the life of the culprit, but they condemn to the galleys for life an assassin or a poisoner, under the fiction that he is not absolutely convicted but only nearly so. This kind of jurisprudence would be natural enough among a people in a half savage state, who look upon the punishment of crimes rather as an act of vengeance regulated by law, than an act of civil justice.

The distinction between the punishment of those who have reached the age of puberty, and those who have not, does not require to be explained by the laws of Lacedemon, or the reasonings of Plato on the laws of the island of Crete: it is founded on this, that those under the age of puberty are supposed not to possess either the full use of reason, or a proper knowledge of the laws of society.

CHAP. XIV *Laws should not be separated from the circumstances in which they were established.*

I MUST acknowledge that it is impossible to see the least connexion between the title of this chapter and the first article.

It is very evident that Montesquieu had collected a number of notes on the laws of all people, and that to form his work, he ranged them under different titles. This is the method for which he has been so much celebrated, and which exists only in the heads of those who model his book according to their own fancy.

If a physician not belonging to a corporation, should not succeed in curing a patient who has freely granted him his confidence, it does not follow that we should punish him; nor does he merit any punishment, when having an exclusive privilege of attending me as a physician, he has prevented me by virtue of his privilege, from applying to another who might have cured me.

Is it in France that the surgeon and apothecary are not interdicted, or condemned to pay damages when ignorant of their profession? If the physicians are not punished, it is because it would be very difficult to prove them to be in the wrong: whereas, it may be very easy to do so with the surgeons and apothecaries?

What is meant by a physician of a lower condition than another? Is this *lower condition* a good reason for condemning the physician to death for the same fault that a physician of a *higher condition* is only condemned to transportation. All this is shocking to the spirit of good laws.

CHAP. XV *It is sometimes proper that the law shall correct itself.*

EVERY man, who kills another, is guilty of murder, if not of assassination, unless he has killed him in self-defence, to save his own life or that of another; and to be considered innocent this excuse should at least be probable.

The laws of the twelve tables were bad.

Besides, does Montesquieu imply any thing more than that a law may require some modifications, and the discrimination of certain circumstances? All this is true and common; but he might have said it in a more simple and useful manner.

CHAP. XVI *Matters to be observed in composing laws.*

THE author begins in this chapter to treat the subject announced by the title of the book. What he says is true in general, but is not sufficiently important nor well explained. See remark in chap. 19.

This sixteenth chapter contains many incongruous things. The testament attributed to Richelieu, employs a vague expression, but that phrase is not a law; and Montesquieu might have found in our laws, or in those of the neighboring people, more remarkable examples. The chancellor de l'Hopital thought it proper to declare Charles IX. of age at fourteen; but neither he nor any other person, ever thought of giving any serious reasons for so doing, or only such as could not be publicly avowed.

Neither the dimensions of the crown nor the Pythagorean numbers are in the laws quoted.

The edict of proscription of Philip II. is not a law.

Although our criminal jurisprudence is fraught with vague laws, which might lead ignorant and ferocious judges to shameful acts of barbarity, yet Montesquieu does not notice them, but seeks examples in laws that no longer exist but in libraries.

He finds fault with the style of the laws of the empire, but this is confounding the preamble with the law itself. When a people enact their own laws, there is no need of explaining the motives, and very often no other but its will can be given; but when a single man dictates laws to a nation, the respect due to human nature imposes upon him the duty of giving reasons for his laws, to shew that he prescribes nothing but what is conformable to justice, to reason, and to the general good. The ministers of the emperor were in the wrong if they wrote the preamble as rhetoricians, but they were right in looking upon them as necessary, and Montesquieu should have made this distinction.

CHAP. XVII *Bad manner of enacting laws.*

LAWS should be directed to general objects, and not to particular cases; the rescripts of the emperors could only be considered as interpretations given by the legislator; now such interpretations could neither have a retrospective effect, nor the force of law, inasmuch as they are not clothed in the authentic form which characterises law.

A law of Caracalla was a law, and might have been an absurd one: a rescript of Marcus Aurelius, or of Julian, though an oracle of wisdom, should not be considered as a law, before an edict had given it the sanction of one.

Justinian may have been in the wrong, by giving the power of laws to several of the rescripts, if they contained absurdities; but it was not because they were made by those lawyers, who wrote in the name of Caracalla, or Comodus. The emperors no more made their rescripts, than Louis XIV. made the regulations of 1670.

This Nacrinus, who was a gladiator and notary, and afterwards the compiler of the rescripts of Caracalla, who reigned a few months, and lost the empire and his life by his folly, is a singular authority to quote in the Spirit of Laws.

CHAP. XVIII *Of ideas of uniformity.*

WE have now arrived at one of the most curious chapters of the work; it is one of those which obtained for Montesquieu the indulgence of all the prejudiced people, of all those who detest light, of all the protectors and participators in abuse: we shall examine it in detail.

1st. Ideas of uniformity and regularity, please all minds, and particularly sound minds.

2d. Can the great mind of Charlemagne be quoted in the eighteenth century, on the discussion of a philosophical question? It is undoubtedly a stroke of ridicule against those who might entertain the idea that Montesquieu was desirous of combating.

3d. We do not understand what is meant by *the same weights in policy, the same measures in commerce.* Commerce employs both weights and measures; policy meddles with both, but should really do so for no other purpose than to see that they have their proper quantity and value, and to keep them so, and to regulate them by standards established for this end.

4th. Uniformity of weights and measures can only displease those disciples of chicane, who fear to see the number of suits diminished, and those traders who apprehend the decrease of profit, from whatever contributes to render commercial transactions easy and simple. That which has been proposed for this purpose, with the common approbation of all enlightened men, is to determine on a natural, uniform, and unchangeable standard; to employ it in forming measures of length, superfices, capacity, and weight, so that the successive divisions in smaller weights and measures may be expressed by simple and commodious numbers; for these divisions and proportions, afterwards to be established, in a public and legal manner, and those exact means which natural philosophy furnishes; the exact relation of all the measures used in the country with the new ones, and which would forever put an end to law suits; at least, on subjects depending on measures of every kind. Such new principles of admeasurement, should be exclusively adopted by the government, the assemblies of the state, the communities, &c. Individuals having the liberty of making use of such measures as they may choose. This change, then, would be effected without any restraint or compulsion, and without troubling commerce; no one has ever proposed another method.

5th. As truth, reason, justice, the rights of man, the interests of property, of liberty, of security, are in all places the same; we cannot discover why all the provinces of a state, or even all states, should not have the same civil and criminal laws, and the same laws relative to commerce. A good law should be good for all men. A true proposition is true every where. Those laws which appear as if it were necessary they should be different in different countries, or exacted on objects which should not be regulated by general laws, consist for the most part of commercial regulations, or are founded on prejudices and habits which should be extinguished, and one of the best means of doing so, is to cease from giving them the countenance of the laws.

6th. Uniformity in laws may be established without trouble, and without producing any evil effects by the change.

This may be admitted for the establishment of a good criminal jurisprudence, but what trouble could a good civil code produce? It would change the order of the distribution of successions, but no succession in expectation is a right of possession, any more than a right to property declared to be bequeathed in a will, can become the property of the legatee, until after the death of the testator. Conventions made before the new law might preserve all their force, unless contrary to natural rights: conventions are of three kinds; their execution is immediate, or a time is fixed, or they are perpetual. In the two first cases, the performance of contracts made before the new law, might be adjudged according to the old jurisprudence without trespassing on the uniformity of laws; in the last case it might be injurious thereto, but the perpetuity of any convention cannot originate from the supposed right of possession, it is altogether founded on the sanction of the law, and consequently the legislator should in the nature of things, possess the right of changing these conventions, by preserving the original and true right of each of the parties or their heirs.

If an uniform and simple jurisprudence were established, the first consequence would be that the advantage of the knowledge of forms would no longer be confined exclusively to lawyers; that all men, capable of reading, would be equally capable of comprehending, and conversant in the subject; and it is difficult to imagine that this equality should be considered as an evil.

7th. It is not hazarding any thing to assume that the establishment of an uniformity in social institutions, would give to all the inhabitants of a country precise ideas on objects of the first importance; a more exact acquaintance with their interests; and would diminish inequality among men in the common conduct of human affairs.

8th. A farmer general also exclaimed in 1775, *Why make changes, are we not very well as we are?* Repugnance to change can only be reasonable in these two cases. 1. When the laws of a country approach so near to reason and justice, and the abuses are so trifling, that no sensible advantage could be expected from a change. 2. When it is supposed that there is no certain principle by which we might direct ourselves in security to the establishment of new laws. Now, all the nations that exist, are far from the first point, and we cannot be any longer of the second opinion.

9th. The *greatness of genius* is one of those vague expressions which strike little minds and impose upon them, which please corrupt men, and are adopted by them. Some men, because they see nothing, are fond of believing that light does not exist: others, who fear light, labor under perpetual apprehension lest the people should open their eyes.

10th. *When citizens follow the laws, of what consequence is it whether they follow the same laws?* It is of consequence to follow good laws, and as it is difficult for two different laws to be equally good, just, and useful, it is of some consequence to them to follow that which is best; it is of consequence that they should follow the same laws, because it tends to establish equality among men. What relation has the ceremonial of the Tartars and Chinese with laws? This article appears to indicate that Montesquieu looked upon legislation as a game, in which it is indifferent whether this or that path be followed, so that the established rule whatever it may be, is adhered to. But this is not true, even of gaming, where the rules, though apparently arbitrary, are almost all founded on reasons which the gamesters indistinctly perceive, and which mathematicians, accustomed to the calculation of probabilities, can explain.

CHAP. XIX *Of legislators.*

MONTESQUIEU here confounds legislators, with political writers who have proposed systems of legislation.

Is it certain that Aristotle had so marked an intention of contradicting Plato? What we know of the Grecian republics gives us reason to believe that their legislation was very imperfect in some respects, and particularly that it was very complicated. The more simple the legislation of a state is, the better it will be governed.

What has Caesar Borgia to do with legislation? The discourse of Machiavel on Titus Livius, and his history of Florence, contain many political views which announce, when we take into consideration the age in which Machiavel lived, a comprehensive and profound mind; but he certainly never dreamt of Caesar Borgia in writing them. The book entitled, *The Prince,* the life of Castracani, &c. are works in which Machiavel explains how a rascal may conduct himself in order to rob, murder, and so forth, with impunity. Caesar Borgia was for some time thought to be an adept of this kind; but there is in this no question involving principles of legislation.

Why has not Montesquieu counted Locke among the number of legislators? Is it because he thought the laws of Carolina too simple?

Were it permitted us to offer a few ideas here, on the subjects of this book, we should, in the first place, distinguish the case wherein it was in agitation to give a new legislation to a people; that wherein laws are only passed on a branch more or less extensive of legislation; and where the law has only a particular object.

In the first case, it is a necessary preliminary to fix the object on which the legislator should act. These objects are: 1. The laws which relate to the defence of the rights of the citizen against violence and fraud: these are the criminal laws. 2. The laws of the police or civil administration; they are divided into two classes; some determine the sacrifices which each citizen may be obliged to make of his liberty for the maintenance of order and public tranquillity. It is a genuine right that man acquires by living in society, and consequently it is not unjust that individuals should make some sacrifices of a part of their liberty to secure it.

The second kind of laws of police, are those which regulate our enjoyments as to things that are public, such as roads, streets, &c.

Thirdly, the civil laws may be divided into five kinds; those which determine what should belong to possessions, as the laws of succession, &c.

Those which regulate the means of acquiring property, as the laws on sales and purchases; those which regulate the exercise of the right of possession in cases where the entrance upon possession was obstructed; those which secure possession, as in cases of mortgages closed, or debts due; those, in short, which affect the condition of individuals.

On all these objects, laws of two kinds are required, the first are such as determine the principles upon which each question should be investigated and decided: the other the forms of decision.

Fourthly, political laws, which regulate, 1. The exercise of the right of legislation. 2. The mode of employing the public force for defence against internal attack. 3. The means of executing the laws internally. 4. The manner of treating with foreigners on behalf of the nation. 5. The public expenditures. 6. Public resources to defray expenditures.

We shall not speak of the laws that relate to commerce, because it should be free, and requires no other laws than those which protect property.

Then, on every subject all the particular questions which present themselves, should be reduced to general and simple propositions, and to as small a number as is consistent with efficacy; then a particular enquiry should be made into each, in order to *determine*.

First: if they should be established by a law. Second: whether, according to the principles of justice, reason does not furnish an answer to the proposition.

If reason furnishes a principle, it should be followed; if not, the course most congenial with public utility, should be pursued.

It is not sufficient that the laws thus framed be clear, they should be couched in language the most simple and precise, and in words of a determinate and known signification; and whenever words of questionable construction are used, they should not be suffered to pass without a definite and scrupulous explanation.

As every legislator may be deceived, the motive for instituting the law should accompany it. This course is necessary in order to attach those who are subject to them, to the laws, and for the information of those who execute them; in short, to prevent pernicious changes, and to facilitate changes that are useful. But the explanation of the motive should be detached from the law, as in a mathematical book, the demonstration is separated from the proposition, and even the work containing them. A law is nothing more than this proposition: *it is just or reasonable,* according to the text of the law.

If desirous only of giving a particular branch of legislation, care should be taken to define, with great exactness, the limits beyond which it should not pass; after having regulated it according to reason and justice, to examine whether it contains any thing contrary to any established law, and carefully to discover all such errors, as the roots of those evils which it is the best interest of society to eradicate. However, it would be better to have a good law, in contradiction to a bad one, which could not be destroyed, than to suffer the bad one to remain alone.

When desirous of being convinced that a particular law is good, it should be examined, but not alone; it should be taken in connexion with all the laws that enter into a good system for the branch of legislation to which it belongs and with its actual situation; it may then be discovered either that the laws we are desirous of making, should enter into and make part of a system, or that they are only useful or necessary by being opposed to the injustice which may result from laws already established, and which cannot otherwise be changed.

In the first case, we should conform ourselves to positive justice: in the second, to relative justice; in the first, the law should be presented as a true law; in the second, as a modification of the bad law for which it is a remedy. The more particular the object of a law is, the more important it is for the legislator to explain his motives. It is much more easy to understand the general spirit of legislation, or a branch of it, than a particular law.

It would be well to regulate, in a general legislature, the means by which the laws are to be reformed, from which abuses result, without being obliged to wait for the excess of abuses, which usually makes the necessity evident, by the calamity that has been produced.

There are laws which should appear to the legislator as formed for perpetuity: there are others, which should be considered as only temporary. These two descriptions of laws should be classed and distinguished in the compilation of the laws.

For example, the law which declares that taxes should always be established in proportion to the clear product of the land, may be considered as a law founded on the nature of things;[33] but the law which fixes the manner of estimating the produce, may require to be changed, because it is possible to render the method more perfect.

It is yet more important to distinguish the laws which are only temporary. The chancellor de l'Hopital, in an edict of pacification, condemned to death any one who should break an image. It is very evident, that this too rigorous law, had only for its object, to prevent such irregularities as might tend to rekindle the civil war; yet it was in virtue of this law, interpreted as perpetual against all reason, that the parliament of Paris had the barbarity to condemn the chevalier de Labarre. Even if the law were just, it should have been declared that it was to expire after a certain number of years, unless the continuation of the troubles should require it to be renewed.

What Montesquieu says, chap. 16, on the emission of money, is not sufficient; not only their valuation should be specific, but the intrinsic value also, should be determined; but this real value should be sufficient, whether in metallic value, or in other goods; as for example according to the mean price of bread in Europe, and of rice in Asia: because the article forming the principal and habitual nourishment of the people, is the only one of which the value can be considered as constant; but if the manner of living should change, the principle of valuation should also change, and a new measure of valuation be established.

We have said there are things which should be valued in metal; such is the interest of a sum of money lent, which should always be some part of a known weight; such is the interest of the purchase money of a house, or furniture, and the like; while the interest of the purchase money of land, should be valued in produce.

33. We may perceive that at the time this was written, Condorcet yet adhered to the opinions of the most exclusive economists.

Laws should be composed according to a systematic order, so that it may be easy to comprehend them all, and follow each of the details.

This is the only method by which it can be discovered whether there are not contradictions or omissions, or if the questions which present themselves in the sequel have been proved or not.

This is the only means of clearly discovering when a reform is necessary, or on what part of the old law it should act, and then the reform ought to be so conducted, that without altering the unity of the system of laws, it may substitute the new law for that which is to be made the object of reform.

These reflections are simple; they contain only a small number of the principles which should enter into the composition of a work, on the manner of instituting laws; they are necessary; but Montesquieu has not thought it worth his while to employ his time upon them.

Letters of Helvetius

ADDRESSED TO

PRESIDENT MONTESQUIEU AND M. SAURIN

ON PERUSING THE MANUSCRIPT

OF

THE SPIRIT OF LAWS.*

ADVERTISEMENT.

[This advertisement and the following letters are extracted from the fifth volume of the works of Helvetius, edited by the abbé de la Roche, and translated for this volume.]

It had been said in several of the public papers, that at the time when the Spirit of Laws acquired great celebrity, Helvetius expressed much surprise at the circumstance, to his intimate friends: the facts, as Helvetius himself has related them, were these:

Helvetius was the friend of president Montesquieu, and whilst he held the station of farmer-general, spent much time at the country residence of Montesquieu at Brede. In the course of their philosophical conversations, the president mentioned to his friend, his work on the Spirit of Laws; and then gave him the manuscript to peruse: before he sent it to the press, Helvetius, who loved the author as much as he loved truth, was alarmed when he read this

---

* These two letters do not appear in the French edition of the text. Moreover, the evidence suggests that the first letter was a forgery. Of importance is Destutt de Tracy's view that government did not simply fall into the categories of good and bad, as Helvetius suggested, but of national and special.

work, at the danger to which the reputation of Montesquieu was about to be exposed. He repeatedly opposed, both in person and by letter, those opinions which he considered the most dangerous, as they were about to be laid down as political maxims, by one of the finest writers in France, in a work illuminated by genius, and inculcating many important truths. His natural modesty, and his admiration of the author of the Persian Letters, however, combating with his judgment, he requested Montesquieu's permission to shew the manuscript to their common friend, M. Saurin, the author of Spartacus; a man of profound and solid understanding, whom they both regarded as a most faithful man, and impartial judge. Saurin coincided in opinion with Helvetius. When the work appeared, and they witnessed its prodigious success, without changing their opinions, they remained silent from a respect for the judgment of the public, and for the honor of their friend.

This silence it might be well to imitate, so far as the errors of president Montesquieu were confined to theory; but now, that those errors have become the support of great prejudices, and that private passions are converting them into practical principles, it becomes important to expose them, and to lay before the public the sentiments which the friends of Montesquieu expressed to himself. Respect for great men after their death, would extend too far, were it to prevent the condemnation of errors, which they would themselves have renounced, if they had observed the dangers attendant upon their dissemination. It is believed, therefore, that the intentions of Helvetius will not be abused, by publishing some of his letters to Montesquieu. They cannot but be useful when the human mind has been awakened to the fatal effects of long established errors.

LETTER I.

Letter of Helvetius to President Montesquieu.

I HAVE perused, even to the third time, my dear president, the manuscript which you communicated to me. You greatly interested me in this work, whilst I was at Brede. I know nothing that resembles it: indeed I know not whether our French heads are steady enough to enable us to discern all its great beauties. For my own part, I am enraptured with them: I admire the vast genius which created them, and the depth of research which you must have accomplished, in order to collect so much knowledge from the rubbish of those barbarian laws, from which I had believed so little could be derived for the instruction or benefit of mankind. I behold you, like the hero of Milton, after having traversed the immensity of chaos, rising illustrious out of darkness. Thanks to you, we shall now be correctly informed of the spirit of laws of the Greeks, Romans, Vandals, and Visigoths; we shall now know through what intricate labyrinths human genius is compelled to pass, in order to relieve those unfortunate people who are oppressed by tyrants and religious oppressors. You bid us behold the world, how it has been governed, and how it is still ruled: but you too often give the world credit for reason and wisdom, which are in fact your own, and of which it will be much surprised at receiving the honors.

You compromise with prejudice, as a young man entering the world, does with certain females, who, although advanced in years, have still some pretensions, and by whom he wishes to be considered polite and well bred. But have you not flattered them too much? Such a course may propitiate the priests; and in dividing the spoil with those Cerberus's of the church, you silence them with respect to your religion: as to the rest, they will not be able to comprehend you. Our lawyers are not able either to read or understand you. As to the aristocrats, and our petty despots of all grades, if they understand you, they cannot praise you too much, and this is the fault I have ever found with the principles of your work. You may recollect, that in our discussions at Brede, I admitted that they might apply to the actual state of things; but I concluded that a writer, anxious to serve mankind, ought rather to lay down just maxims for an improved order of things yet to arise, than to give force or consequence to those which are dangerous, at the moment when prejudice is striving to preserve and perpetuate human ignorance and subjection. To employ philosophy in giving them consequence, is to give human genius a retrograde motion, and to perpetuate those abuses which interest and bad faith, are but too apt to uphold. The idea of perfectibility amuses our contemporaries, offends hypocrites, and men in power; but it instructs our rising generation, and is a light to posterity. If our offspring shall possess common sense, I doubt whether they will accommodate themselves to our principles of government, or adopt in their constitutions, which without doubt will be better than ours, your complicated balances and intermediary powers. Even kings themselves, if they understand their true interests (and why do they not consider them?) would, by dispensing with those pernicious powers, more securely establish their own happiness and the welfare of their subjects.

Instead of this, in Europe, which is now the least oppressed of the four quarters of the globe, where is there a prince, who, when all the streams of public revenue have passed through the hundred thousand channels of feudality, employs them to public advantage? One part of the nation enriches itself by the miseries of the other: the nobility, an insolent cabal: and the monarch, whom it flatters, is himself oppressed without being aware of it. History, well attended to, is a perpetual lesson. A king creates intermediate orders; they soon become his masters, and the tyrants of the people. How are they to maintain their despotism? They must cherish anarchy for their own sakes; they are jealous of nothing but their privileges, which are at variance with the natural rights of those whom they oppress.

I have told you, and I repeat it, my dear friend, that your combinations of balanced powers only tend to separate and complicate individual interests, rather than to unite them. The example of the English government has seduced you: I am far from thinking that constitution perfect: I shall have much to say to you upon that subject. Let us wait, as Locke said to king William, until some great calamities which must originate in the vices of that constitution, shall have made us acquainted with its danger; until that corruption, already become indispensable, to overcome the force of apathy in their upper chamber, shall be established by the ministers in the commons, and until they shall no longer blush at it: then shall we see the danger of an equilibrium, which must be perpetually broken in order to accelerate or retard the movements of so complicated a machine. In effect, do we not see in our own day, that taxes are necessary to corrupt the very parliament, which gives the king the right to levy imposts upon the people?

The very liberty which the English nation enjoys, does it indeed result from the principles of that constitution, rather than from their good laws, which have no dependance upon it; which the French may have, and which alone, perhaps, would render their government supportable. As yet, we have no pretensions to it. Our priests are too fanatical, and our nobles too ignorant, to become citizens, or to perceive the advantages of becoming and forming a nation. Every one of them knows he is a slave, and lives with the hope of one day or another becoming a petty despot in his turn.

A king is also the mere slave of his mistresses, of his favorites, and his ministers. If he gets in a passion, the kicks which his minions receive, place him on a footing with the lowest blackguard: this, I think, is the only use for intermediaries in a government. In a state, ruled by the fantasies of a monarchy, the intermediaries who surround him, are alternately engaged in deceiving him, and in preventing the complaints of the people against the abuses by which they profit from reaching his ears. Is it the people who complain, that are dangerous? No: but *those who are not heard:* in such circumstances, the only persons to be dreaded in a nation, are those who hinder others from being heard. When the sovereign, notwithstanding the flatteries of the intermediaries, is forced to have the clamors of the people borne even to himself, the evil is at its height; if a remedy is not then prompt, the ruin of the empire is at hand; the people may learn, too late, that the chief was imposed upon by his favorites.

You perceive, that by intermediaries, I mean the members of that vast aristocracy of nobles and priests, whose chief resides at Versailles, which usurps almost all the functions of power, and multiplies them at will, by the mere authority of birth; without right, without talents, without merit; and which keeps even the sovereign in dependence, in order that the ministry may be changed as it shall suit their interests.

I will close, my dear friend, by acknowledging to you, that I have never well understood the subtle distinctions, so incessantly repeated, respecting the various forms of government. I know but two descriptions: *the good and the bad.* The good, which is yet to be formed; the bad, the great secret of which is, to draw by a variety of means, the money of the governed into the pockets of the governors. That which the ancient governments acquired by war, our moderns obtain more certainly by financiering: it is only the difference in the means which makes any variety. I believe, notwithstanding, in the possibility of a good government, where the liberty and property of the people being respected, one may see the general good necessarily resulting, without your balances or particular interests. Such would be a simple machine, the springs of which, being easily regulated, would render unnecessary the complicated appendages of wheels and balances, so difficult to be kept in order by those unskilful people who usually meddle with the affairs of government. These people wish to do every thing, and they act upon us as upon an inanimate mass, which they fashion to their fancy, without consulting either our desires or our true interests; a course of conduct, which betrays at once their impertinence and their ignorance: and yet, after all this, they seem surprised, that the excess of their abuses should provoke a desire for reform, and attribute to every thing rather than their own mismanagement, the sudden impulse given to affairs by the diffusion of knowledge and the exercise of public opinion. I dare to predict, that we approach such an epoch. I am, &c.

LETTER II.

Helvetius to A. M. Saurin.

As we had agreed, my dear Saurin, I have written to the president, with regard to the impression which his manuscript made upon you, as well as upon myself. At the same time that I have freely explained my opinions, I have conveyed them in language expressive of interest and friendship. Do not be uneasy, our remarks have not hurt him; he likes to witness in his friends that frankness, which distinguishes him among them; he freely promotes discussion, answers by sallies of wit, and rarely alters his opinion. I never fancied, when delivering our opinions, that they would change his; but we have not been able to say

> . . . . cur ego amicum
> Offendam in nugis? Hæ nugae seria ducent
> In mala derisum semel, exceptum que sinistrè.

Whatever it cost him, he should be sincere with his friends. When the light of truth shall shine forth and displace self love, he will find that they cannot be reproached with having been less sincere than the public.

I send you his answer, since you cannot come and join me in the country. You will find it such as I had foreseen. You will perceive that he had need of method to rally his ideas, and that being unwilling to lose all that he has thought, written, or imagined, since his youth, and according to the various dispositions in which he found himself, he has laid hold of that which least conflicts with received opinions. With that sort of spirit which distinguished Montagne, he adhered to the prejudices of the lawyers and noblesse; this is the source of all his errors. His fine genius had elevated him in his youth, to the production of the Persian Letters; now advanced in years, he seems to repent having given envy that pretext for thwarting his ambition. He is more solicitous to uphold received ideas, than to inculcate others more novel and more useful. His manner is dazzling. It must have required the greatest force of genius to form such a mixture of truths and prejudices. Most of our philosophers may admire it as a *chef-d'oeuvre*. These things are new to all minds, and the less the number of opponents or good judges of his work, the more I fear that he will for a long time lead us astray.

But what the duce would he have us to understand by his treatise upon fiefs? Is it such an affair as to require an enlightened mind to unravel it? What legislation can result from a chaos of barbarian laws, established by force, reverenced only by ignorance, and which will forever be repugnant to a good order of things? Without the conquerors, who have destroyed every thing, what will be our situation with all these motley institutions? Ought we then to inherit all the errors that have been accumulating since the origin of the human race? They would still govern us; and having become the property of the strongest, or of the basest, it would require a more terrible remedy than conquest to release ourselves from them. It is nevertheless, the only remedy, if the voice of wise men is made to mingle with the interest of the powerful, and aid in erecting unnatural usurpations into legitimate properties. And what sort of property is that possessed by a few, injurious to all, even to those possessing it; and which corrupts by producing arrogance and vanity? In truth, if man is happy only when in the practice of the virtues, and in possession of the intelligence which confirms good principles; what virtues and what talents are we to expect from an order of men who engross every thing, and who claim consequence in society, by no other title than that of their birth? The industry of society is for no other end, but for them; all places of honor and profit devolve upon them; the sovereign governs, but through them, and for them alone draws subsidies from his subjects. Is not this totally overturning all ideas of sense and justice? This is the abominable order which misleads so many men of fine genius, and which totally perverts the principles of public and private morality.

L'Esprit de corps assails us on all sides, under the name of established orders: it is a power erected at the expense of the great mass of society. It is by these hereditary usurpations we are ruled. Under the name of the nation, there exist only corporations of individuals, and not citizens who merit that title. Even philosophers wish to form corporate bodies: but if they flatter private interests at the expense of the general welfare, I predict that their reign will not be long: for the knowledge which they circulate, will sooner or later disperse the darkness in which they wish to conceal prejudices; and our friend Montesquieu, deprived of his titles of wise man and legislator, will become no more than the lawyer, the nobleman, and the fine genius. Therefore am I afflicted for him and for humanity.

END OF THE WORK

Acknowledgments

I wish to express my thanks to Christine Dunn Henderson, for suggesting the publication of Destutt de Tracy's almost forgotten masterpiece on Montesquieu's *Spirit of the Laws*. At Liberty Fund I was extremely fortunate to receive the editorial assistance of Laura Goetz. Not only did she provide invaluable help in preparing the final version of the text but our correspondence on the beauty of choral music was a real joy. Finally, I wish to thank Melody Negron of Westchester Publishing Services for seeing this volume through the production stages. She was the very model of efficiency, professionalism, and politeness.

Jeremy Jennings
London
May 2024

Index

Note: Page numbers followed by *n* and note number refer to numbered footnotes. Page numbers followed by *n** refer to footnotes with symbols.

tical, xxv, 23–24, 42, 48, 69;
motives of punishment in, 46,
123; simplicity of law in, 49–50;
typical devolution into aristocracy, xxv, 25
despotic government: as abuse of
monarchy, 22, 47, 69; commerce as counterweight to, xxii;
defense tactics of, 76; fear as
moving principle of, xx, 21–22,
50, 68, 122; as first degree of
civilization, 46, 123, 125; Montesquieu on type of corruption
characteristic of, 68; Montesquieu's examples of, xxi; motives
of punishment in, 46, 123; as
natural for large states, 68; as
type, in Montesquieu, xx, xxiv,
17–18, 47, 122; type of education appropriate to, 28, 35; type
of laws appropriate for, 39
Destutt de Tracy, Antoine Claude
Louis: acquaintance with
Jefferson, xii; admiration of
Jefferson, xi, xvii; *Commentaire
sur l'Esprit des Lois de Montesquieu*, xxxii–xxxiii; correspondence with Jefferson, xii,
xv–xviii; *Élémens d'idéologie*,
x, xi, xii; *Élémens d'Idéologie:
IV partie: Traité de la volonté*,
xi, xxxii; family background,
vii; First Republic and, ix–x;
and French Revolution, vii–ix;
Grammaire, x, xii; and *idéologie*,
invention of study of, ix, x; and
Institut National des Sciences

et des Arts, x–xi; intellectual
influences on, vii, ix; life of,
vii–xi; *Logique*, x; marriage and
children, vii; *M. de Tracy à
M. Burke*, viii; and Napoleon,
x–xi; politics of, viii; *Quels sont
les moyens de fonder la morale
d'un peuple?*, xxxii; on single
vs. plural executive, xvi,
xvii–xviii; textbooks by, x;
Traité de l'économie, xxxii;
Treatise on Political Economy,
xxx, xxxii. See also *Commentary
and Review* (Destutt de Tracy)
Directory, ix–x, xvi
division of labor, benefits of, xxxi,
170–71, 176–79
divorce, right of, in representative
government, 43
domestic servitude of women,
causes of, 159–60
Duane, William, xii–xv, xxxi
Dubos, Jean-Baptiste, Abbé, 211
Dunoyer, Charles, xxxiii
Dupont de Nemours, Pierre
Samuel, vii
Durfort de Civrac, Émilie Louise
de, vii

education: in aristocratic government, xxvi–xxvii, 33–34; in
democracies, 34–35; in despotic
states, 28, 35; in elective monarchy, 33; in hereditary monarchy,
31–33; in monarchies, xxvi, 28;
in national government, 35–36;
need to instill ideas consonant

59, 60; monarchy, Montesquieu on, 211–12; moral factors igniting desire for change in, 61. *See also* French Revolution

Frederick II (Holy Roman Emperor), 202

freedom of individuals. *See* liberty, individual

freedom of speech, in representative government, 44

freedom of the press: as important for happiness and good order, 117; as necessary for political liberty, 118, 119, 125

free will, 85

French Revolution: destruction during, 59; Destutt de Tracy and, vii–ix; economic power unleashed by, 59–61, 60n7; lack of national assembly or transitional authority, 97–98; and *Spirit of the Laws*, xxiii; value of preserving power demonstrated by excesses of, 116

geography's effect on societies, Destutt de Tracy's critique of, xxx

Germanic confederation, source of weakness in, 75

Germany: ancient, Montesquieu's praise of government in, 92; resources wasted on luxury, 60

gold, as currency, 192

government: economical, as best, xxx–xxxi; good, maximization of liberty in, xxviii; good and bad, as types, 18, 234; good produced and evil prevented as criteria for judging, 120; moderate and immoderate, Montesquieu on, xx–xxi; necessity of evaluating reality of, 18

governments two classes in Destutt de Tracy, xxv, 19, 23. *See also* national government; special government

government founded on reason: characteristics of law in, 127–28; freedom to act according to natural law in, 122–23; independence of state and liberty of members as primary functions of, 127; rights of man as basis of, 122, 126–27, 128. *See also* constitution, creation through reason; laws of government based on reason; power distribution within government to maximize liberty

government's three types in Montesquieu, xix–xx, 122; commerce appropriate to each, 179; degrees of civilization of, 46, 123, 125–26; Destutt de Tracy's critique of, xxiv–xxv, 16–20, 23, 29–30, 67; importance to Montesquieu's analysis, 129; as reducible to two types, 46–49, 122; size of country appropriate for, 68–70. *See also* despotic government; monarchy; republican government, as type

moderate government: Montesquieu's examples of, xxi; political liberty as unique to, xxi
moderation as political principle:
Destutt de Tracy's critique of,
xxiv, 22; monarchical government and, xxi; Montesquieu
on, xx
monarchy: appropriate size of
country for, 69–70; characteristics of officeholders in, 41;
corruption characteristic of,
Montesquieu on, 68; cost of
maintaining, 69–70; decrease
in monarchs' powers with
advance of civilization, 106–7;
defense tactics of, 76; Destutt
de Tracy on flaws of, xxix, 23;
and division of society into
class factions, 111; education
appropriate to, 31–33; English,
Destutt de Tracy on, xxviii;
English, Montesquieu's admiration for, xxii; French, Montesquieu on, 211–12; French
views on Destutt de Tracy's
criticism of, xxxii–xxxiii;
hereditary, inherent problems
with, 109–12; honor and
ambition as moving principle
of, xx, xxiv, 22, 49, 50, 68,
122; as inherently opposed to
national supremacy, 110–11;
law in, Montesquieu on, 49;
laws appropriate for, 38–42;
luxury as necessary expense for,

64; and moderation, Montesquieu on, xxi; moral effects
on populace, 64; as natural
for medium-sized states, 68;
necessity of nobility to support, 40; necessity of suppressing inferior orders, 41; as poor
candidates for confederation,
75–76, 79; preservation principles in, 26; simplicity of law
in, 49–50; tempered, as type of
aristocratic government, 47–48,
49; tendency toward immo-
rality and corruption, 111; as
type, Montesquieu on, xx–xxi,
16–17, 122
monarchy, pure: as first degree
of civilization, 48, 69, 125; as
intolerable, 48; typical evolu-
tion into aristocratic government, 48–49
money: absurdity of artificial
control of interest rates, 195,
195n28; arbitrary names for
denominations, 193; copper
currency, 192–93; credit notes
of large companies used as,
196; currency exchange, bankers' profits in, 195–96; effect of
decreased amount in circulation, 58; effects of increasing
amount in circulation, 196;
gold currency, 192–93; government changes in value of
(financiering), 193–94; and
inequality, 163; removing

rapacity, and pursuit of luxury, 56
reason. *See* constitution, creation
through reason; government
founded on reason; laws of government based on reason
religion: aristocratic government
and, xxvi, 33–34, 126; correction of errors in, 119; of
individual, as properly outside
laws' influence, 127, 205; and
inequality, 163; influence in
second degree of society, 119,
126; as lever to achieve power,
48–49; monarchy and, 31–32;
morality of, as contrary to
enlightened principles, 206;
necessary separation from civil
affairs, 205; pernicious aspects
of, 205–6, 206n31
religious education: as appropriate for monarchies, 31–32; in
aristocratic government, 33–34
representative democracy: absorption of conquered peoples
by, 81–82; advantages of, 24;
characteristics of, xxvi, xxvii;
characteristics of office holders in, 45; characteristics of
people in, xxvi; colonies and,
82; confederation and, 74, 127;
confederations as experiments
in, 75; diffusion of knowledge
in, 44; freedom of speech in,
44; free flow of information in,
43; free reign given to normal
inclinations and industry,
42–43; measure to ensure

general equality, 43; measure
to ensure moral citizens, 44;
motives of punishment in, 46,
123; opposition of executive
and legislative power in, 70;
principles sustaining, xxvi,
24–25; printing technology
as prerequisite for, 24, 162;
promotion of freedom in,
xxvii; promotion of knowledge
in, xxvii; as relatively inexpen-
sive, 70; as suitable for any size
country, 70; tendency toward
equality, 43; as third degree of
civilization, 46, 70, 123, 126;
type of education appropriate
to, 35–36; as type of national
government, 19, 24; types of
laws appropriate for, 42–45;
as unknown in Montesquieu's
time, xxvi, 24; virtues of
citizens in, 25; waste of luxury
as foreign to, 64. *See also*
constitution of representative
democracy
republican government, as type:
ancient republics, Montesquieu
on, xx; colonies and, 82; Destutt
de Tracy's critique of, 16; education in, 28–29; inappropriate
linking of democracy and aristocracy in, 47, 67–68, 69; Montesquieu on, xx, 122; as natural
for small states, 68, 74; necessity
of defense through alliance or
confederation, 74, 124; virtue as
moving principle of, xx, 122

and cost of inputs for other
production, 149; distortion
of markets and production
by, 143–49; duties imposed at
time of production, 144–46;
effects of, 134, 136, 141–49;
indirect and interactive effects
of, 148–49; local taxes, 146;
and merchandise's natural vs.
conventional (market) value,
141–42, 146–48; on necessities,
144–45, 146–47; on wine,
134, 144, 145
taxes on persons or businesses,
134; ill effects of, 134; person
bearing burden of, 139–40
taxes on rent of houses, 134; as
effective seizure of interest in
property, 138–39; ill effects of,
135, 135n19; person bearing
burden of, 138
thèse nobiliaire, xxiii
Tocqueville, Alexis de, xxiii
trade. *See* commerce
traders: factors affecting profit of,
172; limits on number needed
for commerce, 173; and morality, 188–89; role in facilitating
commerce, 171–72, 173; types
of external trade, 181–84; work
of, as productive, 173–75
treason against the nation, as
often-abused charge, 120
trial by jury: Destutt de Tracy on,
50–51; as necessary for political
liberty, 118, 119, 125
Turgot, Anne Robert Jacques, vii

United States: and absorption of
Louisiana Territory, 81–82;
assembly of deputies used to
write constitution, 95; causes
of population growth in, 201;
confederative system in, 74,
93; distribution of power in
government of, xxviii, 93; and
prosperity from productive
labor, 59, 62
unproductive labor, damage to
prosperity, 142–43, 174
unproductive spending, public
expenditures as, xxx–xxxi,
132–33

value: conventional (market)
value, 142, 146–48, 191–92;
economists' common errors on,
150–55; of merchandise, compo-
nents of, 154–55; natural value,
141–42, 146–48, 156, 191–92
vanity: and displays of luxury,
56, 63; necessity of exciting, in
monarchy, 64
virtue: good and bad forms of, 22,
29; in Montesquieu, as false
virtue, 25; as moving principle
of republics, xx, 22, 122; in
representative democracy, 25
Voltaire, vii, xxiii, 202, 202n30, 212

war: law of nations and, 78; and
right of conquest, 79, 124; right
to make, 77, 79, 124
wealth: creation of, Destutt de
Tracy on, xxx; diminution

This book is set in Adobe Garamond Pro, a modern adaptation by Robert Slimbach of the typeface originally cut around 1540 by the French typographer and printer Claude Garamond. The Garamond face, with its small lowercase height and restrained contrast between thick and thin strokes, is a classic "old-style" face and has long been one of the most influential and widely used typefaces.

This paper meets the requirements of ANSI/NISO Z39.48-1992 (Permanence of Paper). ∞

Book design by Darryl Keck

Composition by Westchester Publishing Services

Index by Lee Gable

Printed and bound by Sheridan Books, Inc., Chelsea, Michigan